Fountas & Pinnell

Assessment Guide

A Guide to Benchmark Assessment System 2

Irene C. Fountas

Gay Su Pinnell

Heinemann, Portsmouth, NH

Heinemann

361 Hanover St.
Portsmouth, NH 03801-3912
www.heinemann.com

Offices and agents throughout the world.

Fountas & Pinnell Benchmark Assessment Guide 2: A Guide to Assessment System 2

ISBN10: 0-325-04792-8
ISBN13: 978-0-325-04792-8

Printed in Guangzhou, China

0114/CA21400152

4   5   6   7   8   NOR   18   17   16   15   14

TABLE OF CONTENTS

| Section 8 | Frequently Asked Questions | 139 |

| Section 9 | Appendix, Glossary, Index | 149 |

Online Resources Instructions

All forms for the system are also available on the Online Resources site.

To access the site, go to www.fountasandpinnell.com/resources.

If this is your **first time** at the site please click on the **Register** button, enter the product code **FPBAS7239E1** and set up your account.

Registration requires an email address and password that you will use to access the site going forward.

If you **previously registered** at this site, then simply log in and add the product code above. After you are logged in, click on the image of the *Benchmark Assessment System* product to access the necessary forms.

section 1

Getting Started

In this section, we provide background for benchmark assessment in general and its relationship to our work in particular. An overview of the *Fountas & Pinnell Benchmark Assessment System 2* components displays the file box and its contents and gives a brief description of all the parts of the system. Finally, we share ideas about how to prepare for an efficient assessment conference.

▶ Introduction to the *Fountas & Pinnell Benchmark Assessment System 2*

Fountas & Pinnell Benchmark Assessment System 2 provides materials and procedures for observing and assessing the reading levels and behaviors of students in grades 3–8. It is directly linked to Fountas and Pinnell levels L–Z and small-group reading instruction using leveled books.

A *benchmark* is a standard against which to measure something. In *Fountas & Pinnell Benchmark Assessment System 2,* the standard is set by the benchmark books a student reads aloud and talks about during the assessment conference. These books have been written, edited, and extensively field-tested to ensure that they reflect the characteristics of texts and the demands of texts on the reader at each specific Fountas and Pinnell level (*The Continuum of Literacy Learning* [Pinnell and Fountas, Heinemann, 2011, 2008]).

The F&P Text Level Gradient™, created and refined as a teaching and assessment tool over the past twenty years, represent twenty-six points on a gradient of reading difficulty (Figure 1.1). Each point on that gradient, from the easiest at level A to the most challenging at level Z+ (which are books recommended for high school and beyond) represents a small but significant increase in difficulty over the previous level. There are two equivalent benchmark books (one fiction and one nonfiction) for each of the levels from L–Z in *Fountas & Pinnell Benchmark Assessment System 2.* Following the *Benchmark Assessment System's* standardized assessment procedures, you use the leveled benchmark books to identify each student's reading levels. Benchmark results yield optimal levels for independent reading and instructional reading at a given point in time. The results also provide information about the text level that will be too demanding to allow for effective learning by the student (hard level).

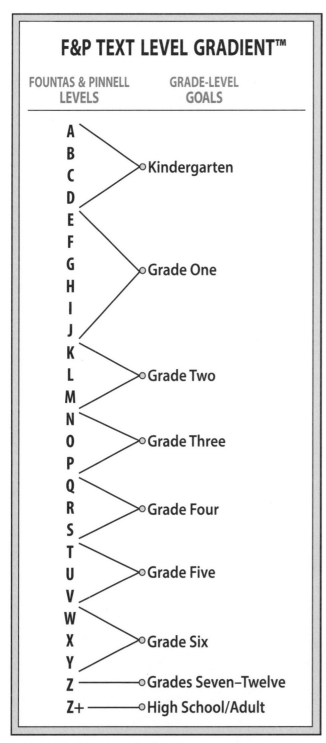

FIGURE 1.1 F&P Text Level Gradient™

The *Fountas & Pinnell Benchmark Assessment System 2* is administered during a one-on-one, student-teacher assessment conference. For about thirty minutes, the student reads aloud and talks about a series of benchmark books while you observe and code the reader's behaviors on carefully constructed Recording Forms. Using established scoring conventions and procedures for analysis, you can not only establish optimal learning levels but also gather valuable information about each individual's processing strategies, fluency, and comprehension—all of which give you insights about how to target your future teaching. Optional diagnostic assessments that focus on phonics/word analysis and vocabulary provide even more data to inform high-quality instruction.

Administered once, *the Fountas & Pinnell Benchmark Assessment System 2* conferences provide information to help you

❑ determine three reading levels for each student: Benchmark Independent, Benchmark Instructional, and Hard

❑ form initial groups for reading instruction

❑ select texts that will be productive for a student's instruction

❑ plan efficient and effective instruction

❑ identify students who need intervention and extra help

❑ diagnose particular areas of reading difficulty

Administered one, two, three, or four times per year, the *Fountas & Pinnell Benchmark Assessment System* can do all of that *plus* document student progress across a school year and across grade levels. As students progress through the levels, becoming increasingly expert readers, the A-Z gradient becomes a "ladder of progress." To document ongoing progress, you can code and score a student's reading of an instructional level text you use in your teaching and have a brief comprehension conversation. We suggest administering the assessment at least once at the beginning of the school year to know where to begin instruction and then again in March. By scheduling this way, you can assess a student's progress across most of the year and also use the March results to inform teaching through the end of the school year.

There are two ways to preview the *Fountas & Pinnell Benchmark Assessment System 2:* by reading through this guide and by exploring the *Professional Development DVD.* You will also find helpful information at *fountasandpinnell.com.*

► Components of the *Fountas & Pinnell Benchmark Assessment System 2*

All components of the system are conveniently packaged in a sturdy box that includes hanging file folders in which to organize the benchmark books and Recording Forms by level for easy access.

Benchmark Assessment System 2 box

Benchmark books

Assessment Guide

The Continuum of Literacy Learning, 3–8

Assessment Forms

Optional Assessments: Student Forms

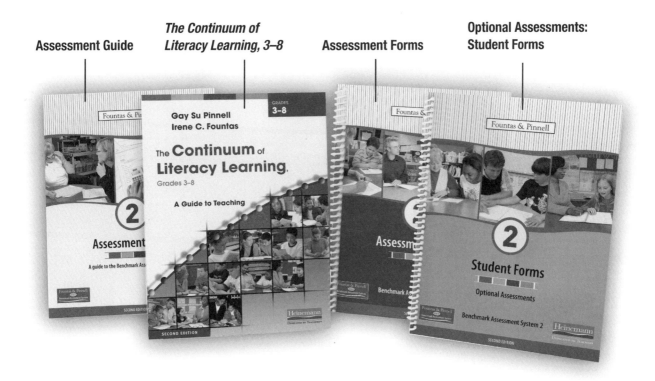

F&P Calculator/Stopwatch

Recording Forms

Student Folders (set of 30)

Professional Development DVD

Assessment Forms CD-ROM

Benchmark Books

Thirty benchmark books, a fiction and a nonfiction text for each level from L–Z, are the centerpiece of the *Fountas & Pinnell Benchmark Assessment System 2* and provide the student reading contexts. They are organized from lowest (L) to highest (Z) level to reflect increasingly challenging texts. Each fiction and nonfiction book has been written to reflect the text characteristics specific to the level. (See *Leveled Books, K–8: Matching Texts to Readers for Effective Teaching* [Fountas and Pinnell, Heinemann, 2006] for a full description of these level characteristics.) In addition, each benchmark book has been field-tested and edited to ensure representation of the designated level, whether fiction or nonfiction. Fiction and nonfiction pairs have been matched so that if a student can read one genre, he should be able to read the other at the same level eliminating the need for reading two books at each level. (See the research report at *fountasandpinnellbenchmarkassessment.com.*)

The characteristics of all thirty benchmark books in the *Fountas & Pinnell Benchmark Assessment System 2* are described in detail in Appendix A. You will notice that these are short stories or informational books with limited picture support. They provide strong evidence of a student's text processing and understanding.

Assessment Forms Book, CD-ROM, and Online Resources

All forms for the system are available in a book of blackline masters as well as in electronic form on a CD-ROM and on the Online Resources site. All three contain resources that can be photocopied or printed in the quantities needed for assessment: Recording Forms and Assessment Summary forms, Class Record forms, Records of Reading Progress, At-a-Glance charts for easy administration, and optional assessments. On the CD-ROM, a simple navigation system allows you to select forms based on book level, title, and genre. You may want to print a large quantity of each to keep in your file box for future use. The Online Resources can be accessed by going to www.fountasandpinnell.com /resources. The product code and instructions for accessing this site are included in the Quick Start Guide.

Professional Development DVD

This DVD provides a foundation for understanding the *Fountas & Pinnell Benchmark Assessment System 2* materials and procedures. Its goal is to provide individualized training in coding, scoring, analyzing, and interpreting oral reading records and using the information to inform teaching. The DVD walks you through the parts of the system and the assessment administration procedures. It includes an overview of the system components, multiple models of real teachers administering the assessment with students, as well as an in-depth discussion of scoring, analyzing, and interpreting an assessment. Practice sessions with sample assessment data provide you with opportunities to train yourself anywhere and anytime on coding oral reading; scoring accuracy, fluency, and comprehension; analyzing and interpreting results; and documenting change over time. The modular structure and interactive design of the DVD allow you to direct your own learning and focus on areas of greatest interest or need.

F & P Calculator/Stopwatch

A specially designed *F & P Calculator/Stopwatch* performs highly specific functions related to the system. See Appendix B for complete operating instructions.

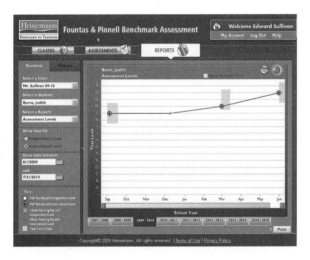

BAS Online Data Management System (ODMS)

The *BAS Online Data Management System* is a secure and efficient way for teachers and school and district administrators to collect, analyze, and report student assessment data according to district requirements. A one-year individual teacher subscription to this secure, web-based data management system is included with the initial purchase of *BAS*. After year one, subscriptions are per teacher per year (for an unlimited number of students) and includes unlimited access for school and district administrators. The product code for accessing *ODMS* is included on the back of your *Technology Package*. For a product tour and downloadable user manual, go to: *fountasandpinnell.com* and scroll down to "Online Data Management System."

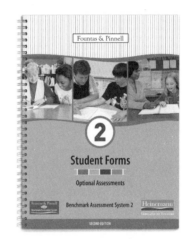

Optional Assessments: Student Forms

This book provides a reusable student copy of the Where-to-Start Word Test and selected optional assessments (Phonics and Word Analysis as well as Vocabulary Assessments). Turned to the appropriate assessment, it can be placed in front of the student for oral assessments. Each student page is coated for durability and set up to make it easy for the reader to follow.

Student Folders

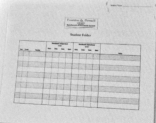

File folders, one for each reader, are a handy place to store recent assessment results and observations; they are printed with a Longitudinal Record of Reading Progress that can be passed from grade to grade, K–8.

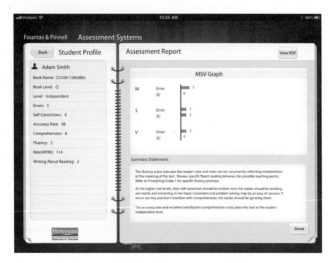

Fountas & Pinnell BAS Reading Record App for iPads (in press)

Reading record software that performs the following functions:

- ❑ Saves individual reading record assesments and summary assessments as PDFs.

- ❑ Times the conference and calculates oral reading and accuracy rate, self-correction ratio, fluency and comprehension scores.

- ❑ Records audio from the assessment conference.

- ❑ Syncs data to the *Online Data Management System (ODMS)*.

▶ Preparing for a Benchmark Assessment Conference

Even before you begin getting ready to administer the assessment, think about when and where you want to conduct the one-on-one conference. If you are the student's literacy teacher, you are the ideal person to conduct the assessment as you will gain, firsthand, a rich set of information to inform your teaching.

Get Started Quickly

Plan to begin your assessment conferences right at the start of the school year and spend about two weeks of your daily reading block time completing them. The assessment conference gives you a chance to spend time with each student. You can get to know your students and begin to develop relationships while you gather critical information. You should think of

the assessment conference as time well spent on reading, thinking, and talking with students about books. You may also decide to have them do the writing portion of the assessment, giving them another opportunity to engage in a worthwhile literacy activity that provides evidence of text understanding.

Use Reading Block Time

We suggest that you conduct your assessments during your reading block times while the children are rotating to centers, reading independently, or engaged in other assigned independent literacy work. Plan to complete about two or three assessments per day. Some assessment conferences will be short, while others will be longer. This schedule will enable you to complete your series of assessment conferences in about two weeks.

Enlist School Support

You may have a teaching assistant, a student teacher, or a rotating substitute teacher in the school who can read aloud to the students, engage them in shared reading, or monitor independent work. This support will free you to conduct two or three assessment conferences each day.

If your school is able to provide one or two days of substitute coverage, you will be able to assess most of your students quickly. The substitute can provide instruction while you take each of your students for an assessment conference.

Another option is to pair with a grade-level colleague so that one of you can teach students from both classes while the other conducts assessments with his or her own students.

Select a Location

Find a place that is reasonably quiet to administer the assessments. You will not want the child to be distracted and you also want to hear the child's responses clearly. Some specialist teachers have their own instructional space that is empty when they do not have students, so they can take the student to a room where it is very quiet. On the other hand, it may not be worth going a long distance down the hall.

We have had good experience with giving the assessment in a quiet corner of the classroom while other students are engaged in independent work. You may want to take this option (or work just outside the room in the corridor) if you have staff support. If you work in the classroom, you can have dedicated space in which you have your materials organized.

Be sure that you are conducting the assessment far enough away from the other students you are going to assess that they cannot hear the reading or conversation about the stories.

Put Materials in Order

The assessment will go more smoothly if you begin with everything prepared and in order.

❑ **Benchmark books** Make sure the fiction and nonfiction benchmark books for each level are in the appropriate level folder in the benchmark box. You can have the entire box available (if you have space), or take out the levels that you plan to use.

❑ **Recording Forms** Also in the hanging file folder, you will want to place multiple copies of the Recording Forms for both the fiction and the nonfiction benchmark books. These forms have the typed texts for each book and the space to record all of your information. Printing out multiple copies from the *Assessment Forms* CD-ROM or the Online Resources site, or copying them from the *Assessment Forms Book* and keeping them in good supply in the hanging folders will save time going to the printer or copy machine for each assessment.

❑ **Assessment Summary Form** You will want to have a supply of these generic forms, also found in the *Assessment Forms Book*, CD-ROM, and Online Resources, in a folder in the front of your box. You'll need at least one copy to summarize the set of text readings for each child you assess.ings for each child you assess.

❑ **F & P Calculator/Stopwatch** While you can do the assessment without the calculator/stopwatch (using the formulas included on the Recording Form), it will be quicker and easier to have your *F & P Calculator/Stopwatch* with you.

❑ **Assessment at-a-Glance chart and Coding and Scoring at-a-Glance chart** Two charts in the *Assessment Forms Book* and *CD-ROM* will be helpful in reminding you of key steps in the assessment process. Make a copy of each to clip on your clipboard or laminate for your assessment corner. The Assessment at-a-Glance chart provides a concise description of the administration procedures. It will remind you of the steps, especially the first year you use the system. The Coding and Scoring at-a-Glance chart provides a quick review of coding and scoring procedures for oral reading. Over time, you will be so familiar with this information that you will not need to use the charts. (Both charts are also found inside the covers of this guide.)

❑ **Writing implements** Have a good supply of writing implements—sharpened pencils or markers—so you will not have to spend time looking for them. We suggest that you use inexpensive mechanical pencils so you can erase if needed. If you choose to have students complete the optional drawing or writing section of the assessment, it will be more efficient to give the students a pencil or a fine marker rather than have them look for their own. A fine marker is ideal, allowing students to simply cross out when needed instead of spending time erasing. You may also want to have clean sheets of paper available for the writing prompt if you are using the condensed version of the Recording Form.

Administering, Coding, and Scoring a Benchmark Assessment Conference

In this section, you will find directions for administering and scoring the *Fountas & Pinnell Benchmark Assessment System 2.* You can print a copy of the Assessment at-a-Glance chart from the inside front cover of this guide or from the *Assessment Forms Book* or *CD-ROM* and place it in front of you as you conduct the assessment. You might want to copy it on card stock and laminate it or tape it in the area in which you conduct your assessment conferences. The *Professional Development* DVD offers additional guidance on how to administer, score, and analyze benchmark assessments.

We begin with a walk-through of the Recording Form, which is the system's primary tool for collecting and recording data about the students' oral reading and comprehension. Each book in the *Fountas & Pinnell Benchmark Assessment System 2* has a corresponding three-part Recording Form that guides the assessment at all levels. It is used to observe and code the reading behavior through Oral Reading (Part One), a Comprehension Conversation (Part Two), and an optional Writing About Reading prompt for responding to the text (Part Three). The first four pages of this section present a brief summary of the form. A detailed explanation follows.

▶ Recording Form Walk-Through

Part One: Oral Reading

The Recording Forms are available as blackline masters in the *Assessment Forms Book* as well as in electronic form on the *Assessment Forms CD-ROM*. The *Assessment Forms Book* contains condensed versions of the Recording Forms, while the CD offers expanded versions with more writing space and blank forms.

The oral reading section of the assessment includes:

❏ Space for the student's name, grade, the date of the assessment, the teacher's name, and the school's name. You'll have a Recording Form for each book a student reads.

❏ A standardized text introduction to read aloud to the student after showing the child the benchmark book cover and reading aloud the title.

❏ A place to record the start and end time. You can use the reading time and the running words (RW) later to calculate reading rate, or use the *F & P Calculator/ Stopwatch.*

❏ The typed text of the benchmark book appears word-for-word, page for page. On this text, you code the oral reading, recording errors (repetitions, substitutions, omissions, insertions), self-corrections, appeals and tolds.

❏ Columns to tally the reader's errors (E) and self-corrections (SC), with additional columns for analysis of these errors and self-corrections. Each of these attempts is analyzed for the source of information the reader likely used to make it: M = meaning, S = structure, and V = visual information.

❏ A summary score box to record final scores when completed.

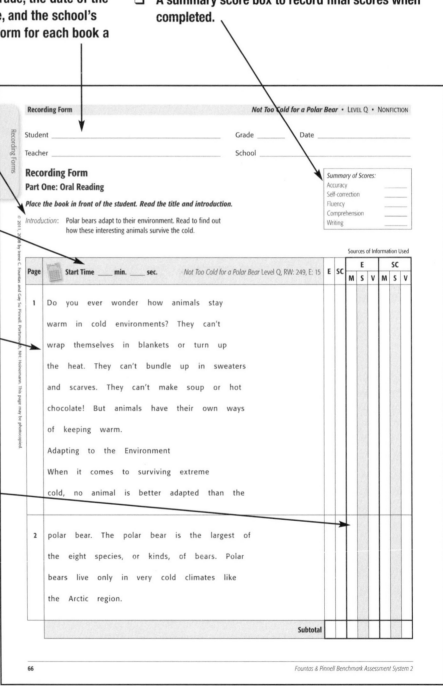

The scoring section summarizes the oral reading: accuracy, self-corrections, and fluency for all levels.

❑ **A chart to help you quickly figure the accuracy rate (the percentage of the total words that the student has read correctly) by tallying the number of errors on the coded text and circling the errors and matching percentage on the scale.**

❑ **A space to record the number of self-corrections (when the reader makes an error and then, without help from the teacher, corrects it).**

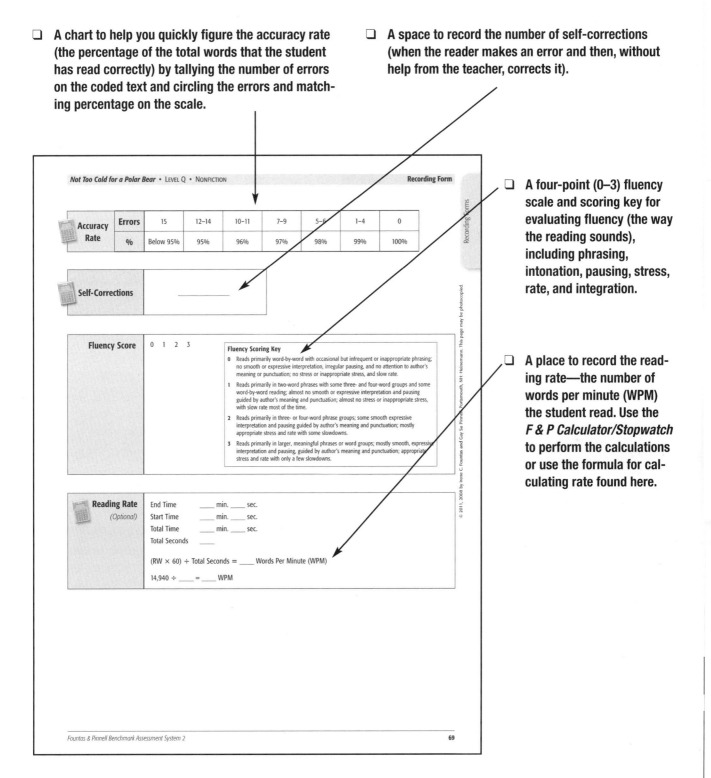

❑ **A four-point (0–3) fluency scale and scoring key for evaluating fluency (the way the reading sounds), including phrasing, intonation, pausing, stress, rate, and integration.**

❑ **A place to record the reading rate—the number of words per minute (WPM) the student read. Use the *F & P Calculator/Stopwatch* to perform the calculations or use the formula for calculating rate found here.**

Not Too Cold for a Polar Bear • LEVEL Q • NONFICTION   Recording Form

Accuracy Rate	Errors	15	12–14	10–11	7–9	5–6	1–4	0
	%	Below 95%	95%	96%	97%	98%	99%	100%

Self-Corrections _____

Fluency Score   0 1 2 3

Fluency Scoring Key

0 Reads primarily word-by-word with occasional but infrequent or inappropriate phrasing; no smooth or expressive interpretation, irregular pausing, and no attention to author's meaning or punctuation; no stress or inappropriate stress, and slow rate.

1 Reads primarily in two-word phrases with some three- and four-word groups and some word-by-word reading; almost no smooth or expressive interpretation and pausing guided by author's meaning and punctuation; almost no stress or inappropriate stress, with slow rate most of the time.

2 Reads primarily in three- or four-word phrase groups; some smooth expressive interpretation and pausing guided by author's meaning and punctuation; mostly appropriate stress and rate with some slowdowns.

3 Reads primarily in larger, meaningful phrases or word groups; mostly smooth, expressive interpretation and pausing, guided by author's meaning and punctuation; appropriate stress and rate with only a few slowdowns.

Reading Rate *(Optional)*

End Time   _____ min. _____ sec.
Start Time   _____ min. _____ sec.
Total Time   _____ min. _____ sec.
Total Seconds _____

(RW × 60) ÷ Total Seconds = _____ Words Per Minute (WPM)

14,940 ÷ _____ = _____ WPM

Recording Forms

Part Two: Comprehension Conversation

Immediately after the oral reading, and before the scoring is complete, you will engage the reader in a comprehension conversation about the benchmark book.

❑ **An open-ended invitation to talk to begin the comprehension conversation**

❑ **A column containing prompts (or probes) to help you elicit the key understandings the reader may not have mentioned.**

❑ **A chart of key understandings, important ideas, or thinking that the reader should have gained from *within* the text (getting the literal meaning by processing words and stated ideas), *beyond* the text (getting the implied meaning and synthesizing information), and *about* the text (engaging in critical analysis and responding to the writer's craft). The chart includes space to write in additional understandings the student demonstrates.**

❑ **A comprehension scoring key that will guide you in scoring each category of key understandings on a four-point (0–3) scale in the score column.**

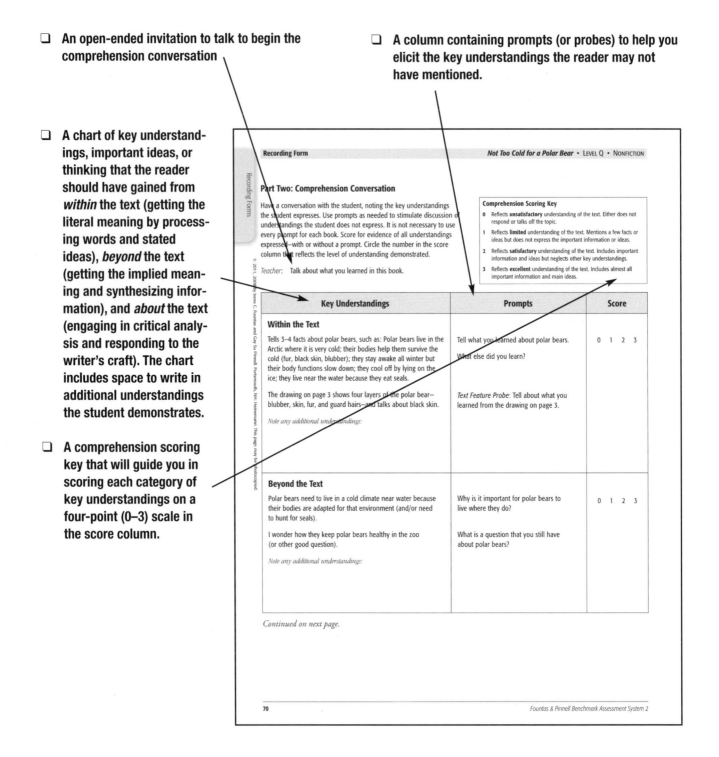

Recording Form

Not Too Cold for a Polar Bear • Level Q • Nonfiction

Recording Forms

Part Two: Comprehension Conversation

Have a conversation with the student, noting the key understandings the student expresses. Use prompts as needed to stimulate discussion of understandings the student does not express. It is not necessary to use every prompt for each book. Score for evidence of all understandings expressed—with or without a prompt. Circle the number in the score column that reflects the level of understanding demonstrated.

Teacher: Talk about what you learned in this book.

Comprehension Scoring Key

0 Reflects **unsatisfactory** understanding of the text. Either does not respond or talks off the topic.

1 Reflects **limited** understanding of the text. Mentions a few facts or ideas but does not express the important information or ideas.

2 Reflects **satisfactory** understanding of the text. Includes important information and ideas but neglects other key understandings.

3 Reflects **excellent** understanding of the text. Includes almost all important information and main ideas.

© 2011, 2008 by Irene C. Fountas and Gay Su Pinnell. Portsmouth, NH: Heinemann. This page may be photocopied.

Key Understandings	Prompts	Score
Within the Text Tells 3–4 facts about polar bears, such as: Polar bears live in the Arctic where it is very cold; their bodies help them survive the cold (fur, black skin, blubber); they stay awake all winter but their body functions slow down; they cool off by lying on the ice; they live near the water because they eat seals. The drawing on page 3 shows four layers of the polar bear—blubber, skin, fur, and guard hairs—and talks about black skin. *Note any additional understandings:*	Tell what you learned about polar bears. What else did you learn? *Text Feature Probe*: Tell about what you learned from the drawing on page 3.	0 1 2 3
Beyond the Text Polar bears need to live in a cold climate near water because their bodies are adapted for that environment (and/or need to hunt for seals). I wonder how they keep polar bears healthy in the zoo (or other good question). *Note any additional understandings:*	Why is it important for polar bears to live where they do? What is a question that you still have about polar bears?	0 1 2 3

Continued on next page.

70

Fountas & Pinnell Benchmark Assessment System 2

Part Three: Writing About Reading

In the condensed version of the Recording Form found in the *Assessment Forms Book*, the writing prompt appears at the bottom of the previous page. In the expanded version, which you can print from the *Assessment Forms CD-ROM*, the prompt appears on its own page, following the introduction shown below.

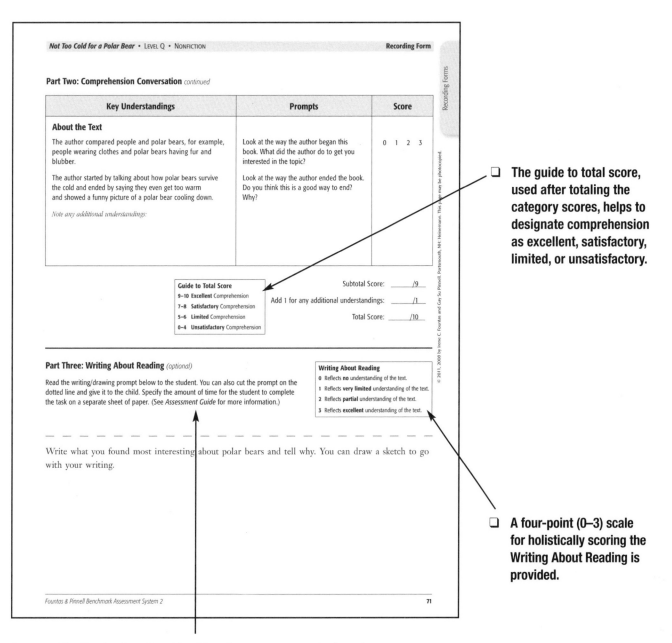

Not Too Cold for a Polar Bear • LEVEL Q • NONFICTION ------ Recording Form

Part Two: Comprehension Conversation *continued*

Key Understandings	Prompts	Score
About the Text		
The author compared people and polar bears, for example, people wearing clothes and polar bears having fur and blubber.	Look at the way the author began this book. What did the author do to get you interested in the topic?	0 1 2 3
The author started by talking about how polar bears survive the cold and ended by saying they even get too warm and showed a funny picture of a polar bear cooling down.	Look at the way the author ended the book. Do you think this is a good way to end? Why?	
Note any additional understandings:		

Guide to Total Score

9–10 **Excellent** Comprehension

7–8 **Satisfactory** Comprehension

5–6 **Limited** Comprehension

0–4 **Unsatisfactory** Comprehension

Subtotal Score: ____ /9

Add 1 for any additional understandings: ____ /1

Total Score: ____ /10

Part Three: Writing About Reading *(optional)*

Read the writing/drawing prompt below to the student. You can also cut the prompt on the dotted line and give it to the child. Specify the amount of time for the student to complete the task on a separate sheet of paper. (See *Assessment Guide* for more information.)

Writing About Reading

0 Reflects **no** understanding of the text.

1 Reflects **very limited** understanding of the text.

2 Reflects **partial** understanding of the text.

3 Reflects **excellent** understanding of the text.

- - - - - - - - - - - - -

Write what you found most interesting about polar bears and tell why. You can draw a sketch to go with your writing.

Fountas & Pinnell Benchmark Assessment System 2 ------ 71

❏ **The guide to total score, used after totaling the category scores, helps to designate comprehension as excellent, satisfactory, limited, or unsatisfactory.**

❏ **A four-point (0–3) scale for holistically scoring the Writing About Reading is provided.**

A prompt for the (optional) writing/drawing assessment designed to provide additional evidence of text comprehension.

▶ Finding a Place to Start

One way to save time and still get excellent assessment data from benchmark testing is to find a good level at which to start. If you do not have sufficient information from the student's previous teacher or school records to judge the starting point for the assessment, you may want to use the Where-to-Start Word Test in the *Assessment Forms Book* or *CD-ROM*. It is a series of lists of increasingly difficult words, organized by grade level and designed to help you approximate the starting point.

You will always have the student read at least three texts as you determine his independent and instructional levels. The hard level is a decision based on all the data.

- ❑ *Independent*—98–100% accuracy with excellent or satisfactory comprehension

- ❑ *Instructional*—95–97% accuracy with excellent or satisfactory comprehension or 98–100% accuracy with limited comprehension

- ❑ *Hard*—below 95% accuracy with any comprehension score

These levels are necessarily relational to each other.

Ideally, you will start the assessment on a level that is easy for the reader. This text:

- ❑ is likely to support effective processing, including comprehension

- ❑ allows the reader to process smoothly and with phrasing

- ❑ allows the reader to start with success

Ideally, you will start with a text that the student can read with 98% accuracy or better. If you do not have an easy level, move down the levels until you do. Then continue the assessment with increasingly more difficult books (higher levels).

You want to find the level at which the student reads with 95–97% accuracy and excellent or satisfactory comprehension (instructional level). Have the student continue to read until he reads with less than 95% accuracy or until he makes the number of errors (E) noted on the front cover of the book he is reading. If the student's comprehension drops below the criterion for limited comprehension, you can also stop moving up the levels.

When that happens, you will usually have three levels: (1) the highest level read independently, (2) the highest level read at an instructional level, and (3) the level that is too difficult for the student (hard text). *Then*, you can use all the information to make a decision about the Recommended Placement level—the best level for instructional reading.

We summarize the kinds of starting-point information you can use from two different kinds of literacy programs in Figure 2.1. If your students have been learning to read in a leveled books program, use the column on the left. If they are learning to read in a core or basal program, refer to the right column.

If you are assessing the student at the beginning of the school year or when a student first enters your classroom, first consider information from last year's teacher and the student records. In Figure 2.2 we provide some thinking that will help you choose a place to start. Remember that students are reading previously *unseen* text with only a minimal introduction to the text. The reading level they are able to achieve will give you a very good idea of the kind of texts they can read without teacher support. If you are working with an English language learner at the beginning of the year (or one who is new to the school), you may not have enough information about language proficiency to determine a place to start. Conversing with the student over several days and informally trying out a few leveled texts will provide more information. You will want to follow your district policy regarding language proficiency requirements and the administration of standardized tests prior to administering the *Benchmark Assessment System 2*. We believe you will find the small, precise differences in the benchmark book levels very useful in gathering information about the reading skills of English language learners.

If you are assessing at the middle or end of the school year, one of the best sources of information about where to start comes from the student's current reading performance in the classroom. If you are the classroom or literacy teacher and you have worked with the student recently, then you probably have a good idea of his instructional level. If you are not the classroom or literacy teacher, you can ask for advice about the level the student is reading. Figure 2.2 shows how you might determine a starting level at the beginning,

Sources of Information for Determining a Starting Point

Leveled Books Program	Core or Basal Program
Use records or book charts from previous school year.	Use records from previous school year (see Figure 2.3 for conversion to Fountas and Pinnell level).
Identify books the student is reading independently *(see Fountas & Pinnell Leveled Book List, K–8+* [Heinemann, 2009] or *fountasandpinnellleveledbooks.com*) for level, and start one level lower.	Identify books the student is reading independently (see *Fountas & Pinnell Leveled Book List, K–8+* [Heinemann 2009] or *fountasandpinnellleveledbooks.com*) for level, and start one level lower.
Identify instructional-level books the student is reading in a reading group and start one level lower.	Identify instructional-level books the student is reading (see Figure for conversion to Fountas & Pinnell levels).
Use the Where-to-Start Word Test (*Assessment Forms Book* and *CD-ROM*; Optional Assessments: Student Forms book).	Use the Where-to-Start Word Test (*Assessment Forms Book* and *CD-ROM; Optional Assessments: Student Forms* book).
For English language learners, consider any information you have on language proficiency assessments. All of the above information will also be helpful in determining where to start.	For English language learners, consider any information you have on language proficiency assessments. All of the above information will also be helpful in determining where to start.

FIGURE 2.1 Determining a starting point

Approximate Start Level Based on Grade-Level Performance

Grade	Reading Performance *(how the child is reading relative to expected grade-level performance)*	Time of Year			Approximate Benchmark Assessment Starting Level
		Beg.	Mid.	End	
Grade 3	Below level	X			J
	Below level		X		K
	Below level			X	L
	On level	X			M
	On level		X		N
	On level			X	O
	Above level	X			P
	Above level		X		Q
	Above level			X	Q

FIGURE 2.2 Approximate start level based on grade-level performance

continues

Grade	Reading Performance *(how the child is reading relative to expected grade-level performance)*	Time of Year			Approximate Benchmark Assessment Starting Level
		Beg.	Mid.	End	
Grade 4	Below level	X			N
	Below level		X		O
	Below level			X	P
	On level	X			P
	On level		X		Q
	On level			X	R
	Above level	X			S
	Above level		X		T
	Above level			X	U
Grade 5	Below level	X			Q
	Below level		X		R
	Below level			X	S
	On level	X			S
	On level		X		T
	On level			X	U
	Above level	X			V
	Above level		X		W
	Above level			X	X
Grade 6	Below level	X			S
	Below level		X		T
	Below level			X	U
	On level	X			V
	On level		X		W
	On level			X	X
	Above level	X			X
	Above level		X		Y
	Above level			X	Y

FIGURE 2.2 *continued*

Grade	Reading Performance *(how the child is reading relative to expected grade-level performance)*	Time of Year			Approximate Benchmark Assessment Starting Level
		Beg.	Mid.	End	
Grade 7/8	Below level	X			T
	Below level		X		U
	Below level			X	V
	On level	X			W
	On level		X		X
	On level			X	Y
	Above level	X			X
	Above level		X		Y
	Above level			X	Y

* If L is too difficult for the reader, go to *Benchmark Assessment System 1* and select a starting point based on the classroom teacher's estimate of student performance.

** If a student can read level Z with 98% or greater accuracy, satisfactory or excellent comprehension, and satisfactory fluency (Independent level), you will want to give the student opportunities to read a variety of books at X, Y, Z, or Z+ that offer interesting topics and a broad array of genres. Be sure to consider appropriateness of content for the age group.

middle, and end of the school year when the student's general reading performance is known.

If you are using a basal or core program, you can also use Figure 2.3 to help you decide where to start. It will be helpful to think about the level of the basal core text or anthology your students have completed successfully and its correspondence to the Fountas and Pinnell levels.

After determining the starting level—the highest level at which you expect the student will read with relative ease—locate the appropriate books in the box and make sure you have copies of the Recording Forms for books at the selected level and for the levels before and after. The fiction and nonfiction texts for each level are listed in Figure 2.4.

At each level, there is a fiction and a nonfiction text. The level of the book appears in two places: (1)

on the front cover in the lower left corner (Figure 2.5) and (2) on the back cover in the lower left corner. These labels will help you easily locate the appropriate book for the levels you have chosen. The genre of the book (fiction or nonfiction) is printed under the level on the lower left corner of the back cover. Fiction and nonfiction pairs have been matched so that if a student can read one genre, he is likely to be able to read the other. We recommend that you alternate the fiction and nonfiction texts as you move up the gradient during an assessment conference, so if you begin with the fiction title, move on to a nonfiction title at the next level tested. This will give you a picture of how the student is performing in both genres and provide a reliable instructional level. It is not necessary (or recommended) to have a student read both fiction and nonfiction texts on a level.

Approximate Start Level for Basal or Core Texts	
Last Basal/Core Level the Student Completed	**Approximate Fountas & Pinnell Level to Start Testing**
Kindergarten	A
Grade 1 pre-primer (1)	B
Grade 1 pre-primer (2)	B
Grade 1 pre-primer (3)	C
Grade 1 primer	D
Grade 1 late	E
Grade 2 early	G
Grade 2 late	K
Grade 3 early	L
Grade 3 late	N
Grade 4 early	O
Grade 4 late	Q
Grade 5 early	R
Grade 5 late	T
Grade 6 early	U
Grade 6 late	V
Grade 7–8	W

FIGURE 2.3 Approximate start level for basal or core texts

Benchmark 2 Assessment System Books		
Level	**Fiction**	**Nonfiction**
L	Ernie Learns	Hang On, Baby Monkey
M	Saving Up	City Hawks
N	Vanessa's Butterfly	Dogs at Work
O	The New Girl	Snake Myths
P	Plenty of Pets	Animal Instincts
Q	A Secret Home	Not Too Cold for a Polar Bear
R	The Election	Fishing Smarts
S	Could Be Worse	Amazing Animal Adaptations
T	"Get a Horse!"	Why Do Wolves Howl?
U	Canyon Mystery	Earthquakes
V	A Call for Change	Tsunamis: Mighty Ocean Waves
W	How I Spent My Summer Vacation	Obituary: Coretta Scott King 1927–2006
X	A Weighty Decision	The Internet: Getting Connected
Y	Saying Goodbye	The International Space Station
Z	Surviving the Blitz	The Train at the Top of the World

FIGURE 2.4 Benchmark Assessment System 2 books

▶ Using the Assessment at-a-Glance Chart

For a quick reference, we suggest you copy the Assessment at-a-Glance chart on the inside cover of this book, or print it from the *Assessment Forms Book* or *CD-ROM*. The following sections take you step-by-step through the assessment conference.

▶ Introducing the Benchmark Book

Read the title of the book. Then read the standardized introduction to the reader. The standardized introduction to the text is printed on the colored wave at the bottom of the front cover (Figure 2.5) and on the Recording Form. The introductions were created and field-tested to give the reader a start on the book and to ensure that each student would begin the assessment with the same introductory material. For the assessment to be standardized, take care not to embellish the introduction or enter into any additional conversation with the student about the text.

If you are using the *F & P Calculator/ Stopwatch*, enter the number of running words (RW), which is printed on the book cover (Figure 2.5) and the Recording Form. The number of running words is the exact number of words that the student reads orally. A black square, or a stopping point, appears in the text at the point the child should stop reading orally (Figure 2.6). The RW *does not* include the title of the book, captions under pictures, or diagram labels. In nonfiction books, it *does* include headings and subheadings. This number is used to calculate the percentage of accuracy with which the student has read and the reading rate, which is the words per minute. The back cover has the total running words (TRW) for the book.

Note the number of errors printed under the running words on the front cover (Figure 2.5). It indicates the point at which the reader's accuracy has gone below 95%. When the accuracy rate goes below 95%, the text is probably too hard. Keeping track of the number of errors as a student reads will allow you to switch to a lower level if the reader is having much difficulty. When it is evident the student is reading a hard text, discontinue the reading because the text is much too difficult.

Not Too Cold for a Polar Bear
by Kitty Colton

Polar bears adapt to their environment. Read to find out how these interesting animals survive the cold.

Q
RW 249
E 15
Fountas and Pinnell Benchmark Assessment System 2

Introduction

Number of errors

Running words

FIGURE 2.5 Benchmark book cover

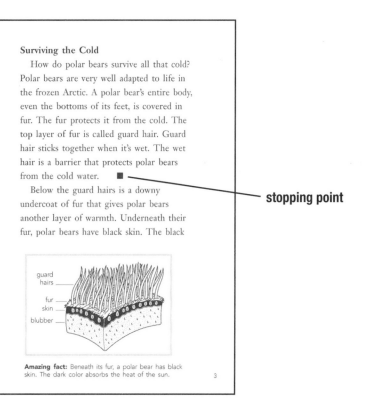

polar bear. The polar bear is the largest of the eight species, or kinds, of bears. Polar bears live only in very cold climates like the Arctic region.

The word Arctic tells you that the polar bear's environment is icy cold. In the winter, temperatures can drop to minus 50 degrees. As if that's not enough reason to shiver, polar bears also spend a great deal of time in the icy Arctic Ocean. Polar bears are the largest predators on land. They mainly hunt and eat seals, and because seals are usually found in the ocean, polar bears are often found in or near the ocean, too. They are excellent swimmers.

Polar bears are classified as marine mammals.

2

Surviving the Cold

How do polar bears survive all that cold? Polar bears are very well adapted to life in the frozen Arctic. A polar bear's entire body, even the bottoms of its feet, is covered in fur. The fur protects it from the cold. The top layer of fur is called guard hair. Guard hair sticks together when it's wet. The wet hair is a barrier that protects polar bears from the cold water. ■

Below the guard hairs is a downy undercoat of fur that gives polar bears another layer of warmth. Underneath their fur, polar bears have black skin. The black

stopping point

guard hairs
fur
skin
blubber

Amazing fact: Beneath its fur, a polar bear has black skin. The dark color absorbs the heat of the sun.

3

FIGURE 2.6 Stopping point for oral reading

▶ Coding Oral Reading

Have the student begin to read the text orally. If you want to measure reading rate, start the time on the *F & P Calculator/Stopwatch*. Alternatively, you can start your stopwatch or use a clock with a second hand and record the starting time on the Recording Form. Have the student read to the stopping point and then continue to read silently.

You can use this time to write comments and summarize the reading behaviors you observe.

Code the oral reading behavior on the Recording Form as the student reads. The page number and typed text on the Recording Form correspond exactly to the benchmark book, and there is space to record the student's errors and self-corrections (Figure 2.7). Record your observations using the conventions from Figure 2.8. (The *Professional Development DVD* provides individualized training on the coding conventions.) Figure 2.7 shows how the coding might look partway through a student's oral reading of *Not Too Cold for a Polar Bear*. In this case, the teacher did not place a check mark over

each word read correctly. You may choose to use a check mark to indicate that the child has read a word correctly, but usually the child reads too fast so marking errors, repetitions, and tolds is more efficient.

Be sure to listen to how the reading sounds while you code errors, since you will simultaneously be evaluating accuracy (percentage of errors), judging fluency (the way the reading sounds), and using the timer to determine reading time. With especially fluent readers, you may get behind in your coding. If you get very far behind, you can ask the reader to stop and wait a moment at the end of a page. Or, if your coding is mixed up, you can ask the student to start over at a good point.

When the student has reached the stopping point, stop timing and record the time on the form.

▶ Counting Errors to Get an Accuracy Score

Accuracy, or the percentage of total words the student has read correctly, is only one indicator of a reader's ability to process a text, but it is an important one. Students may read a text with high accuracy but understand it only superficially. They may read a text with lower accuracy but remember enough details to get the gist. But in general, there is a clear, positive relationship between accuracy and understanding.

Since this is a standardized assessment, use established guidelines to count errors and assess all of your students in the same way. In fact, it is important for all teachers in a school and district to use the same system. The error-counting conventions in Figure 2.8 will help you standardize the assessment for all students so that progress can be accurately documented. The chart shows the conventions and how to look at each behavior to count errors and self-corrections.

Total the errors and self-corrections in each line of text separately. A self-correction is *not* an error. Then count the errors by going down the column (Figure 2.9).

Next, figure out the accuracy score. Enter the number of errors into the calculator and tap the accuracy button to get the percentage of words read accurately. Alternatively, on each Recording Form, you will find an accuracy rate bar (Figure 2.10). This will help you instantly find the accuracy rate. Just count the errors and circle the accuracy that is relevant. Next,

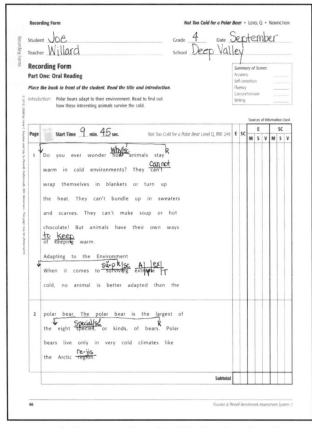

FIGURE 2.7 Coding oral reading of *Not Too Cold for a Polar Bear*

Coding Errors and Self-Corrections in Oral Reading

Behavior	Coding	Error Counting
Accurate reading	no mark OR environments ✓	No error
Substitution, not corrected	worry / wonder	One error
Substitution, self-corrected	worry / wonder |SC	No error; one SC
Multiple substitutions, not corrected	adopt | adopted / adapted	One error per word in the text
Missing the same word several times in a text	Speckles / Species spiced / species	One error each time missed
Errors on names and proper nouns—repeated during the reading	area / Arctic ark / Arctic	One error the first time; no error after that even if different substitutions are made for the nouns
Contractions (reads as two words or reads two words as contraction)	Cannot / Can't they're / they are	One error
Multiple substitutions, self-corrected	adopt | adopted |SC / adapted	No error; one SC
Insertion of a word	✓ very ✓ / ∧	One error per word inserted
Omission of a word	✓ only̅ ✓	One error per word
Skipping a line	f̅rom t̅he c̅old w̅ater	One error per word
Repetition	R R2	No error
Appeal followed by "You try it" then student reads word correctly	A environments |Y |✓	No error
Appeal followed by "You try it" then student makes substitution	A environments |Y | endings	One error
Appeal followed by "You try it" then a Told	A environments |Y | T	One error
Told (teacher supplied word)	environments |T	One error
"Sounding out" followed by correct reading	O-n-ly ✓ / Only	No error; no SC
"Sounding out" followed by incorrect or no further reading	O-n-ly | once / only	One error
Sounding the first letter and then saying the word correctly	O ✓ / only Sp ✓ / Species	No error; no SC
Sounding the first letter incorrectly and then saying the word correctly	W |SC / only	No error; no SC

Coding system developed by Marie Clay as part of the running record system in *An Observation Survey of Early Literacy Achievement. Revised Second Edition,* Heinemann. 2006

FIGURE 2.8 Error and self-correction coding

count the self-corrections and write the total number on the self-corrections line.

If you determine the student is reading a level with less than 95% accuracy, consider whether or not to continue with the comprehension conversation. If accuracy is below but close to 95% and there are repeated errors, the student may have understood enough that the comprehension conversation will provide important information. However, if the accuracy rate is well below the criterion and the student had much difficulty, end the assessment. If you determine she made enough errors to make the text hard early in the reading, there is no need to have her finish reading the text.

Special Cases for Assessing Accuracy

❏ If the student skips a full page of print, intervene and tell him to read the page. Do not count this as an error.

❏ If the student inserts many words, you could have more errors than the running words on a page. This is likely to happen only at the lower levels. In this case, score the page as having the same number of errors as words on the page.

❏ No matter how many attempts a student makes at a word, score only one error for each word.

❏ Occasionally, especially at the lower levels, a student will begin to "invent" text, that is, tell the story by making up his own language, disregarding the print. If this happens, write inventing at the top of the sheet and stop the assessment. In this case, the text is a hard text.

❏ When a reader is processing the text satisfactorily but gets mixed up and loses his place, just ask him to start over at a good starting point and begin your coding again. Do not count this as an error.

❏ If you are using this assessment with a student who is an English language learner, you will need to be sure that the student speaks English well enough to understand the directions and the introduction, enter into conversation with you, process the print, and understand the text. Estimate the level and move down if necessary. If the student seems confused, read the introduction again. You can also paraphrase directions as well as the comprehension conversation to support greater understanding.

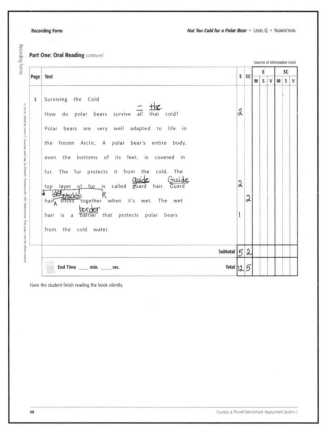

FIGURE 2.9 Counting errors and self-corrections

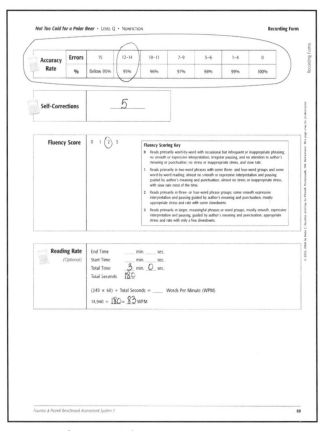

FIGURE 2.10 Accuracy rate bar

▶ Evaluating Fluency

Immediately after the student finishes reading orally, rate fluency by making a note at the bottom of the coded text about how the reading sounded and circling the rating on the fluency scoring key.

A fluency score reflects how consistently students are interpreting the meaning of the text with their voices. When reading at the independent or instructional level, students should read along at a reasonable pace (not too slow or too fast). At the instructional level, you can expect fluent, phrased reading, though at the independent level, reading will be more consistently fluent throughout the text. Use the following guidelines to rate readers' fluency. A high score indicates that the reader is

❏ phrasing, or grouping words, as evident through intonation, stress, and pauses as well as through emphasizing the beginnings and endings of phrases by rise and fall of pitch or by pausing

❏ adhering to the author's syntax or sentence structure, reflecting their comprehension of the language

❏ being expressive; the student's reading reflects feeling, anticipation, and character development as well as stress on the appropriate words

❏ using punctuation to cue pausing or altering the voice.

A simple four-point (0–3) fluency scoring key is included on the form and shown in Figure 2.11. Score fluency from 0–3 according to this key. (An optional, expanded Six Dimensions Fluency Rubric is included in the *Assessment Forms Book* and *CD-ROM*.)

For reliable assessment across your school or district, view the examples of oral readings on the *Professional Development DVD* with a group of colleagues. Reach agreement on typical examples of ratings and then check with the ratings we have given. Once your group has built an internal sense of what each rating means, you can quickly write down a rating for each record. Remember that the rating is not a label for an individual reader. It evaluates a single reading of a particular text.

Typically, a reader will demonstrate fluency and phrasing on texts that are easier (a score of 3). On more challenging texts, the same reader will slow down occasionally for problem solving but become more fluent on easier stretches of text (a score of 2). On texts that are too hard for the reader, the process will break down so that it sounds dysfluent most of the time (a score of 1). There are some readers, however, who have developed a habit of very slow reading. These readers may read with high accuracy but get low scores for fluency (a score of 0 or 1). On the other hand, some readers may gloss over errors or make careless errors, sounding fluent (a score of 3) but read with low accuracy (below 95%). Each of these readers needs different instruction. Your diagnosis of a reader's fluency, viewed from the perspective of accuracy and comprehension scores, will provide information to inform teaching. Think about the reading as a whole and make a judgment as to the extent it was fluent and phrased. Remember that on an instructional-level text, the reader may slow down to problem solve and then speed up again.

Fluency Scoring Key

0   Reads primarily word-by-word with occasional but infrequent or inappropriate phrasing; no smooth or expressive interpretation, irregular pausing, and no attention to author's meaning or punctuation; no stress or inappropriate stress, and slow rate.

1   Reads primarily in two-word phrases with some three- and four- word groups and some word-by-word reading; almost no smooth, expressive interpretation or pausing guided by author's meaning and punctuation; almost no stress or inappropriate stress, with slow rate most of the time.

2   Reads primarily in three- or four-word phrase groups; some smooth, expressive interpretation and pausing guided by author's meaning and punctuation; mostly appropriate stress and rate with some slowdowns.

3   Reads primarily in larger, meaningful phrases or word groups; mostly smooth, expressive interpretation and pausing, guided by author's meaning and punctuation; appropriate stress and rate with only a few slowdowns.

FIGURE 2.11 Benchmark Assessment System fluency scoring key

Fluency and English Language Learners

It is important to note that when they read orally, many English language learners will not sound precisely the same as native speakers of the language. The cadence of the reading may vary slightly, or different words may be stressed. There may be pauses to search for the meaning of an English word or to think in the individual's first language. Phonetic variations that do not interfere greatly with comprehension or fluency can be ignored. Judge based on knowledge of the student.

Also, it is good to remember that sometimes an individual may sound fluent when reading in a new language because she has learned to decode the words. You will want to check understanding very carefully. The fact that a reader can decode the words and read with a fair amount of fluency does not guarantee understanding, and that is true of all learners.

▶ Guiding the Comprehension Conversation

Too often, comprehension is assessed by asking a student a series of questions which are checked against a series of answers provided in a teacher guide. This can lead to students' thinking that their purpose for reading is to answer their teacher's questions correctly. For *Benchmark Assessment System 2*, we have constructed a different process—one that will allow you to gather evidence of comprehension while engaging in a conversation with the student about the text.

The purpose of the comprehension conversation is to gain behavioral evidence of a student's understanding. Similar to a reading conference, in the comprehension conversation portion of this assessment a student reads texts, converses with you about them, then he may write in response to what he's read. As a general rule, you only need to complete the comprehension conversation on an independent and instructional level for each student. You will usually decide not to complete it for his hard level, especially if you have strong evidence that he did not understand it (e.g., meaningless errors). Also, consider the accuracy rate.

The comprehension conversation can be found in Part Two of the Recording Form. Begin with a general prompt provided on the form to elicit the student's thinking. It will either ask him to "talk about what you learned in this book" or "talk about what happened in this story." (Figure 2.12) The idea is to open a conversation that will allow you to see what the text has prompted him to think. Be sure he understands that he is expected to talk—some readers may think they are supposed to just listen or answer questions. You can make general comments like "Say more about that," "Tell more," "What else?," or "Why?" to get a student to talk more easily. Often, just pausing a few seconds more to listen will prompt a student to say more.

Following the general prompt, the Recording Form for each benchmark book provides a list of key understandings and prompts. If you already have ample evidence of understanding, you will not want to use all of the prompts. The key understandings are categorized and provide evidence that a reader is thinking:

- ❑ *Within the Text:* The reader is gaining the literal meaning of the text through solving the words; monitoring her own understanding and accuracy; searching for and using information; remembering information in summary form; adjusting for purpose and type of text; and sustaining fluent reading.

- ❑ *Beyond the Text:* The reader is making predictions; making connections with prior knowledge, personal experience, and other texts; inferring what is implied but not stated; and synthesizing new information by changing her own ideas.

- ❑ *About the Text:* The reader is thinking about the literary elements of the text; recognizing elements of the writer's craft; and thinking critically about the text.

The prompts are written to parallel the key understandings and are designed to help facilitate the conversation if students don't mention them on their own. But if a student has already provided details, you will not need to prompt for the information again.

As a student shares what she's learned from a book or tells what a story is about, place a check next to the key understandings she mentions (Figure 2.13). Remember, you are not looking for word-for-word repetition of the understanding, but rather for an indication that she understands a key idea. If she does

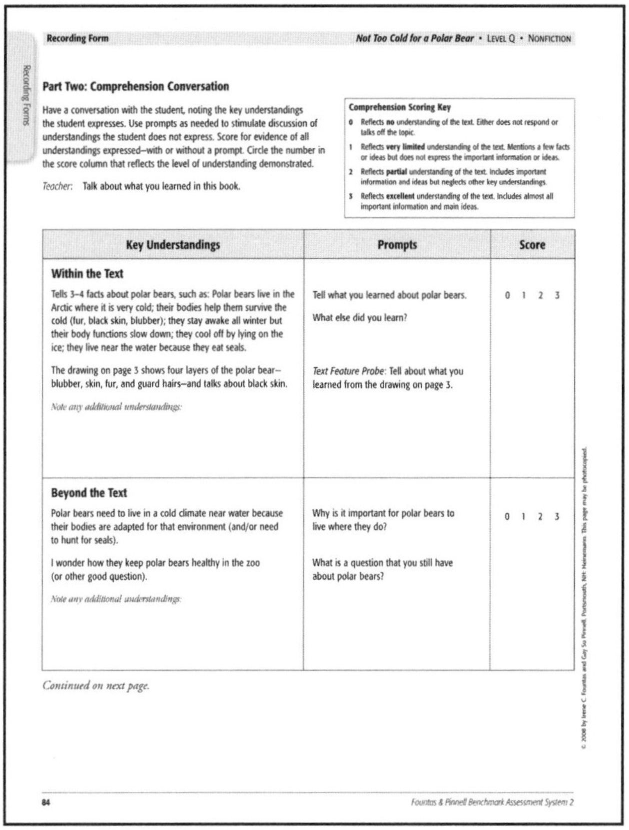

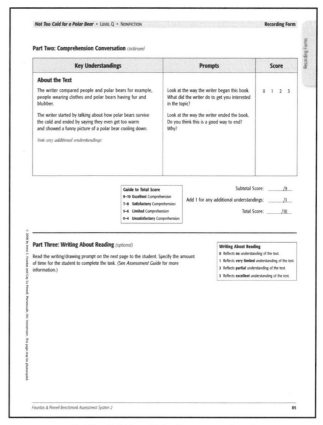

FIGURE 2.12a *Not Too Cold for a Polar Bear* comprehension conversation

FIGURE 2.12b *Not Too Cold for a Polar Bear* comprehension conversation

not mention some of the key understandings on her own, use the prompts to probe further. Feel free to paraphrase the prompts if needed. Ask the student to talk more about a topic if needed, then check it off the form. Do not judge her response lower because you needed to prompt her thinking. Prompted responses are just as correct as spontaneous ones. At the same time, avoid "leading" the student to an answer. Just use the prompts in a conversational way and if they don't elicit a response, move on.

Note: It is acceptable for a student to search back in the book for answers to prompts if he initiates the action. Leave the book in front of him but don't make the suggestion. If he reads the text directly from the book in response to a prompt, ask him to answer in his own words.

If during a comprehension conversation, a student discusses insights and information that are not reflected in the key understandings provided, jot down the additional understandings he volunteers on the form. You can evaluate them later as part of the scoring.

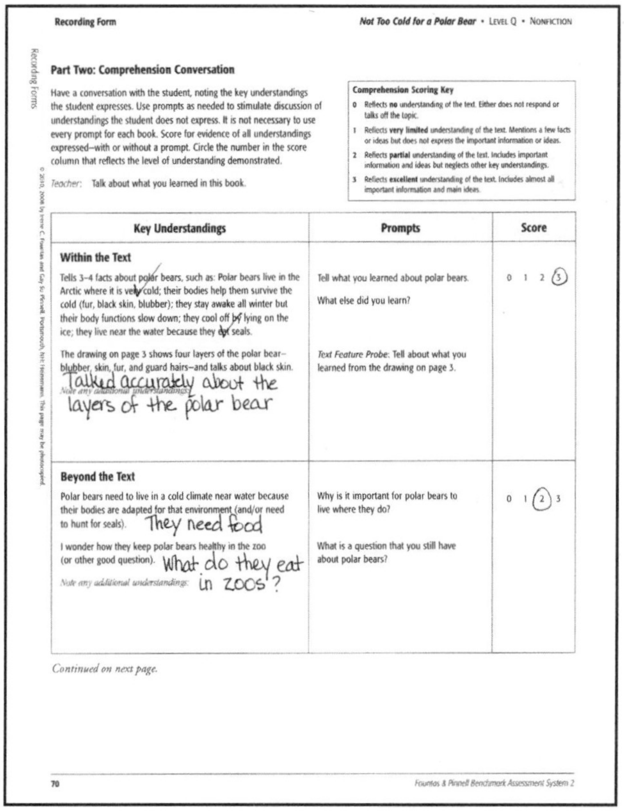

FIGURE 2.13 Recording evidence during the comprehension conversation

As you engage in this process with English language learners, make an extra effort to draw them into a conversation, keeping in mind that they may understand more than they can explain in English. If you understand a student's native language, it is a great idea to converse for a few minutes using that language. She may even respond first in her native language if it helps her process the information. If that happens, make a note of it on the form. Your primary task is to determine whether or not she understands the material well enough, not the language she uses to express that understanding. Sketching or writing may also be helpful to English language learners in expressing understandings. You can consider either of these in making a final decision about a student's comprehension.

▶ Scoring the Comprehension Conversation

After the comprehension conversation, use the scoring rubric in the Comprehension Scoring Key provided on the Recording Form (Figure 2.14) to judge the degree to which a student has demonstrated understanding of the key ideas in thinking within, beyond, and about the text. This key is not designed for you to "count" the number of correct answers in each category. Instead, make an overall judgment using the evidence in each of the areas as to whether the child showed unsatisfactory, limited, satisfactory, or excellent understanding of the information. As you circle the scores on the rubric, be sure that you have clear evidence of understanding, as this score will be an important indicator of the kind of teaching you need to do later.

Next, score additional understandings. Comprehension is such an individual factor that it is difficult to list the exact understandings that every reader should have. Each of us may take something different from a text depending on our own life experiences. If a student comes up with one or more unique and valuable understandings, add an additional point to their final score.

Note: At levels L–Z, the total possible score is 10 points: 3 points for *Within the Text*, 3 points for *Beyond the Text*, 3 points for *About the Text*, and 1 point for any *additional understandings*.

As a final step, add up the subscores and use the Guide to Total Score (Figure 2.15) to determine if the student's overall understanding is unsatisfactory, limited, satisfactory, or excellent.

Comprehension Scoring Key

0   Reflects **unsatisfactory** understanding of the text. Either does not respond or talks off the topic.

1   Reflects **limited** understanding of the text. Mentions a few facts or ideas but does not express the important information or ideas.

2   Reflects **satisfactory** understanding of the text. Includes important information and ideas but neglects other key understandings.

3   Reflects **excellent** understanding of the text. Includes almost all important information and main ideas.

FIGURE 2.14 Comprehension scoring key

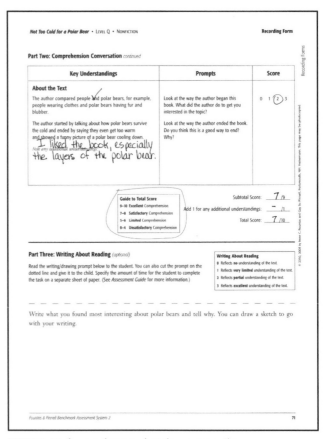

FIGURE 2.15 A scored comprehension conversation

Making the Most of the Comprehension Conversation

After practicing a few of these comprehension conversations, you will find that the process is both easy and enjoyable. They are similar to the kinds of conversations you have every day with students in reading groups or reading conferences. Over time, your students will learn how to spontaneously offer their thinking about a text—and that is a valuable ability to have.

What is a conversation like? If we observed you and a friend, we would likely see something like this:

1. You say something.

2. Your friend comments on what you said.

3. You add more.

4. Your friend asks a question.

5. You answer and make another comment.

6. Your friend says more.

We contrast this scene with a series of continuous questions that are asked one after another. The point is that real conversation does involve some questions but not a steady barrage. The conversation is a flow of talk, back and forth. Figure 2.16 summarizes some of the ways to have a good conversation.

We summarize some of the keys to a good comprehension conversation about *City Hawks* in Figure 2.17. The transcript of the conversation is followed by a coded Recording Form reflecting that conversation. Afterwards, we explain the teacher's intentions as she participated in this conversation.

As she initiated this conversation, the teacher was looking for evidence of thinking within the text, that the student understood and remembered the important information from the text by telling three to four important facts. For example:

❏ A hawk built a nest on a building in New York.

❏ He raised baby birds.

❏ People liked to watch them.

❏ Some people didn't like so many people watching the building.

❏ They took the nest down.

❏ People made them put the nest back.

❏ The graphic on page 4 of *City Hawks* shows that the building is across the street from the park. This is important because Pale Male can hunt for food in the park.

Keys to a Good Comprehension Conversation

- Be sure you have read and thought about the information in the book. If you know the text well, you can discuss it better. (The benchmark books text characteristics in Appendix A will help here.)

- Read the key understandings and prompts prior to the assessment so you are very familiar with them. You need not use every prompt with each student.

- Tell students beforehand that you are going to be meeting with each one of them to listen to them read, so you will be able to help them as readers. Explain that you will ask them to read a short book and then you want them to tell all their thinking about what they read. Sometimes you will ask questions to help them talk more about the book, but you want them to do as much talking about the book as they can.

- Invite the student to share his thinking and be sure to leave some silence before jumping in. It is very important to provide enough "wait time" for students, especially English language learners, to muster their thoughts and put them into words.

- Pick and choose prompts that get the child talking more.

- Rephrase comments or prompt questions to be sure the student understands.

- Use open-ended probes such as "tell more," "say more," "why?" or "what else?"

- Think of different ways to ask the same question or get at the information.

- Allow the child to look back in the text if the student initiates it. If he starts to read the book again, stop him by saying, "Just tell about the ideas in your own words."

- Use an encouraging tone when inviting the student to talk more.

FIGURE 2.16 Keys to a good comprehension conversation

Teacher — Student Interaction	Teacher Scoring
Invites conversation	**Within the Text**
T: Talk about what happened in the story.	
S: There was a hawk. I think his name was Pale Male. He couldn't find a place to build his nest in the country, so he went to a big apartment building and built a nest.	0 1 2 ③
Probes further.	
T: What else?	
S: He wasn't supposed to have a nest on the building and they took it down—or the stuff it was on, they took it down.	
Probes further.	
T: Then what happened?	
S: They got mad—the people who liked the hawks—and so they had to put it up again.	
Asks for information about the end.	
T: And what happened at the end?	
S: He gets to stay there and build a nest and have baby hawks.	
Asks for interpretation of a graphic.	
T: Tell what you learned from the drawing on page 4.	
S: You can see here that the building is right next to the park, so that's how he found it.	
Asks for inference.	**Beyond the Text**
T: Why did some people want the nest taken down?	
S: They were maybe scared because all those people were looking at them with binoculars. They were really looking at the hawks but also the people who lived there.	0 1 2 ③
Asks for inference.	
T: I wonder why they wanted to look at Pale Male and his babies.	
S: They don't get to see baby birds because normally he would build the nest in the country. So it was neat to see them.	
Asks for comparison.	
T: So, what were the two different sides in the argument—the two ways different people felt about Pale Male?	
S: Some people liked him and wanted him to stay so they could watch him, but people who lived there didn't want the nest so the crowds would go away.	
Probes further.	
T: Anything else?	
S: Some people like birds but some people don't.	

FIGURE 2.17 Sample comprehension conversation, *City Hawks,* level M

The student does not have to remember every detail of the text. That would not be efficient. If readers are struggling to remember everything, their minds will work only on literal comprehension. They will remember both important and irrelevant details; enjoyment will be decreased and higher level comprehension will suffer. But it is important for them to grasp essential information.

The teacher was also looking for evidence of thinking beyond the text—what the reader inferred, connected to prior knowledge, predicted from context, and synthesized new knowledge. For example:

- ❑ Hawks live in the country, but Pale Male built his nest in the city.
- ❑ Pale Male built his nest on the building because it was near the park but safe.
- ❑ People liked to watch Pale Male and his babies because they do not get to see hawks in the city (or other reason consistent with the text).
- ❑ The nest was removed because people in the building didn't like being watched all the time with binoculars.
- ❑ Some people liked Pale Male and his nest, and some people didn't like him.

Finally, in the comprehension conversation, the teacher was looking for evidence that the student could think *about the text.* For example:

- ❑ The writer first gave some information about hawks and then told the story in chronological order.
- ❑ The writer presented two sides of an argument.
- ❑ The writer seems to support the idea that the nest should stay on the building.

Figure 2.18 shows how the teacher scored this conversation.

Recording Form — *City Hawks* • Level M • Nonfiction

Recording Forms

Part Two: Comprehension Conversation

Have a conversation with the student, noting the key understandings the student expresses. Use prompts as needed to stimulate discussion of understandings the student does not express. Score for evidence of all understandings expressed–with or without a prompt. Circle the number in the score column that reflects the level of understanding demonstrated.

Teacher: Talk about what you learned in this book.

Comprehension Scoring Key
0 Reflects **no** understanding of the text. Either does not respond or talks off the topic.
1 Reflects **very limited** understanding of the text. Mentions a few facts or ideas but does not express the important information or ideas.
2 Reflects **partial** understanding of the text. Includes important information and ideas but neglects other key understandings.
3 Reflects **excellent** understanding of the text. Includes almost all important information and main ideas.

Key Understandings	Prompts	Score
Within the Text		
✓Summarizes the story, including 3–4 important facts in sequence, such as: ✓A hawk built a nest on a building in New York; ✓he raised baby birds; people liked to watch them; ✓some people didn't like so many people watching the building; ✓they took the nest down; people made them put the nest back.	Explain what happened in this story. What was the problem? What else happened? What happened at the end?	0 1 2 (3)
✓The drawing on page 4 shows that the tall buildings are just across from the park.	*Text Feature Probe*: Tell what you learned from the drawing on page 4.	
Note any additional understandings: The hawk couldn't find anywhere to build his nest in the country.		
Beyond the Text		
✓Hawks usually live in the country, but Pale Male built his nest in the city.	What was unusual about Pale Male's nest in this true story?	0 1 2 (3)
Pale Male built his nest on the building because it was near the park but safe.	Why did Pale Male build his nest on the building?	
✓People liked to watch Pale Male and his babies because they do not get to see hawks in the city (or other reason consistent with the text).	Why did people like to watch the hawks so much?	
✓The nest was removed because people in the building didn't like being watched all the time with binoculars.	Why did some people want the nest taken down?	
✓Some people liked Pale Male and his nest and some people did not like him.	What was the disagreement different people had about Pale Male?	
Note any additional understandings:		

Continued on next page.

© 2008 by Irene C. Fountas and Gay Su Pinnell. Portsmouth, NH: Heinemann. This page may be photocopied.

28 — *Fountas & Pinnell Benchmark Assessment System 2*

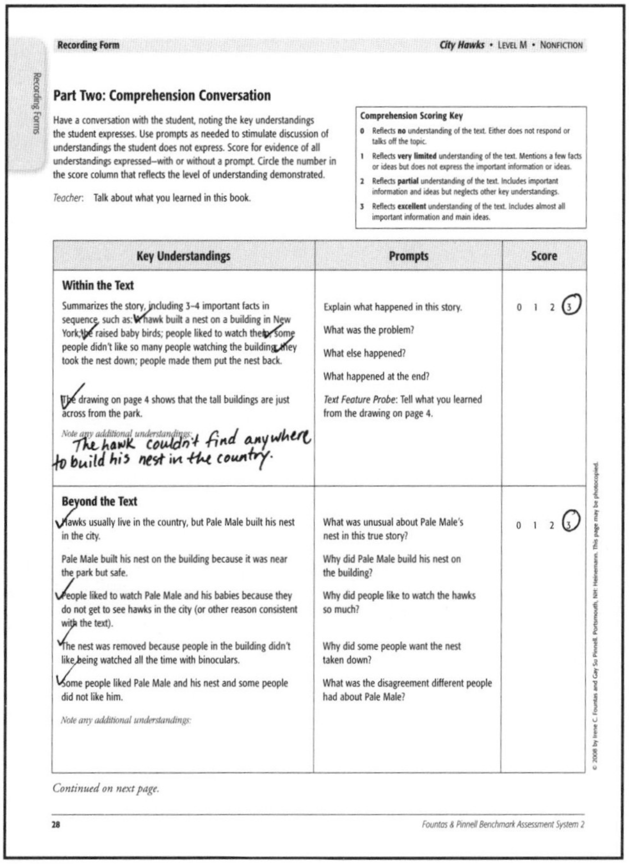

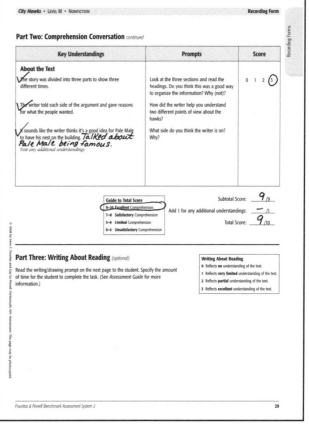

FIGURE 2.18a Coded Comprehension Conversation for *City Hawks*

City Hawks • Level M • Nonfiction — Recording Form

Recording Forms

Part Two: Comprehension Conversation *continued*

Key Understandings	Prompts	Score
About the Text		
✓The story was divided into three parts to show three different times.	Look at the three sections and read the headings. Do you think this was a good way to organize the information? Why (not)?	0 1 2 (3)
✓The writer told each side of the argument and gave reasons for what the people wanted.	How did the writer help you understand two different points of view about the hawks?	
✓It sounds like the writer thinks it's a good idea for Pale Male to have his nest on the building. Talked about Pale Male being famous.	What side do you think the writer is on? Why?	
Note any additional understandings:		

Guide to Total Score
(9–10 **Excellent** Comprehension)
7–8 **Satisfactory** Comprehension
5–6 **Limited** Comprehension
0–4 **Unsatisfactory** Comprehension

Subtotal Score: 9 /9
Add 1 for any additional understandings: – /1
Total Score: 9 /10

Part Three: Writing About Reading *(optional)*

Read the writing/drawing prompt on the next page to the student. Specify the amount of time for the student to complete the task. (See *Assessment Guide* for more information.)

Writing About Reading
0 Reflects **no** understanding of the text.
1 Reflects **very limited** understanding of the text.
2 Reflects **partial** understanding of the text.
3 Reflects **excellent** understanding of the text.

© 2008 by Irene C. Fountas and Gay Su Pinnell. Portsmouth, NH: Heinemann. This page may be photocopied.

Fountas & Pinnell Benchmark Assessment System 2 — 29

FIGURE 2.18b Coded Comprehension Conversation for *City Hawks*

▶ Choosing the Writing About Reading Assessment

After you've finished assessing a student's oral reading, you may want to have her write in response to the prompt in Part Three of the Recording Form for one of the books she read, ideally for the instructional-level text (Figure 2.19). The writing is an optional part of the assessment. It provides additional evidence of the reader's understanding and a concrete sample of thinking that can go in the student's folder. The writing assessment is best completed immediately after the comprehension conversation, but the instructional-level text may not be the last one the student read. Allow her to look back at the book, but make sure she understands that she should write in her own words, not copy from the book. If you are using the condensed Recording Form from *Assessment Forms Book*, children will need blank paper to write on.

Figure 2.19 is an example of Shreya's writing about the level Z text, *Surviving the Blitz*. Shreya was asked to take the point of view of a newscaster in writing about the Blitz. Notice that she not only reported on the devastation but also worked in an interview with the young girl writing the memoir.

Some students perform better if they have a chance to reflect and think about the text in the process of sketching and/or writing. They may reveal in writing greater understanding than they do in the initial conversation. On the other hand, some students have far better ability to talk about a text than to write about it. If a student has only sketched a picture, invite him to tell about it while you record the ideas. You will find that the writing prompt provides a very useful opportunity for your students to share their thinking through writing in a way similar to that required in many standardized tests.

Specify an amount of time for the writing and drawing. At levels L–Q, give the student a maximum of twenty minutes. Levels R–U may require a little more time; and levels V–Z may require up to thirty minutes (Figure 2.20). If you choose to specify different maximum time limits for each level of the writing assessment, be sure to be consistent with all students at the level.

If you are conducting the assessment in the classroom, the student can complete this assignment as independent work, but you may want to ask him to work quietly at a location near you—but not so near that he can hear the content of your conversation. This will allow you to control the time he spends on the task and to ensure concentration. While one student is working on the written response, you can begin assessing the next student on your list or complete the scoring on the Recording Form.

Everything you do to help writers develop effective writing strategies will also contribute to reading proficiency. It is especially helpful for learners who

FIGURE 2.19 Sample writing prompt and student response

Recommended Writing About Reading Time	
Text Level	**Recommended Maximum Time for Writing About Reading**
L–Q	Twenty minutes
R–U	Twenty-five minutes
V–Z	Thirty minutes

FIGURE 2.20 Recommended Writing About Reading time

are finding reading difficult to write as often as possible, preferably every day. But just giving them the opportunity to write will not be enough. Often they do not have the resources to make the writing experience productive.

Writing that is based on reading an enjoyable book provides a strong language base and good models for student writers. Writing to a prompt directs a student's attention to an interesting or outstanding aspect of the story, which he can return to the book to check if necessary. This is excellent preparation for writing to the prompt in standardized tests. Giving students the opportunity to draw or sketch in response to texts they read may lead to fresh insights and deeper connections. Learning effective writing behaviors will give readers the support they need to use writing as a resource for building their processing systems.

▶ Continuing the Benchmark Assessment Conference

You have now learned how to administer, code, and score a student's reading of one benchmark book. To complete the assessment conference, you want to gather more information about the student's ability to read independent, instructional, and hard texts. Your goal is to determine how the student reads all three types of

text. The hard and independent texts help you identify the instructional text. You can use Figure 2.21 to help you find all three types of text to conclude the assessment conference.

▶ Completing the Scoring on Each Recording Form

Before compiling the results of the an assessment conference on the Assessment Summary Form, complete scoring you may not have done during administering the assessment. You should already have an oral reading accuracy rate, a general evaluation of fluency, and a comprehension conversation score (Figure 2.22). Recording the number of self-corrections and calculating reading rate (and Writing About Reading if you chose to assign it), will provide additional information for decision making.

Counting the Number of Self-Corrections

If you haven't already done so, count the number of self-corrections and write that number on the line provided on the score page. The self-correction number quantifies the extent to which the student is monitoring or noticing errors in his own reading. For older students at levels L–Z

Finding Easy, Instructional, and Hard Texts	
If the first book is . . .	**Then . . .**
Easy Student reads at 98–100% accuracy with excellent or satisfactory comprehension.	Move to a higher level text and repeat the same process until the student reads a text that is hard.
Instructional Student reads at 95–97% accuracy with excellent or satisfactory comprehension or 98–100% accuracy with limited comprehension.	Move to a lower level text and repeat the same process until the student reads a text that is easy; then move to a higher level text until the student reads a text that is hard.
Hard Student reads below 95% accuracy with any score on comprehension.	Move to a lower level text and repeat the same process until the student reads a text at an instructional level; then move to a lower level until the student reads a text that is easy.

FIGURE 2.21 Finding easy, instructional, and hard texts

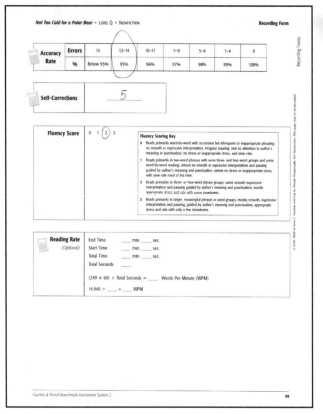

Fluency Scoring Key

0 Reads primarily word-by-word with occasional but infrequent or inappropriate phrasing; no smooth or expressive interpretation, irregular pausing, and no attention to author's meaning or punctuation; no stress or inappropriate stress, and slow rate.

1 Reads primarily in two-word phrases with some three- and four-word groups and some word-by-word reading; almost no smooth or expressive interpretation and pausing guided by author's meaning and punctuation; almost no stress or inappropriate stress, with slow rate most of the time.

2 Reads primarily in three- or four-word phrase groups; some smooth expressive interpretation and pausing guided by author's meaning and punctuation; mostly appropriate stress and rate with some slowdowns.

3 Reads primarily in larger, meaningful phrases or word groups; mostly smooth, expressive interpretation and pausing, guided by author's meaning and punctuation; appropriate stress and rate with only a few slowdowns.

FIGURE 2.22 Oral reading score page for *Not Too Cold for a Polar Bear*

we want the kind of reading that ignores small errors and/or mentally corrects responses before saying them out loud. This is why we switch from reporting self-correction as a ratio in *Benchmark Assessment System 1* to reporting just the number for *Benchmark Assessment System 2*.

If you haven't already done so, count the number of self-corrections and write them on the line on the score page.

Calculating Reading Rate

Reading rate is a measure of how many words per minutes a student reads. Rate is important because it is one indicator of the reader's ability to process with ease. When the reader processes the print at a satisfactory pace, he is more likely to be able to attend to the meaning of the text. He is also more likely to group words as they are naturally spoken instead of reading one word at a time. It is possible for a reader to read individual words—one at a time—quickly, so it will be important for you to notice speed along with the other dimensions of fluency. Phrasing, or grouping words, is critical to effective processing of the text.

If you use the *F & P Calculator/ Stopwatch* to time the reading, you need only enter the number of running words (RW) from the front cover of the benchmark book. The calculator will give you the words-per-minute (WPM) to enter on the Recording Form. If you use a clock or stopwatch, figure the total reading time in seconds and divide this into the RW number provided on the Recording Form to get the WPM.

Readers will develop individual styles for oral reading, so do not try to identify a precise reading rate that all must achieve. Use Figure 2.23 only to identify whether a student's reading is within a desired range. It may also help to think about the range of reading rate you want by the end of the grade level. Remember that rate is a good indicator only if the student is reading a text that is not too difficult. On hard texts, all readers will read more slowly. Also, be sure to remember that all the dimensions of fluent reading are as important as rate. Reading rate is only one aspect of integrated and orchestrated processing of text.

Scoring the Writing-About-Reading Assessment

After the student has finished writing about reading, collect it for scoring. The purpose of this writing is to examine it for evidence of the student's understanding of the instructional level text, so you will not be scoring it for conventions or craft, although you may want to notice her use of these. Look at the ideas

Expected Oral Reading Rates	
End of Grade	**Oral Reading Rates (WPM)**
2 (L–M–N)	90–120
3 (N–O–P)	100–140
4 (Q–R–S)	120–160
5 (T–U–V)	160–180
6 (W–X–Y)	180–200
7–8 (Y–Z)	180–220

FIGURE 2.23 Expected oral reading rates

Rubric for Scoring Writing About Reading

	Scoring Key	Rubric
0	Reflects **no** understanding of the text	The writing is not connected with text or is connected only in a very peripheral way (for example, about the same topic). The student's writing does not reflect any of the information in the text (thinking within the text) or of thinking beyond or about the text.
1	Reflects **very limited** understanding of the text	The writing is connected with the text but reveals either very little understanding or confusion. The student's writing does not reflect thinking beyond or about the text.
2	Reflects **partial** understanding of the text	The writing provides evidence that the student understands the literal meaning of the text (within), including key understandings, and in addition, is thinking beyond the text. It is not necessary for the writing to "retell" the text, but examples from it may be used as evidence.
3	Reflects **excellent** understanding of the text	The writing provides evidence that the student not only understands the literal meaning of the text (within) but grasps the author's message and is thinking beyond and about the text. It is not necessary for the writing to "retell" the text, but summaries, quotes, or examples may be offered in support of points.

FIGURE 2.24 Rubric for scoring Writing About Reading

that the writing reflects and assign a score using the guide shown in Figure 2.24. The Writing About Reading scoring key on your Recording Form is an abbreviated version of this rubric. (Keep in mind that the prompt influences the writing. Some prompts may not call for thinking beyond and about the text. If the student has fully met the demand of the prompt, then you would score her writing as a 3.)

When Jan wrote about *Not Too Cold for a Polar Bear,* her writing reflected excellent understanding of the text (Figure 2.25). Referring to *The Continuum of Literacy Learning* for level Q, Jan exhibited "thinking within the text" when she wrote appropriate and important details when summarizing the text and used new vocabulary in her writing in an appropriate way. She exhibited "thinking beyond the text" when she described a connection between background knowledge (the heat at the local zoo) and new information in the story as well as when she formulated a valid question based on information in the story. She exhibited "thinking about the text" when she showed an awareness of cause and effect. This is why Jan's writing merited the top score of 3.

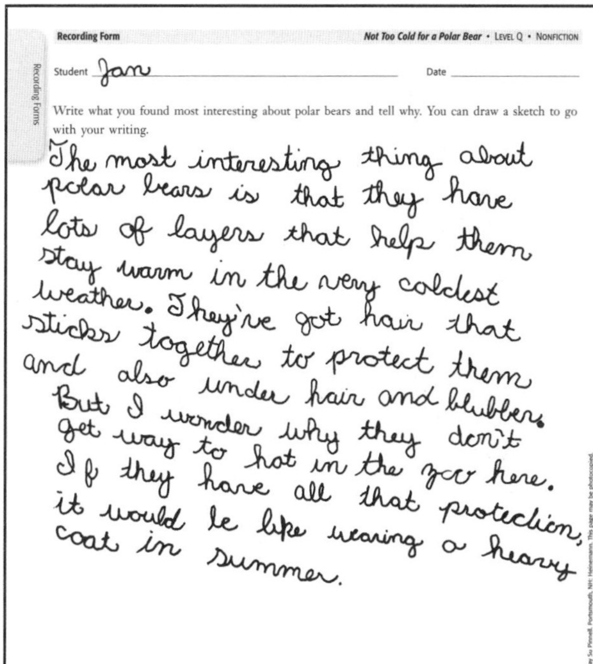
Recording Form — *Not Too Cold for a Polar Bear* • Level Q • Nonfiction

Recording Forms

Student Jan Date

Write what you found most interesting about polar bears and tell why. You can draw a sketch to go with your writing.

The most interesting thing about polar bears is that they have lots of layers that help them stay warm in the very coldest weather. They've got hair that sticks together to protect them and also under hair and blubbers. But I wonder why they don't get way to hot in the zoo here. If they have all that protection, it would be like wearing a heavy coat in summer.

© 2008 by Irene C. Fountas and Gay Su Pinnell. Portsmouth, NH: Heinemann. This page may be photocopied.

86 Fountas & Pinnell Benchmark Assessment System 2

FIGURE 2.25 Jan wrote about *Not Too Cold for a Polar Bear*

▶ Choosing Optional Literacy Assessments

If your district requires particular assessments in the areas of phonics, word analysis, or vocabulary, the *Assessment Forms Book* and *CD-ROM* provide a variety of optional assessments from which to choose, depending on the local need. In addition, a student's previous records or his oral reading performance on *Benchmark Assessment System* may suggest areas you want to explore further. A High-Frequency Word assessment, for example, may confirm your hypothesis that a reader's fluency is due to her lack of automatic recognition of high-frequency words. A Vocabulary-in-Context assessment may provide insight into her use of meaning cues. For more information about Optional Assessments, see Section 4 of this guide.

▶ Making Your Assessment Conference Efficient

The key to an efficient assessment is starting at a point where the student is reading successfully, but the text is not too easy. Use information you have about his previous reading to help you judge. You might even ask what book he has read himself recently.

When you have given the assessment many times, you will find that you know the texts and the prompts well. Your administration will go faster as you have smooth, efficient comprehension conversations. If the student is struggling, that is, he has reached the maximum number of errors (E) as designated on the book cover, there is no need to continue since you have the information you need; the book is too hard.

Of course, when a student reads fluently, the assessment will go faster. Place a great deal of emphasis on the importance of fluency in your instructional program. Figure 2.26 offers some suggestions for saving time and making efficient use of your assessment conference.

Making the Assessment Conference Efficient

To save time, consider the following suggestions.

✔ **Starting Point** Knowing where to start will save the student from having to read numerous texts. Use last year's reading records to get an indication of where to start, or what will be "easy" for a student. Then have in mind the next text, an instructional text, for the student.

✔ **Organized Materials** Keep your assessment books and Recording Forms well organized in a hanging file next to you so you can "hit the ground running."

✔ **Familiarity with Books** When you know the assessment books and key understandings well, you can move the comprehension conversation along briskly.

✔ **Fluency** If your readers are fluent, the reading will take less time.

✔ **Hard Text** As soon as a student's text reading shows the number of errors indicative of hard text, discontinue the reading. There is no need for the student to struggle through the whole text.

✔ **Comprehension Conversation** If the text is hard, do not include the comprehension conversation.

FIGURE 2.26 Making the assessment conference efficient

section 3

Summarizing, Analyzing, and Interpreting Results

In this section, you will find step-by-step instructions for using the Assessment Summary Form to compile assessment results as well as guidance in determining implications for instruction. You'll fill out an Assessment Summary Form for each reader you assess.

The Assessment Summary is a summary record of key information from each of the individual Recording Forms you used with a student. It provides an overall snapshot of a child's reading and summarizes the Benchmark Assessment conference. Information from the Assessment Summary Form can be entered into the *Online Data Management System* for individual and group data analysis and reporting. The first two pages of this section present a walk-through of the form. A detailed explanation follows.

▶ Assessment Summary Form Walk-Through

The Assessment Summary Form contains:

❑ **Space at the top for student, grade, date, teacher, and school information.**

❑ **A results summary box to record the independent, instructional, and recommended placement level for the student.**

❑ **A place to list, from easiest to hardest, the titles, genres, and levels of books the student read during the assessment conference.**

❑ **Columns for recording subscores from Recording Forms for up to five benchmark books.**

❑ **Boxes to check either independent, instructional, or hard level for each book read.**

❑ **A summary of criteria for independent, instructional, or hard levels.**

❑ **Space to record comments about specific reading behaviors you noticed during the assessment conference as well as any instructional implications the assessment data may suggest.**

Summary Form

Student _____ Grade _____

Teacher _____ Date _____

School _____

Benchmark Independent Level* _____
Benchmark Instructional Level** _____
Recommended Placement Level _____

Assessment Summary Form *List the titles read by the student from lowest to highest level.*

Title	System 1 or 2	Fiction/Nonfiction	Level	Accuracy	Comprehension	Independent * (check one)	Instructional ** (check one)	Hard *** (check one)	Self-Correction	Fluency Levels C–Z	Rate Levels J–Z (optional)	Writing About Reading (optional)

***Independent Level**
Levels A–K: Highest level read with 95–100% accuracy and excellent or satisfactory comprehension.
Levels L–Z: Highest level read with 98–100% accuracy and excellent or satisfactory comprehension.

****Instructional Level**
Levels A–K: Highest level read with 90–94% accuracy and excellent or satisfactory comprehension or 95–100% accuracy and limited comprehension.
Levels L–Z: Highest level read with 95–97% accuracy and excellent or satisfactory comprehension or 98–100% accuracy and limited comprehension.

*****Hard Level**
Levels A–K: Highest level read at which accuracy is below 90% with any level of comprehension.
Levels L–Z: Highest level read at which accuracy is below 95% with any level of comprehension.

Comprehension			
Levels A–K		**Levels L–Z**	
6–7	Excellent	9–10	Excellent
5	Satisfactory	7–8	Satisfactory
4	Limited	5–6	Limited
0–3	Unsatisfactory	0–4	Unsatisfactory

Behaviors and Understandings to Notice, Teach, and Support (See *The Continuum of Literacy Learning*)

Fountas & Pinnell Benchmark Assessment System 2   **167**

Summary Forms

▶ Three Levels Defined

Benchmark Independent Level

The Benchmark Independent level is the highest level at which a student can read independently. The benchmark texts at this level are "easy" for the student. The student can read 98–100% of the words accurately with excellent or satisfactory comprehension.

Benchmark Instructional Level

The Benchmark Instructional level is the highest level at which a student can read with good opportunities for learning through teaching. For the level to be instructional, one of the following should be true:

❑ The student reads 95–97% of the words accurately with excellent or satisfactory comprehension.

❑ The student reads 98–100% of the words accurately with limited comprehension.

In both cases, word solving is sufficient. In the second case, word solving is excellent but the student needs instruction to help him understand the texts at the level.

Recommended Placement Level

The Recommended Placement level is the level you decide is appropriate for reading instruction. It reflects your thinking about all of the data gathered during the assessment. Most of the time, this level will be the same as the instructional level, but sometimes a look at the reading behaviors and the specific data will lead you to a different decision.

▶ Filling Out the Assessment Summary Form

Fill out an Assessment Summary Form for each reader you assess. Start by gathering the Recording Forms for the books she read in the order of book level from lowest to highest text level and then completing the information at the top of the Assessment Summary Form. List the book titles, genres, and levels on the form in this order. Then transfer from the Recording Forms to the Assessment Summary Form the accuracy rate, comprehension score, and any other data you have figured on the reading of each book (Figure 3.1).

FIGURE 3.1 Sample completed Assessment Summary Form

Finding Three Levels

Altogether, you will determine three different levels for each of your students: independent, instructional, and recommended placement. Figure 3.2 provides a quick summary of the criteria for independent-level and instructional-level identification. Remember that the instructional level is the highest level before the hard level.

Finding the Benchmark Independent Level To determine this level, look first at the accuracy and comprehension scores you already recorded on the Assessment Summary Form. Check the independent column next to the highest level at which a student reads 98–100% of the words accurately with excellent or satisfactory comprehension.

Finding the Benchmark Instructional Level To determine this level, once again look at the accuracy and comprehension scores you recorded on the Assessment Summary Form. Check the instructional column next to the highest level at which a student reads 95–97% of the words accurately with excellent or satisfactory comprehension or

Finding the Levels, L–Z

Benchmark Criteria for Levels L–Z	Comprehension			
Accuracy	Excellent 9–10	Satisfactory 7–8	Limited 5–6	Unsatisfactory 0–4
98–100%	Independent	Independent	Instructional	Hard
95–97%	Instructional	Instructional	Hard	Hard
Below 95%	Hard	Hard	Hard	Hard

FIGURE 3.2 Finding the levels, L–Z

98–100% of the words accurately with limited comprehension.

Finding the Recommended Placement Level
Finding the recommended placement level requires considering and interpreting accuracy and comprehension scores as well as looking across the rich range of information you gain from a benchmark assessment.

In fact, no matter what the test shows, it *always* requires qualitative judgment on the part of the teacher. When you finish the assessment for an individual, you have an important set of numbers: (1) a percentage of words read accurately and (2) a comprehension score. You also have additional information on the reader's

❑ use of sources of information

❑ oral reading behaviors (errors, substitutions, self-corrections), or the way the reader processed the text

❑ ability to write about the meaning of the text

Looking Beyond the Numbers

You can draw on all of these sources of information to help you look beyond the numbers to make a decision about a student's recommended placement level. The recommended placement level may be the same as the instructional level, but it may differ because of other factors that come out of your analysis. Look again at the accuracy and comprehension scores. Think beyond the categories and numbers you considered for benchmark levels to make a good decision regarding each student's placement for small-group instruction.

The following are some general factors to think about when using data to select a recommended placement level for a student.

ACTUAL SCORES

Look at the actual scores as well as the categories. While we have to establish "cutoffs" for logistical reasons, consider how close to the cutoff point a reader is. In real terms, there really is very little difference between 94% and 95%. However, it does make a difference whether the accuracy rate is 90% or 50% or whether the comprehension score is 4 or 0. These scores can make big differences and can figure into your placement decisions.

FLUENCY AND PHRASING

Look at the student's fluency and phrasing. Some students read accurately but very slowly; slow reading generally interferes with comprehension. On the other hand, students may read fluently but carelessly, making many errors and losing comprehension. If a student reads a text with high accuracy but very slowly with almost no phrasing or recognition of the punctuation, then meaning will be affected. This kind of pattern suggests that you should teach intensively for fluency and phrasing at that level. It is important to prioritize teaching for phrasing and fluency with all students when needed.

TEXT CONTENT

Look at the content of the material. The student's background experience is a critical factor in comprehension. If a student has a great deal of background in an area, she may be able to answer questions or talk about the content even if the text is hard, so the comprehension score may be artificially high. Conversely, if the student lacks background knowledge or has a cultural misunderstanding, her scores may be artificially low. The student may or may not be able to read other books at the level.

SOURCES OF INFORMATION

Take a quick look at sources of information the reader used as she read the text: meaning (M), language structure (S), and visual information (V). As you analyze errors and self-corrections, you can make hypotheses about the extent to which a reader is using different sources of information. For example, a student might read a text at an instructional level for accuracy but make substitutions that indicate using only the first letter of a word without evidence of trying to make sense of a text. Another student might read the same text with just below instructional-level accuracy but show effective use of word-analysis strategies and good comprehension.

PROBLEM-SOLVING ACTIONS

Look at the reader's use of processing strategies or problem-solving actions. Observe to see if he makes several attempts or notices and corrects errors independently. Notice if he has a variety of ways to solve words. Think about whether these actions are effective and efficient. Some repeated errors signal a lack of self-monitoring, but they also can make the accuracy percentage artificially low.

LEVEL OF INDEPENDENCE

Look at the reader's independence in problem solving while reading the text. It makes a difference whether she is actively problem solving or simply waiting to be told a word. For example, she might read a text with high accuracy but stop and appeal at every unfamiliar word. This student is not demonstrating the ability to take risks and to actively search for and use information to solve words.

To make this decision-making process clearer, we provide examples and explanations of how additional considerations might influence recommended placement levels.

Josiah's benchmark scores (Figure 3.3) lead directly to his placement level. They fall neatly within the expected ranges, and the recommended placement level matches the instructional level of N. The teacher

realizes, however, that Josiah needs very supportive teaching to effectively process level N. His accuracy and comprehension are both borderline, and his processing breaks down at level O.

Kaitlin's benchmark scores (Figure 3.4) indicate level T placement, but her teacher has a rationale for placing her at level S. Kaitlin's instructional level is T but her teacher notes that her independent level is borderline (98% accuracy with satisfactory comprehension). Her teacher decided to drop down a level for a short time and begin instruction at level S, knowing that Kaitlin will gain fluency and firm up her processing prior to moving to level T.

The box in the upper right corner of the Assessment Summary Form provides a place to summarize the three levels. To summarize, the levels you determine for each student are shown in Figure 3.5.

Once you determine a student's recommended placement level, you can use the information to form guided reading groups and select texts for your lessons. Once you begin instruction and gain more

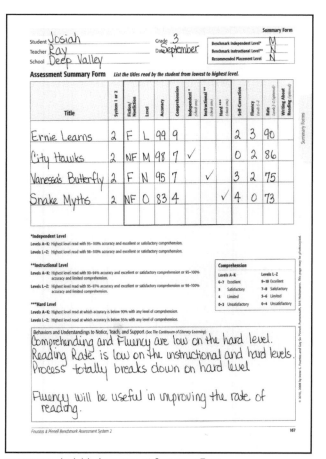

FIGURE 3.3 Josiah's Assessment Summary Form

evidence, you can always adjust the students' grouping if a placement is not working well. Figure 3.5 summarizes the three levels you need to determine for each student.

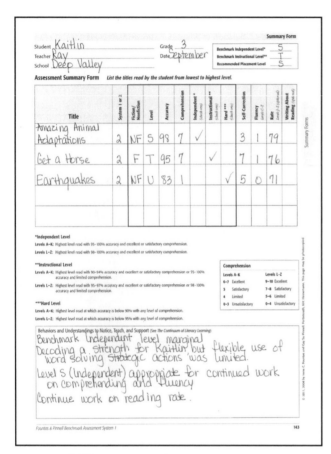

FIGURE 3.4 Kaitlin's Assessment Summary Form

Determining Three Levels	
Benchmark Independent level	98–100% accuracy with excellent or satisfactory comprehension
Benchmark Instructional level	95–97% accuracy with excellent or satisfactory comprehension, or 98–100% accuracy with limited comprehension
Recommended Placement Level	Best level for instruction after considering accuracy, comprehension, fluency, and processing strategies

FIGURE 3.5 Determining three levels

▶ Looking More Closely at Benchmark Text Reading

Now that you have determined the three levels, you know the level to recommend for each student for independent reading and the level at which you will begin instruction. At this point, examine the assessment results for additional information to inform instruction. We recommend looking carefully at the student's reading of the instructional level text. Using the instructional-level text, analyze the reading behaviors that the student controls, partially controls, or does not yet control. You can also examine the reader's ability to use the sources of information in the text.

Analyzing Sources of Information

To inform teaching, analyze the student's errors and self-corrections on her instructional-level text to find out what kinds of information the reader is using and what kinds of information are being neglected. For example, a reader who consistently makes substitution errors like *whole* for *entire* may be thinking about the meaning of the text but neglecting to check with the letters in the word. A reader who consistently makes errors like *serve* for *survive* may be noticing the letters but neglecting to think about whether the reading sounds right and makes sense. (**Note:** the *Professional Development DVD* provides support in decision making based on this information.)

After tallying each error and self-correction on the Recording Form (Figure 3.6), look at the number and kinds of errors and self-corrections the student has made. Look at the far right sources of information columns. Begin by writing *MSV* next to each error in the error column. For self-corrections, write *MSV* in the error column and in the self-correction column. For both the errors (E) and the self-corrections (SC), you are going to hypothesize and record the sources of information that the reader was using when he made the error or self-correction, determining if the student was using meaning (*M*), structure (*S*), or visual information (*V*) at the time (Figure 3.7).

❑ *Meaning* Readers often make substitutions that indicate they are thinking about the meaning of the text. For example, a reader might say *ballet*

for *dance*. Ask yourself: Did the meaning of the text influence the error? Does the substitution make sense? If so, circle the *M* in the sources of information column under error (E).

❑ *Structure* A powerful source of information for a reader is the structure of language. From our knowledge of oral language, we have implicit understanding of the way words are put together to form phrases and sentences. It "sounds right" to us. Readers often substitute nouns for nouns or verbs for verbs, indicating an awareness of the structure of language. For example, a reader might say *I imagine we two sitting across a table* for *I imagine that the two of us are sitting across a table*. The reader has made several errors in reading one sentence but moves right on. For each error, ask yourself: Does the error fit an acceptable English language structure up to the point of error? Did structure influence the error? If so, circle the *S* in the sources of information column under error (E).

Note: Readers often use multiple sources of information as they process texts. You might code some of these errors as both *S* (the student substituted one verb construction for another) and M. Not self-correcting these relatively minor errors might make sense in terms of efficiency; however, it signals that the reader is neglecting visual information, which may lead to loss of meaning at other places in the text.

❑ *Visual information* Readers use the visual features of print—the letters and words—to read. They connect these features to phonetic information that exists in their heads. For example, looking at the picture, a reader might say *serve* for *survive*. Ask yourself: Did the visual information from the print influence the error (letter, part, word)? If so, circle *V* in the error column.

❑ *Using sources of information in combination* Sometimes readers sample only some of the visual information in a word, for example, reading *porch* for *podium* in the sentence: *Later that morning, Jill walked slowly across the auditorium stage and stood behind the podium.* A reader who makes this kind of error may not be looking beyond the first letter of the word. Only one

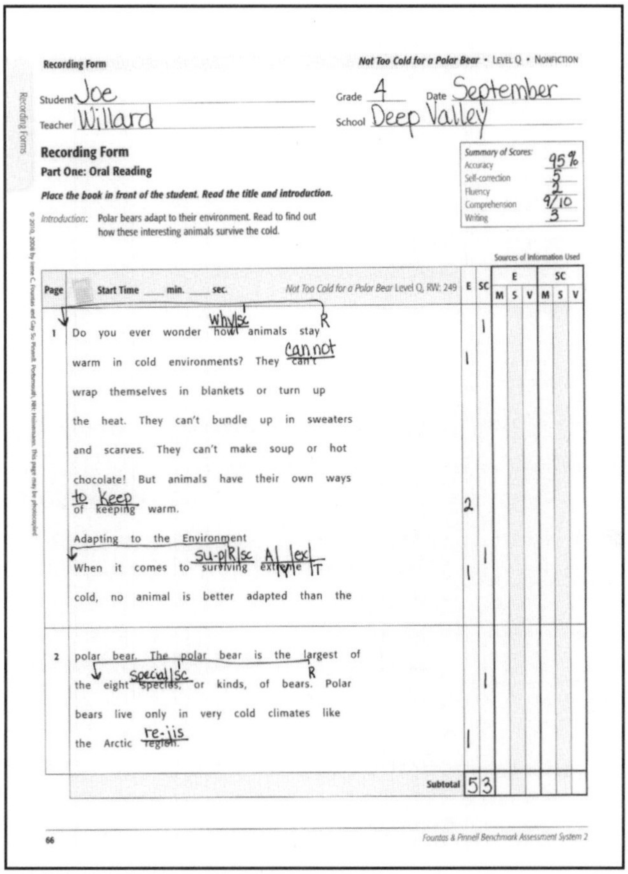

FIGURE 3.6 Coded oral reading of *Not Too Cold for a Polar Bear*

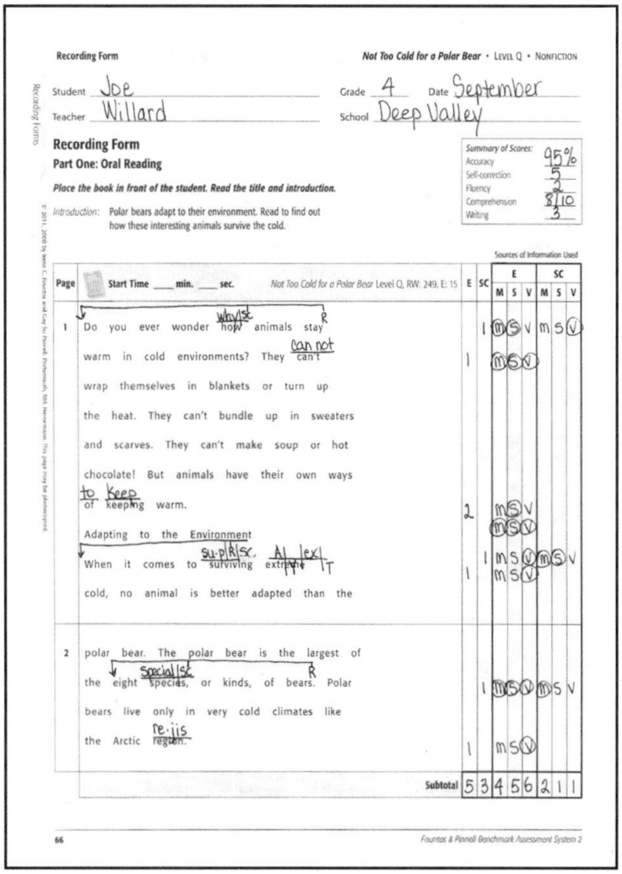

FIGURE 3.7 Analyzing errors for sources of information

error has been made, and in this case the reader might comprehend the text despite the error. But perpetuating this kind of error will inevitably lead to loss of comprehension. Something should trigger the reader to notice a mismatch, and it could be the combined knowledge that "something doesn't make sense here" and "*porch* doesn't match the last part of the word."

Use a similar procedure for coding a student's self-corrections. Here, you are hypothesizing the additional information that he might have used to correct the error. The self-correction of course indicates use of all three sources of information—meaning, language structure, and visual information—because it is the accurate word. But you are searching here for what he might have used as *additional* information to correct the error.

If he made the error *ballet* for *dance*, for example, and then self-corrected, the error would be analyzed as *M*, and in the self-correction column you would circle *S* and *V,* because he might have thought about the way the language sounded and might have noticed the *d* or another part of the word. If he said *porch* for *podium* and then self-corrected, you would circle *M* in the self-correction column, because the meaning of the text likely influenced the correction.

These analyses will help you look qualitatively at the student's use of these different sources of information. Think about what he is neglecting. You can help him attend to the information sources needed as you listen to him read orally during reading lessons or do some teaching after the reading. If readers in a group are neglecting to think about what might make sense, you can prompt them to do so. If they are not noticing the first letter or other part of a word that would be helpful, you can draw the visual information to their attention.

▶ When the Numbers Don't Line Up Perfectly

When you determine Benchmark independent and instructional levels, you are considering several variables rather than simply accuracy. It is worth the extra trouble it may take to look in this complex way because some students are extraordinarily competent

as word solvers, but they do not think actively enough or they do not have enough background experience to understand what they are reading. There may be figurative language or big ideas that they do not understand. This kind of reading reveals strengths but does not add up to effective processing. In addition, it provides an unreliable view of the reader. A student who is "word calling" without understanding will not be able to function well on tests and will find it hard to learn from reading.

Occasionally, a student will read with low accuracy but be able to respond to questions—either from getting the gist of the story or from previously acquired background knowledge. This kind of reader may be merely careless about errors or have word-solving difficulties that will affect his future ability to process harder texts.

Because we have introduced a high criterion for accuracy as well as for comprehension at levels L–Z, you may find that occasionally numbers do not exactly match the criteria for each of these levels. This situation will not be a problem when you are using the benchmark criteria for your own information and grouping. For example, you can have two independent levels (slightly different from each other) and then a hard text. You would simply make a decision on the placement level based on all the information. The instructional level would be the highest level with 95–97% accuracy and satisfactory or excellent comprehension.

However, you may need to report two or three of the levels to the principal or the central office of your district. In this case, consult the chart in Figure 3.8. Here you will find some cases in which the numbers do not match neatly. The third column shows the teacher's solution to the problem. Find the one that most closely matches your own case and use it to help you make decisions about recording levels. After you have solved many of these problems, you will find that you can make these decisions quickly.

Noting Strategic Actions

Look again at the errors you have marked on the text in the Recording Form for the student's instructional-level book. Think about her as a problem solver. Noting problem areas will be helpful in your thinking:

Finding an Instructional Level When the Numbers Do Not Line Up Perfectly

Problem	Example of Student Scores	Solution

The student has 2+ independent levels and no instructional level.	P at 98% accuracy with excellent comprehension
	
	Q at 98% accuracy with satisfactory comprehension
	
	R at 97% accuracy with limited comprehension
		Take the highest level read independently and make it the placement level. Expect the student to move quickly.
		
		    P = Independent level
		
		    Q = Independent level
		
		    Q = Recommended Placement level
		
		Remember that students reading at this level will *always* have many independent levels (all below the instructional level).

The student has 2+ instructional levels.	P at 97% accuracy with excellent comprehension
	
	Q at 97% accuracy with satisfactory comprehension
	
	R at 97% accuracy with satisfactory comprehension (with many self-corrections)
		Take the highest level instructional text that shows evidence of processing.
		
		    P = Instructional level
		
		    Q = Instructional level
		
		    Q = Recommended Placement level
		
		Expect this student to move quickly to level R as you work on word-solving strategies.

The student has no instructional level because the reading is uneven.	M at 98% accuracy with satisfactory comprehension
	
	N at 94% accuracy with satisfactory comprehension
	
	O at 98% accuracy with satisfactory comprehension (with many self-corrections and low fluency)
	
	P at 90% accuracy with limited comprehension
		For instruction, you want to be sure you are on firm ground. With uneven reading like this, select the level you are most sure that the student can process with your help. Monitor placement carefully.
		
		    M = Independent level
		
		    N = Hard level (but just below instructional)
		
		    O = Independent level (but inefficient)
		
		    P = Hard level
		
		    N = Recommended Placement level

The student has no instructional level because of very high accuracy on one level, limited comprehension on the next highest level, and low accuracy and limited comprehension on the next.	K at 100% accuracy with satisfactory comprehension
	
	L at 99% accuracy with limited comprehension
	
	M at 75% accuracy with limited comprehension
		For instruction, use a text that the student can comprehend with your support. Select level L and work on active thinking. You should be able to move quickly to M.
		
		    K = Independent level
		
		    L = Instructional level
		
		    L = Recommended Placement level

FIGURE 3.8 Finding an instructional level when the numbers do not line up perfectly,

continues

Problem	Example of Student Scores	Solution

The reader's comprehension is uneven, with unsatisfactory comprehension at a particular level.	L at 98% accuracy with satisfactory comprehension
	
	M at 95% accuracy with unsatisfactory comprehension
	
	N at 91% accuracy with satisfactory comprehension
		Select M for instruction, but observe the reader closely to move to N if level is too easy.
		
		   L = Independent level
		   M = Instructional level

The student does not have an independent level.	R at 98% accuracy with limited comprehension S at 92% accuracy with limited comprehension	You need to try levels Q and perhaps P to get a level the reader can process with satisfactory comprehension (independent level). R = Instructional level (be prepared to move to Q if text is too hard)

The student does not have an instructional level because there appears to be a large gap between two readings.	Q at 99% accuracy with excellent comprehension
	
	R at 85% accuracy with limited comprehension
	
	S at 72% accuracy with limited comprehension
		R is too hard for instructing this reader, and Q is obviously an easy text. You may wait to try the reader on the alternate level R book, but probably Q is the best level.
		
		   Q = Independent level
		   Q = Instructional level
		   Q = Placement level
		
		The student may read some books on level P as independent reading. Observe closely and work to move the student quickly to R for instructional level.

All the texts seem too hard for the reader	L at 75% accuracy with limited comprehension M at 60% accuracy with limited comprehension N at 55% accuracy with limited comprehension	You need to keep going down in level. If the *Benchmark Assessment System 1* is available in your school, switch to that system to use easier texts.
All the texts seem too hard for the reader to understand.	P at 98% accuracy with unsatisfactory comprehension Q at 100% accuracy with unsatisfactory comprehension R at 97% accuracy with unsatisfactory comprehension	You need to keep going down in level until you find a text that the reader can comprehend with limited comprehension (and 98%–100% accuracy) or satisfactory or excellent comprehension (and 95%–97% accuracy).
The student has no instructional level because all levels appear to be easy.	X at 98% accuracy with excellent comprehension Y at 98% accuracy with satisfactory comprehension Z at 98% accuracy with satisfactory comprehension	This is a good problem to have! Just indicate Z as instructional level and Y as independent level. This student will benefit from small group discussion, extending understanding through writing, and wide reading experience. Select age-appropriate material.

FIGURE 3.8 Finding an instructional level when the numbers do not line up perfectly, *continued*

❏ *Searching for and using information* Effective readers actively search for the information they need to read with accuracy, fluency, and understanding. They make attempts that, even if not right, show you they are trying out what they know. You can teach students many ways to search for and use multiple sources of information in the text. For nonfiction texts, searching for and using information very often includes using text features such as table of contents, glossary, and headings. Students are also expected to interpret graphics such as labeled photographs and drawings, maps, diagrams, and charts.

❏ *Solving words* You want students to have and use many ways to solve words. As they learn more, they will recognize many words automatically, but they also need to be able to use phonics and word analysis strategies so that they can learn many more. Then you can teach them many different ways to solve words.

❏ *Self-monitoring* Rather than reading along and ignoring errors, you want her to notice when something doesn't fit. Effective readers are constantly monitoring their own reading accuracy. If she does not show signs of checking on herself or self-monitoring, you can draw attention to mismatches and show her how to fix them.

❏ *Self-correcting* Self-correction is a sign that a reader is monitoring his reading and working actively to make everything fit—meaning, structure, visual information, and the way the reading sounds.

❏ *Maintaining fluency* Effective readers put all sources of information together so that their reading sounds fluent and expressive. They read in word groups and stop at punctuation; they stress words in bold and italic type. You can think about how the reading sounded. If a student is not fluent and the text is easy enough, you can demonstrate fluent reading and show him how to put words together so that it sounds good, reading with intonation and logical word groupings.

The questions in Figure 3.9 will be helpful in guiding your thinking as you look at your coding and think about the reading behaviors you observed. Notice how Mrs. Willard has used the guide to note important behaviors that Joe evidenced in his reading of *Not Too Cold for a Polar Bear*. This guide can be copied or printed from the *Assessment Forms Book* or *CD-ROM*

for easy reference. The questions will help you focus on the actions a student takes and give you insight into how he uses different kinds of information and problem solves his way through the text. You will be able to notice effective and ineffective processing and listen for his ability to maintain fluency. By using the guide regularly, you can train yourself to look beyond the numbers to the reading behaviors that will provide critical information for your teaching.

Using this as your guide, make notes on your Assessment Summary Form in the box at the bottom of the form. Your observations of the processing or problem-solving actions a student is able to use will have important implications for the instruction you provide in your lessons.

Once you have completed an Assessment Summary Form, enter the data into the *Online Data Management System*. Doing so will allow you to track progress over time, analyze trends in reading performance, and compare data within your class in order to inform your instructional plans. See Section 7 of this guide for more information.

After you review and analyze the scores and the strategic actions, note your thinking about areas of the reading process that have important instructional implications. See Section 6 of this guide for a summary of ways the assessment can inform instruction.

▶ Expanding Performance Evidence or Diagnosis with Optional Literacy Assessments

The extensive information gathered through the basic Benchmark Assessment procedures described in this section provide clear direction for instruction, but you may also wish to get more diagnostic evidence about the student's literacy knowledge with the optional assessments found in the *Assessment Forms Book* and *CD-ROM*. A reading interview, an array of phonics and word analysis assessments, and a variety of vocabulary assessments will provide targeted information about the learner's knowledge in specific areas of literacy learning. For more information, see Section 4 of this guide.

Name: _Joe_   Date: _September_

Key: C=Consistent
      P=Partial
      N=Not evident

Guide for Observing and Noting Reading Behaviors	C P N	Notes
1. Early Reading Behaviors *Does the reader:* • Move left to right across a line of print? • Return to the left for a new line? • Match voice to print while reading a line or more of print? • Recognize a few easy high-frequency words?	C	*under control*
2. Searching for and Using Information **Meaning** *Does the reader:* • Make meaningful attempts at unknown words? • Use the meaning of the story or text to predict unknown words? • Reread to gather more information to solve a word? • Reread and use the meaning of the sentence? • Reread to search for more details—information, characters, plot? • Reread to gather information to clarify confusions? • Use headings and titles to think about the meaning of a section of text? • Use information in the pictures to help in understanding a text? • Use knowledge of the genre (and its characteristics) to help in understanding a text? • Use knowledge of the genre (and its characteristics) to help in finding information? • Use readers' tools to help in finding information (glossary, index)? **Structure** *Does the reader:* • Use knowledge of oral language to solve unknown words? • Reread to see if a word "sounds right" in a sentence? • Reread to correct using language structure? **Visual Information** *Does the reader:* • Use the visual information to solve words? • Use the sound of the first letter(s) to attempt or solve a word? • Use some, most, or all of the visual information to solve words? • Use sound analysis to solve a word? • Make attempts that are visually similar? • Use knowledge of a high-frequency word to problem solve? • Search for more visual information within a word to solve it? • Use analogy to solve unknown words? • Use syllables to solve words? • Use prefixes and suffixes to take apart and recognize words? • Use inflectional endings to problem solve words? • Recognize words quickly and easily? • Reread and use the sound of the first letter to solve a word? • Problem solve unknown words quickly and efficiently? • Work actively to solve words? • Use multiple sources of information together in attempts at words? • Use all sources of information flexibly to solve words? • Use all sources of information in an orchestrated way?	C C C E P P N P	*p.2 specials/sc species* R *p.1, p.2* *p.2 reason* ✓ *a few appeals*
3. Solving Words *Does the reader:* • Recognize a core of high-frequency words quickly? • Recognize words quickly and easily? • Use a variety of flexible ways to take words apart? • Use the meaning of the sentences to solve words? • Use the structure of the sentence to solve words? • Use some of the visual information to solve words? • Use known word parts to solve words?	C C P	

354

Fountas & Pinnell Benchmark Assessment System 2

FIGURE 3.9 Guide for Observing and Noting Reading Behaviors

Key: C=Consistent
P=Partial
N=Not evident

© 2010, 2008 by Irene C. (Fountas and Gay Su Pinnell. Portsmouth, NH: Heinemann. This page may be photocopied.

Guide for Observing . . . (cont.)	C P N	Notes
3. Solving Words *(cont.)* *Does the reader:* • Use sound analysis (sounding out)? • Use analogy to solve words? • Make attempts that are visually similar? • Use the sound of the first letter to solve words? • Work actively to solve words? • Use known words or parts to solve unknown words? • Use syllables to problem solve? • Use prefixes and suffixes to take words apart? • Use inflectional endings to take words apart? • Use sentence context to derive the meaning of words? • Use base words and root words to derive the meaning of words? • Make connections among words to understand their meaning?	P N N N	p.2 rea-sonv
4. Self-Monitoring *Does the reader:* • Hesitate at an unknown word? • Stop at an unknown word? • Stop at an unknown word and appeal for help? • Stop after an error? • Notice mismatches? • Notice when an attempt does not look right? • Notice when an attempt does not sound right? • Notice when an attempt does not make sense? • Reread to confirm reading? • Use knowledge of some high-frequency words to check on reading? • Check one source of information with another? • Check an attempt that makes sense with language? • Check an attempt that makes sense with the letters (visual information)? • Use language structure to check on reading? • Request help after making several attempts?	P P	usually makes an attempt before appealing p.1 why/how/sc p.2 minutes/minus/sc p.2 earth/land/sc
5. Self-Correcting *Does the reader:* • Reread and try again until accurate? • Stop after an error and make another attempt? • Stop after an error and make multiple attempts until accurate? • Reread to self-correct? • Work actively to solve mismatches? • Self-correct errors?	C P	rereading often results in self-correcting about ⅓ of time
6. Maintaining Fluency *Does the reader:* • Read without pointing? • Read word groups (phrases)? • Put words together? • Read smoothly? • Read the punctuation? • Make the voice go down at periods? • Make the voice go up at question marks? • Pause briefly at commas, dashes, and hyphens? • Read dialogue with intonation or expression? • Stress the appropriate words to convey accurate meaning? • Read at a good rate—not too fast and not too slow?	C C C C C C	
7. Other Behaviors		

Fountas & Pinnell Benchmark Assessment System 2   355

Resources

FIGURE 3.9 Guide for Observing and Noting Reading Behaviors, *continued*

Using Optional Literacy Assessments

The extensive information gathered through the standard Benchmark Assessment procedures provides clear direction for instruction, but you may also wish to get more diagnostic evidence about a particular student's literacy knowledge through the optional assessments in the *Assessment Forms Book* and *CD-ROM*. A reading interview, an array of phonics and word analysis assessments, and a variety of vocabulary assessments will provide targeted information about the learner's knowledge in specific areas of literacy learning. The primary purpose for most of these assessments is diagnosis to inform teaching literacy.

Using Optional Literacy Assessments

To gather additional information on a student or a group of students, we have provided a range of tools and assessments from which to choose. All optional assessment forms described in this section are available in the *Assessment Forms Book* and *CD-ROM*.

We have also included an Optional Assessment Summary Form for you to record the student's score each time you administer the assessment. Be sure to look for growth over time. There may be one or two assessments that your school or district wants to administer to all students. For example, you may want to administer the High-Frequency Word Assessment to all Grade 3 students. *Remember to minimize the amount of assessment by selecting assessments only when you feel additional information is needed in a particular area.*

Notice the suggested grade level criteria in the charts in Appendix C of this guide. These charts summarize the different assessments and provide reasonable goals that may be adjusted to fit your district standards. Be sure to consult *fountasandpinnell.com* for any revisions or updates to these forms. If you find specific areas of need, you may find the targeted lessons in *Phonics Lessons* K, 1, or 2 (Fountas and Pinnell, Heinemann, 2003) or *Word Study Lessons* 3 (Pinnell and Fountas, Heinemann, 2004) helpful for whole group phonics and word study instruction.

A Tool for Determining Where to Start

The Where-to-Start Word Test is a quick way to find a starting place for Benchmark Assessment. If you do not have sufficient, dependable information from the previous teacher or school records or your own observations to judge the starting point for the assessments, this test should save you from having the student read a large number of texts.

Ask the student to read the Where-to-Start Word List that you give her. Third graders should begin with the Level 2 list, fourth graders with the Level 3 list, and so on. Place a card under each word and have the student move it down the list as she reads. Do not coach or prompt. Score as errors words that the student cannot

read, substitutes with other words or sounds, says several different ways because she is unsure of the pronunciation, reads incompletely, or adds sounds to (such as a final *s*). Record the number of words read accurately at the bottom of each list. If the student reads 16–20 words on a list correctly, then move to the next level. If a student reads fewer than 16 words correctly, then stop and begin the assessment at the appropriate level shown on the Where-to-Start chart (Figure 4.1).

Where-to-Start Chart							
Number Correct	**List Read**						
	Level 2	Level 3	Level 4	Level 5	Level 6	Level 7	Level 8
0–5	E	I	M	P	R	T	U
6–10	F	J	M	P	R	T	V
11–15	G	K	N	Q	S	U	V
16–20	H	L	O	Q	S	U	V

FIGURE 4.1 Where-to-Start Chart

Getting to Know Your Students

The Reading Interview is a form you can use to learn more about a student's preferences and reading history. It takes about five minutes to administer. This assessment will enable you to help students find titles that they will be interested in reading. It will also show you how aware they are of their own reading strengths and weaknesses. You can also look at the interviews across a whole class to decide which titles would be good for the whole group and which would be better suited to small groups or individuals.

Ask each question on the Reading Interview sheet and record the student's response or let students complete the interview sheet on their own, depending on the grade level you are working with. In addition to reading strengths and weaknesses, you are looking for whether students have a difficult time thinking of books they enjoy and the variety of topics, genres, and authors they have experienced.

Analysis of Fluency

The Six Dimensions Fluency Rubric (Figure 4.2) lets you take a detailed look at oral reading fluency. It targets five dimensions of fluency—pausing, phrasing, stress, intonation, and rate—and a sixth dimension,

Student _____   Date _____

Six Dimensions Fluency Rubric

1. Pausing Pausing refers to the way the reader's voice is guided by punctuation (for example, short breath at a comma; full stop with voice going down at periods and up at question marks; full stop at dashes).

0	1	2	3
Almost no pausing to reflect punctuation or meaning of the text *Needs intensive teaching and/or text not appropriate*	Some pausing to reflect the punctuation and meaning of the text *Needs explicit teaching, prompting, and reinforcing*	Most of the reading evidences appropriate pausing to reflect the punctuation and meaning of the text. *Needs some prompting and reinforcing*	Almost all the reading is characterized by pausing to reflect punctuation and meaning of the text. *Teaching not needed*

2. Phrasing Phrasing refers to the way readers put words together in groups to represent the meaningful units of language. Sometimes phrases are cued by punctuation such as commas, but often they are not. Phrased reading sounds like oral language, though more formal.

0	1	2	3
No evidence of appropriate phrasing during the reading *Needs intensive teaching and/or text not appropriate*	Some evidence of appropriate phrasing during the reading *Needs explicit teaching, prompting, and reinforcing*	Much of the reading evidences appropriate phrasing. *Needs some prompting and reinforcing*	Almost all the reading is appropriately phrased. *Teaching not needed*

3. Stress Stress refers to the emphasis readers place on particular words (louder tone) to reflect the meaning as speakers would do in oral language.

0	1	2	3
Almost no stress on appropriate words to reflect the meaning of the text *Needs intensive teaching and/or text not appropriate*	Some stress on appropriate words to reflect the meaning of the text *Needs explicit teaching, prompting, and reinforcing*	Most of the reading evidences stress on appropriate words to reflect the meaning of the text. *Needs some prompting and reinforcing*	Almost all of the reading is characterized by stress on appropriate words to reflect the meaning of the text. *Teaching not needed*

4. Intonation Intonation refers to the way the reader varies the voice in tone, pitch, and volume to reflect the meaning of the text—sometimes called expression.

0	1	2	3
Almost no variation in voice or tone (pitch) to reflect the meaning of the text *Needs intensive teaching and/or text not appropriate*	Some evidence of variation in voice or tone (pitch) to reflect the meaning of the text *Needs explicit teaching, prompting, and reinforcing*	Most of the reading evidences variation in voice or tone (pitch) to reflect the meaning of the text. *Needs some prompting and reinforcing*	Almost all of the reading evidences variation in voice or tone (pitch) to reflect the meaning of the text. *Teaching not needed*

5. Rate Rate refers to the pace at which a reader moves through the text—not too fast and not too slow. The reader moves along steadily with few slow-downs, stops, or pauses to solve words. If the reader has only a few short pauses for word solving and picks up the pace again, look at the overall rate.

0	1	2	3
Almost no evidence of appropriate rate during the reading *Needs intensive teaching and/or text not appropriate*	Some evidence of appropriate rate during the reading *Needs explicit teaching, prompting, and reinforcing*	Most of the reading evidences appropriate rate. *Needs some prompting and reinforcing*	Almost all of the reading evidences appropriate rate. *Teaching not needed*

6. Integration Integration involves the way a reader consistently and evenly orchestrates rate, phrasing, pausing, intonation, and stress.

0	1	2	3
Almost none of the reading is fluent. *Needs intensive teaching and/or text not appropriate*	Some of the reading is fluent. *Needs explicit teaching, prompting, and reinforcing*	Most of the reading is fluent. *Needs some prompting and reinforcing*	Almost all of the reading is fluent. *Teaching not needed*

Guiding Principles for Rating Try to focus on one aspect at a time but give your overall impression.

Assessing Fluency and Phrasing

FIGURE 4.2 Six Dimensions Fluency Rubric

integration, which refers to the way the reader orchestrates the other five dimensions.

Use this form to observe and record a student's oral reading of a benchmark book or other leveled text. The fluency assessment helps you notice and think about the dimensions of oral reading that a student controls and needs to develop. To begin, have the student read aloud the selected text. Consider the student's rate, phrasing, pausing, intonation, and stress as separate dimensions and rate each from 0–3 on the rubric. Then rate your overall impression of the student's integration of all the elements in the reading.

Note those dimensions of fluency the reader is demonstrating and those he is neglecting. For more information on fluency, you may want to refer to *Teaching for Comprehending and Fluency, K–8* (Fountas and Pinnell, Heinemann, 2006).

Phonics, Word Analysis, and Vocabulary Assessments

The primary value of these assessments is in diagnosis of particular items related to phonics, word study, or vocabulary. If you re-administer the assessment, you can look for growth in a student's control of the element at a later date. Eighteen word-analysis assessments focus on specific reading-processing skills, letter knowledge, high-frequency words, letter-sound relationships, and word structure. Your school or district may want to select optional assessments that are most important for a particular grade level. Or, you may want to diagnosis a particular area of learning (such as reading words with vowel clusters) when a student, small group, or class is having difficulty. In any case, select only assessments that are needed for a particular purpose.

READING HIGH-FREQUENCY WORDS: 100–200 WORDS

These two assessments give you a range of high-frequency words to work with, from 100 to 200 words. Which of the assessments you use and when you use it will depend on your students' needs. Each of the high-frequency assessments includes words that gradually increase in difficulty level. You may choose to begin with the easier high-frequency words included on Lists 1, 2, and 3 and move up through

each one to Lists 4 and 5, or you can choose the list that best suits your students.

Administer each assessment individually by asking the student to read down the list of words. On the Individual Record, mark his correct responses as well as substitutions. Record the results of the assessment on the form. Notice the number of high-frequency words he reads accurately, the speed of word recognition, partially correct attempts or parts of words known, and the degree of difficulty of his known words.

PHONOGRAMS I AND II

In these assessments, students read words with simple phonogram patterns. Knowing both simple and complex patterns helps them decode new words. Use this assessment to learn which phonograms most of your students can already read, those they can almost read, and those they need to learn. Notice the number of specific phonogram patterns they can recognize accurately; the spelling patterns they know, almost know, or do not know; and their speed in recognizing words and patterns.

You may also administer these assessments individually. Start with List 1, 2, or 3 depending on how advanced your students are. Check a student's reading of between ten and fifteen words at a time over several days with the Phonogram I assessment. In the Phonogram II assessment, administer twenty-five words, which will give you enough information to get started on spelling pattern minilessons. Show the words one at a time. Use the Individual Record to keep an ongoing record of each student's ability to read words with these regular phonogram patterns.

CONSONANT BLENDS

During this assessment, notice each student's ability to use consonant blends to read words, the number of consonant-blend words she can read, and the specific consonant blends she controls in reading.

Administer this assessment individually using the Consonant Blends Word List. Ask the student to read the list of words, going down the column. Score for accuracy and note any substitutions on the Word List, which can be used as her Individual Record. Record the results for all students on the Class Record.

VOWEL CLUSTERS

Students need to learn the various vowel combinations that often appear together in words in order to remember how words "look." Knowing this will help them read new words. Begin by reviewing the list of words found on the Individual Record. Use the list that best suits each student if they read the list individually, or select the list that is most appropriate for the whole class. Record individual responses on the Individual Record. Consider the principle learned if there is a high level of accuracy. Notice the number of words with vowel clusters the student can read and the particular vowel clusters she controls in reading.

SUFFIXES I AND II

These two assessments help you know whether the students understand that a suffix can change the part of speech and whether they can apply their knowledge of suffixes to read words. Administer the assessments individually by giving the student a copy of the Words with Suffixes sheet. Say the base word in column 1 and then ask him to read the word with the suffix. Alternatively, use the base word with the suffix in a sentence and ask him to circle the word you used. Record the results on the Class Record. During this assessment, notice the number of words with suffixes he can read, the particular words and suffixes he recognizes, and the speed with which he reads words with suffixes.

COMPOUND WORDS

This assessment helps you learn whether students can read simple compound words and identify the component parts. Administer this assessment individually and have the student read the words on the Compound Words list. If she finds a word too difficult, prompt her to look for a part she knows. Record accurate responses. Then ask her to make a slash between the two compound words. Notice the number of compound words she recognizes, the specific compound words she recognizes and those she can take apart.

ONE- AND TWO-SYLLABLE WORDS

These assessments provide evidence as to whether students hear word parts and syllable breaks. Use this formation to form small groups of students who have difficulty hearing syllables and need more work. Use the sheet with one- and two-syllable words. Be sure students know the meaning of the words. Ask them to say each word and write the number of syllables or parts they hear. Notice the number of words for which students can identify the correct number of syllables, their ability to identify one- and two-syllable words, to represent sounds with letters, and to represent syllables.

SYLLABLES IN LONGER WORDS

The purpose of this assessment is to demonstrate if students understand the concept of syllables, can hear syllable breaks, can count the number of syllables in a word, and have a beginning understanding of where to divide a word when hyphenating. Most students will be able to hear syllable breaks easily and count the number of syllables in a word. For others, administer the assessment individually. Using the Syllables in Longer Words sheet, read each word aloud and have the student say it softly to herself. Have her place a line between syllables and circle the number of parts of syllables she hears. Notice the number of words in which she can hear and identify syllables, the particular words she can read accurately, the particular words that cause her difficulty, the ability to follow directions, and the speed with which she takes words apart.

GRADES 3–8 WORD FEATURES TEST

There are six different tests with six lists of thirty grade-appropriate words provided. These assessments give you information about which features of words students are able to attend to. The substitutions students make provide information about their knowledge of letter/sound relationships, spelling patterns, and word structure. Ask each student to read the appropriate list of words. Record responses on the Class Record. Notice the word features they can read correctly and those with which they have difficulty.

CONCEPT WORDS

In this assessment, students read concept words and sort them into appropriate categories. Begin by reviewing the Concept Word Lists, and choose lists appropriate for your students. Have each student read a list of words and tell how they are alike. Record the results. You may also ask students to locate concept words in text during reading or have them sort concept words into categories. Notice their ability to read specific words in categories, their speed in recognizing words in categories, and the number of words known in each category.

SYNONYMS I AND II

In these two assessments, students read and identify words that mean the same or almost the same. Administer the assessment either individually or with the whole class, using the Synonyms Word Lists. From choices given at the bottom of each page, students find a synonym for each word on the list and write it next to the word. Notice students' understanding of the concept of synonyms, the number of synonym pairs they form accurately, and the specific synonyms they know.

ANTONYMS I AND II

In these two assessments, students read and identify words that mean the opposite or almost the opposite. Have students read each word and find an antonym from the bottom of the page. Have them write it next to the correct word. Record the results. Notice the number of word pairs students can identify correctly, their understanding of the principle of antonyms, the specific antonyms they know, and their ability to read words accurately.

HOMOPHONES I AND II

In these two assessments, students practice recognizing and using homophones, which many find challenging. In the first assessment, give students the Student Homophone sheet. Read over the list with them, perhaps 5–10 at a time, reminding them that these words sound the same but are spelled differently and have different meanings. Read each sentence to them and have them circle the correct word. Record the results. In the second assessment, students read a sentence and think about which word fits. They write the word in the blank space from two choices given. Expect a fairly high score on this assessment to determine whether students understand the principle and are not just guessing. Notice the number of homophones they correctly represent in sentence context, the ease with which they perform the task, the homophones they can read and understand, and those they find difficult.

HOMOGRAPHS

This assessment shows whether students understand the principle that two words can be spelled the same but be pronounced differently and have different meanings. It also provides information about students' ability to choose between two meanings using sentence context and to reflect meaning through pronunciation. Administer this assessment individually. It is not necessary to use all of the sentences at once. Just five sentence pairs will give you an idea of student understanding. Notice the student's ability to pronounce words accurately to reflect the meaning of the word in context, the speed with which he performs this task, the number of homographs he identifies correctly, and his ability to read specific words.

GREEK AND LATIN WORD ROOTS

This assessment shows whether students understand the meanings of common Greek and Latin roots. Knowledge of these roots will help them improve their vocabulary and apply their knowledge to understanding the meanings of less familiar words. Administer this assessment individually or to the whole class using either the first or second Greek and Latin Roots word sheet. Ask students to read the list of words that goes with each Greek or Latin root and think about what the words have in common. On the blank line, have them write the meaning of the root. Record the results. Notice the words students can read and understand, their ability to identify what the words in each list have in common, the roots they know, and the roots they almost know.

ANALOGIES

This assessment shows whether students understand the relationships between words. The words you use are slightly easier because you want them to concentrate on the relationships. Administer the assessment individually or to the whole class. Make sure students understand the format of analogies. Students need to select from the answer choices the pair of words that share the same relationship. If students have difficulty, ask them to think out loud about word relationships so you can determine if they are having trouble with the format of the analogies or the vocabulary itself. Notice whether students understand the format of analogies, words they understand, words they almost understand, and whether they can identify the relationships between words.

VOCABULARY IN CONTEXT

In this assessment, students use context to correctly identify the meaning of words from a benchmark book at their instructional or independent level. Choosing a book from one of these levels (or both), select words from the list on the corresponding Individual Record, checking those that you used. For each word, have the student turn to the page where the word appears. Then ask, "What does [*word*] mean in this book?" Score answers using the 0–3 rubric provided. Using the chart provided, determine whether his vocabulary in context score is unsatisfactory, satisfactory, or excellent. Notice the number of words known or almost known and the student's use of context to determine which meaning of a word is appropriate.

▶ *Assessment Forms Book* and *CD-ROM*

All of the Optional Assessment forms and materials are available either in reproducible form in the *Assessment Forms Book* or as printable PDF files on the *Assessment Forms CD-ROM*. On the CD-ROM, you can navigate to different tabs for Recording Forms, Summary Forms, Optional Assessments, and Resources (Figure 4.3). Then you can select which forms you want, view the files, and print them as needed. (Coming in 2013, *F&P Online Resources* will be available for printing all BAS forms.)

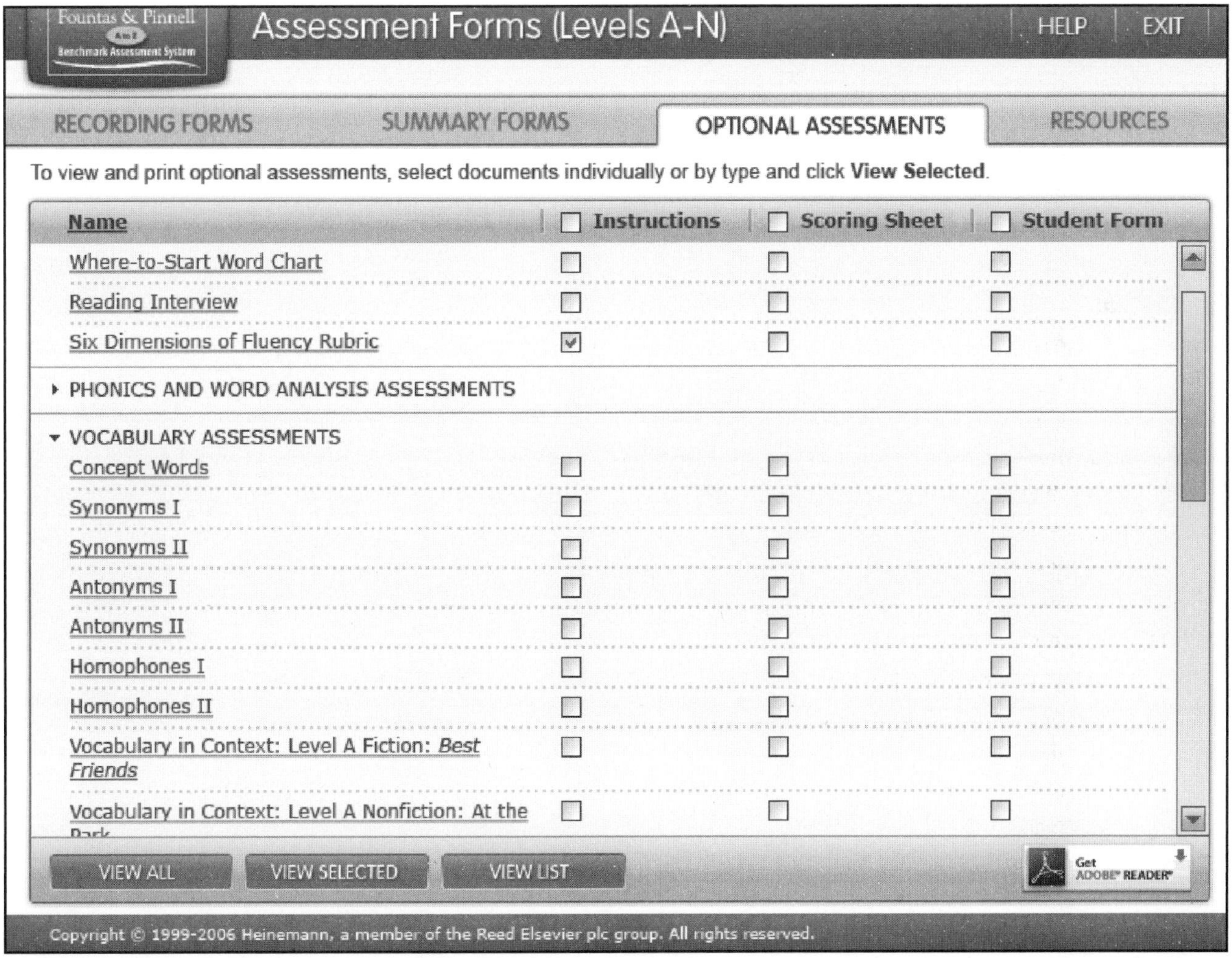

FIGURE 4.3 Optional Assessment menu from *Assessment Forms CD-ROM*

Monitoring Progress and Case Studies

An assessment conference in the *Fountas & Pinnell Benchmark Assessment System 2* represents a student's reading at that point in time. Using standardized procedures and multiple-leveled texts, the conference provides a reliable picture of the student's reading strengths and weaknesses at that moment. Benchmark assessments that are taken two, three, or four times during a year provide a good picture of a student's progress in the instructional program. Nevertheless, assessment results must always be understood within the perspective of the ongoing observation you do every day during reading instruction. By using Benchmark Assessment as a baseline, conducting informal observations, and coding oral reading on reading records at specific intervals, you can track the growth of individuals over time and gain valuable instructional information. You can also identify students who are going off track and provide planned intervention.

In this section, we examine ways of looking at individual progress over time, and monitoring adequate progress. The interpretation and use of Benchmark Assessment data are more important than the scores themselves. In this section we also present eight case studies of individual students, along with our interpretation and commentary.

▶ Monitoring Progress

Looking at Individual Progress

The Summary Forms in the *Assessment Forms Book* and *CD-ROM* provide a place to record a student's Benchmark independent and instructional levels. There are versions for recording scores two times (Bi-annual Assessment Summary), three times (Tri-annual Assessment Summary), or four times (Quarterly Assessment Summary) a year. These scores plot a student's progress over time and provide a clear picture of how the educational system is bringing the student forward as a reader.

In addition, two reading graphs can chart an individual's reading progress. The Annual Record of Reading Progress provides opportunities for noting the levels from Benchmark Assessment conferences and interim reading records. The date and title of the book with the accuracy rate of the reading are entered onto the form and a symbol is placed on a grid; a line connecting the symbols provides a graph of progress. The Longitudinal Record of Reading Progress (which is also printed on the Student Folder) plots a student's Benchmark level (either independent or instructional) four times a year across all eight grades. The *Data Management System* creates these graphs for you once you have entered the data.

Monitoring Adequate Progress

With typical progress, we would expect third graders at the beginning of the year to independently read texts at levels J, K, and L. They may select books at lower levels with content that is interesting to them. At the same time, they would be participating in small-group reading instruction using books around levels M and N. By the end of the year, they should be reading these levels independently and reaching levels O or P with teacher support. Fourth graders at the beginning of the year should be independently reading levels N and O and participating in instruction at about levels P and Q, progressing by the end of the year to level S or T. Grade 5 students typically move from about levels S to V or W across a year, and grade 6 students from levels V to Y or Z.

In grades 7 and 8, students are typically able to read widely across levels W, X, Y, and Z. At levels V–Z, text difficulty is related to very complex interrelated factors. There may be high-level, technical vocabulary words and/or the sentences may be long and very complex. On the other hand, the words and sentences may be relatively easy, but the characters and plot can be complex. Many texts at these levels assume that the reader has prior knowledge of the topic or understands significant aspects of the setting. At the highest levels, students need deep understanding of genres and their characteristics; based on that knowledge, they form expectations that support them in comprehending the text. And, the issues texts explore are often mature, requiring background knowledge and experience to understand. Except for the age-appropriate content, texts at level Y or Z are equivalent to or even more difficult than typical adult reading. Students who can read at these levels can probably also read adult material although often with limited understanding.

What all of this means is that effective reading at all levels, especially the higher levels, is much more than decoding the words. Sometimes you will find that students can read high levels with a high degree of accuracy, but their understanding of the ideas and content is only superficial. For a level to be appropriate, a student must be able to think deeply and to articulate understandings in oral language or writing.

A student's instructional level is important to know. Reading texts that demand a little more than a student's independent level—and instructional support—makes it possible to expand the reading processing system. The independent level is also important to know. It is on independent-level texts that students can read with high accuracy that they have the opportunity to smoothly orchestrate systems of strategic actions. Students who have formed the habit of reading dysfluently need to engage in a great deal of easy reading. Through independently reading books of their choice, they can:

❑ increase vocabulary

❑ build content knowledge that will be helpful in reading informational texts

- ❑ increase fluency

- ❑ build up their knowledge of how texts are organized

- ❑ learn how to select appropriate texts for themselves

- ❑ choose their independent reading books according to interest rather than by level; but if they have learned how to select books appropriately, they can explore topics across a range of levels that they can read independently.

Daily observations of reading behavior and systematic administration of the *Benchmark Assessment System 2* will help you notice and document progress to determine when students need intervention. Students who are reading just below grade level need daily small-group instruction using a gradient of text. It will also be helpful to them to do a great deal of easy reading, supported by individual conferences in which you can support depth of thinking and coach for fluency. Those students who are reading a year or more below grade level need intervention in the form of tutoring or small groups in addition to intensive classroom instruction. Some characteristics of effective interventions are:

- ❑ daily reading of continuous text at instructional level

- ❑ reading and rereading easier texts at independent level

- ❑ phonics and word work appropriate to the level

- ❑ writing in connection with reading

- ❑ intensive teaching by an individual with specialized skills.

We do not recommend that students who are having difficulty be turned over to paraprofessionals or volunteers. These students need the most skilled teaching of all.

▶ Instructional Level Expectations and Goals

Think about a student's present grade level and where you are in the school year to determine whether his performance meets grade level expectations. Teach at the instructional level and take him as far as you can in a given year. To give you some perspective on your goals for each grade level, we provide a chart to help you consider the marking quarter (Figure 5.1) Be sure not to be too rigid, as students' reading levels tend to fall into a range. You may also want to consult with your administrator to adjust any of these levels to conform to school or district standards.

In Figure 5.1, each level indicates the instructional level; that is, the level that a student can read with instructional support (for example, with text introduction). The instructional level at levels L–Z is the highest level a student can read with a minimum of 95% accuracy and satisfactory comprehension or a minimum of 98% accuracy with limited comprehension. A student's independent reading level is usually one or two levels lower than the instructional level. It is one at which a student can read without teacher support.

If a student's instructional level matches the indicated level at the particular point in time, he can be considered to be reading on grade level. If his level is higher, then he can be considered to be reading above grade level. In this case, the student may be reading independently at the level.

You can also download this chart at *www.fountasandpinnell.com* by clicking on "Supporting Materials."

Fountas & Pinnell

INSTRUCTIONAL LEVEL EXPECTATIONS FOR READING

	Beginning of Year (Aug.–Sept.)	1st Interval of Year (Nov.–Dec.)	2nd Interval of Year (Feb.–Mar.)	End of Year (May–June)
Grade K		C+	D+	E+
		B	C	D
		A	B	C
				Below C
Grade 1	E+	G+	I+	K+
	D/E	F	H	J
	C	E	G	I
	Below C	Below E	Below G	Below I
Grade 2	K+	L+	M+	N+
	J/K	K	L	M
	I	J	K	L
	Below I	Below J	Below K	Below L
Grade 3	N+	O+	P+	Q+
	M/N	N	O	P
	L	M	N	O
	Below L	Below M	Below N	Below O
Grade 4	Q+	R+	S+	T+
	P/Q	Q	R	S
	O	P	Q	R
	Below O	Below P	Below Q	Below R
Grade 5	T+	U+	V+	W+
	S/T	T	U	V
	R	S	T	U
	Below R	Below S	Below T	Below U
Grade 6	W+	X+	Y+	Z
	V/W	W	X	Y
	U	V	W	X
	Below U	Below V	Below W	Below X
Grade 7	Z	Z	Z+	Z+
	Y	Y	Z	Z
	X	X	Y	Y
	Below X	Below X	Below Y	Below Y
Grade 8+	Z+	Z+	Z+	Z+
	Z	Z	Z	Z
	Y	Y	Y	Y
	Below Y	Below Y	Below Y	Below Y

KEY

Exceeds Expectations

Meets Expectations

Approaches Expectations: Needs Short-Term Intervention

Does Not Meet Expectations: Needs Intensive Intervention

The Instructional Level Expectations for Reading chart is intended to provide general guidelines for grade-level goals, which should be adjusted based on school/district requirements and professional teacher judgement.

06/26/2013

Heinemann

DEDICATED TO TEACHERS

© 2012 by Irene C. Fountas and Gay Su Pinnell. Portsmouth, NH: Heinemann.

FIGURE 5.1 Quarterly instructional level expectations for reading

▶ Peti, Grade 4 Student

Background and Assessment Summary

Peti was a fourth grader who came to the United States from Cambodia 15 months ago. She began learning English when she arrived.

Peti's spring benchmark scores showed evidence that she read level L texts independently and level M texts at an instructional level. (Figure 5.2) These results placed Peti well below grade level for the end of fourth grade.

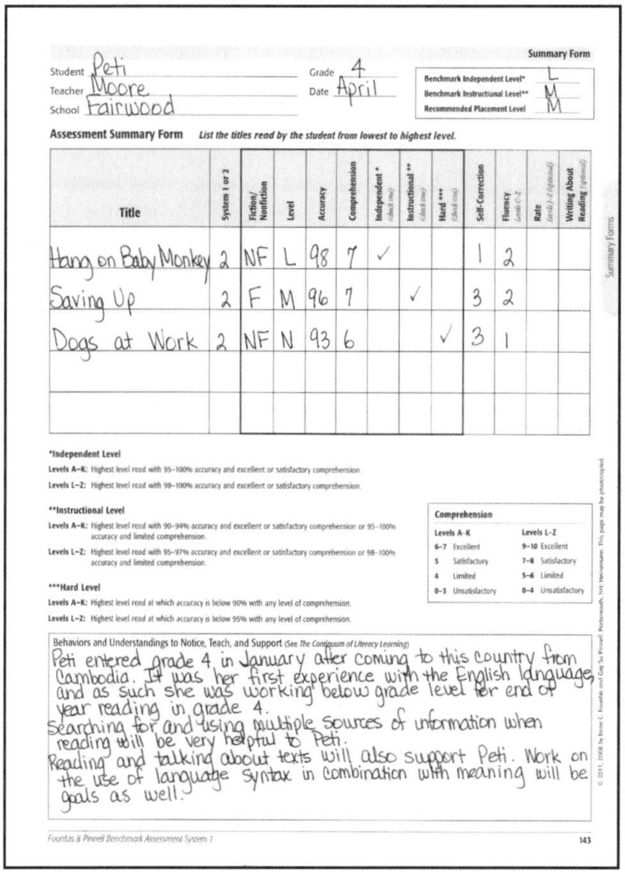

Peti's scores on the level L nonfiction text *Hang On, Baby Monkey,* showed that she read with 98% accuracy and 1 self-correction. Her fluency score was 2 and her comprehension score was 7, placing it at her independent level. In Peti's instructional level M reading of *Saving Up* (Figure 5.3), she scored a 96% for accuracy, with 3 self-corrections, a 2 for fluency and a 7 for comprehension, which was in the satisfactory range. Peti reached her hard level with the level N nonfiction reading of *Dogs at Work,* with scores of 93% accuracy, 3 self-corrections, a fluency score of 1, and a comprehension score of 6, indicating limited understanding.*

---

* To print full-page versions of all case study reading records go to: *www.fountasandpinnell.com* and click on the link for "Case Study Reading Records."

FIGURE 5.2 Peti's Assessment Summary Form

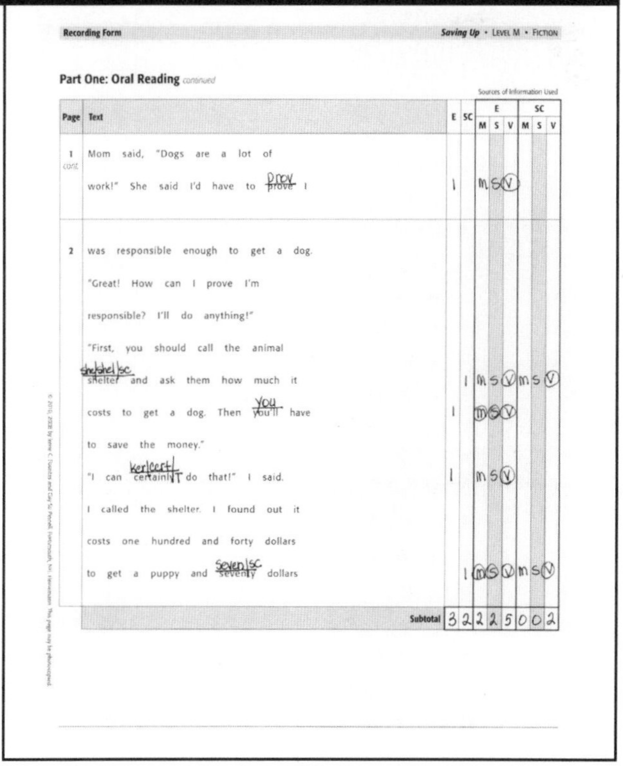

Peti's Level M Recording Form—Instructional Level

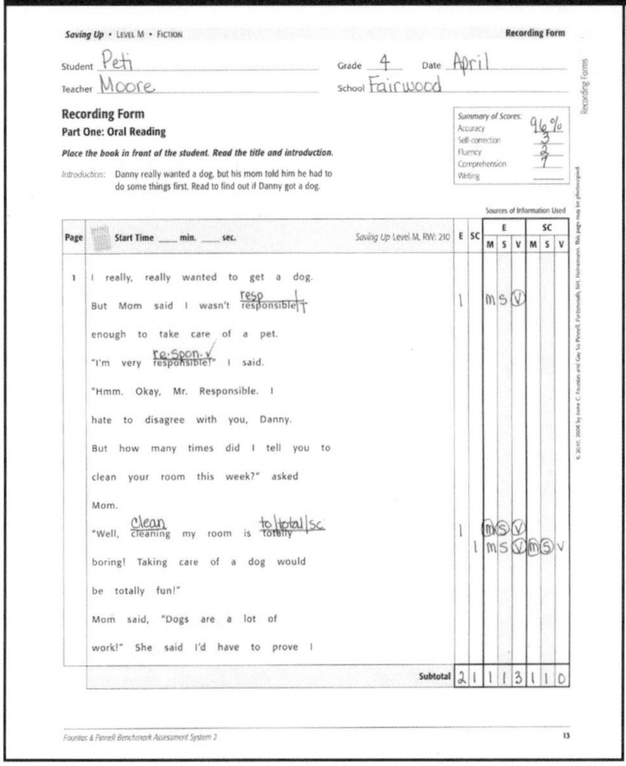

FIGURE 5.3a Peti's Instructional Level Recording Form

FIGURE 5.3b Peti's Instructional Level Recording Form

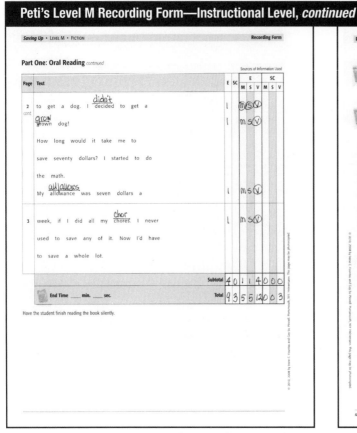

FIGURE 5.3c Peti's Instructional Level Recording Form

Saving Up • LEVEL M • FICTION — Recording Form

Accuracy Rate	Errors	12	10–11	8–9	6–7	4–5	1–3	0
	%	Below 95%	95%	96%	97%	98%	99%	100%

(8–9 / 96% circled)

Self-Corrections — 3

Fluency Score — 0 1 (2) 3

Read quickly. Some attention to expression and pausing.

Reading Rate (Optional)
End Time — 1 min. 10 sec.
Start Time — 0 min. 0 sec.
Total Time — 1 min. 10 sec.
Total Seconds — 70

(RW × 60) ÷ Total Seconds = Words Per Minute (WPM)
12,600 ÷ 70 = 180 WPM

FIGURE 5.3d Peti's Instructional Level Recording Form

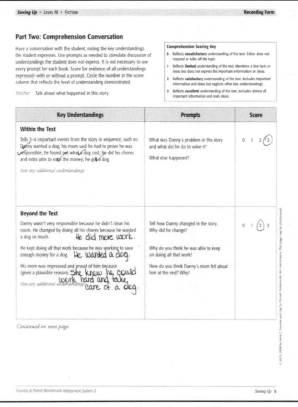

FIGURE 5.3e Peti's Instructional Level Recording Form

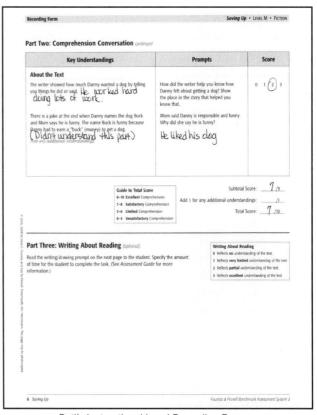

FIGURE 5.3f Peti's Instructional Level Recording Form

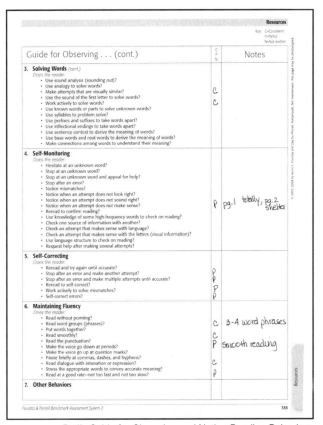

FIGURE 5.4a Peti's Guide for Observing and Noting Reading Behaviors

FIGURE 5.4b Peti's Guide for Observing and Noting Reading Behaviors

Analysis of Processing Strategies

Using the Guide for Observing and Noting Reading Behaviors (Figure 5.4) along with Peti's instructional level M reading of *Saving Up* (Figure 5.3), her teacher noticed the following.

Section 1, Early Reading Behaviors: Peti's early reading behaviors were under control.

Section 2, Searching for and Using Information: Peti made meaningful attempts at unknown words using the story to predict words. She had a strong awareness of visual features of words. For example, she substituted *seven* for *seventy* and *grow* for *grown*. It is possible that Peti was not noticing the ends of words, but it's more likely that she was not monitoring the syntax of English. Her substitutions may have reflected her oral language at that time. Syntactically, when an error didn't sound right, Peti did not reread to search for more information.

Section 3, Solving Words: Peti read many high-frequency words and showed good word-solving ability. She used known word parts (syllables) to solve words, sometimes making several attempts that were visually similar.

Section 4, Self-Monitoring: At times, Peti checked an attempt that made sense with the letters in the word.

Section 5, Self-Correcting: Peti's self-corrections were close to the point of error, indicating attention to meaning and visual sources of information. Her self-correction score showed she was self-correcting some errors, but not all. The errors she did not self-correct may have affected her comprehension.

Section 6, Maintaining Fluency: Peti read primarily in three- or four-word phrase groups. There was some smooth and expressive interpretation and pausing with mostly appropriate rate.

Overall, Peti used some meaning and visual information to support her word-solving. She appeared to focus on solving words at the point of the problem rather than actively thinking about the text. As a result, her comprehending suffered. She needed to read texts that allowed her to work on what sounded right (with English syntax) in connection with the meaning of the text.

Evidence of Comprehension

In Peti's comprehension conversation for the instructional level M fiction text (Figures 5.3e–f), she was able to recall important details from the story. She understood that the character Danny did his chores to earn money to get a dog. She also understood that Danny had to show his mother that he was responsible enough to take care of a dog. Peti explained how Danny changed in the story and why Danny's mother thought he was ready to have a pet. She was able to think within, beyond, and about the text.

Implications for Instruction

Using *The Continuum of Literacy Learning, Prompting Guide 1, Teaching for Comprehending and Fluency: Thinking, Talking, and Writing about Reading, K-8*, and *When Readers Struggle: Teaching that Works* as resources, the following information was important to consider when instructing Peti.

FROM *THE CONTINUUM OF LITERACY LEARNING*

The Guided Reading section for Peti's instructional level M contains a description of readers who process texts successfully at that level. Peti was capable of some of this, but to deeply understand this level of text, she needed specific instruction in word-solving strategies and fluency. She also benefitted from more prompting in the areas of searching for and using multiple sources of information.

Specifically, the following goals were identified for Peti's instructional program:

- ❑ use multiple sources of information to solve new words
- ❑ demonstrate knowledge of flexible ways to solve words (noticing word parts, noticing endings and prefixes)
- ❑ use the context of a sentence, paragraph, or whole text to determine the meaning of a word
- ❑ demonstrate competent, active word solving while reading at a good pace-less overt problem solving
- ❑ self-correct when errors detract from the meaning of the text

- ❑ consistently check on understanding and search for information when meaning breaks down
- ❑ demonstrate appropriate stress on words, pausing and phrasing, intonation, and use of punctuation
- ❑ express changes in ideas after reading a text
- ❑ infer the big ideas of a text
- ❑ identify important aspects of illustrations
- ❑ notice and interpret figurative language and discuss how it adds to enjoyment or understanding.

FROM *PROMPTING GUIDE, PART 1*

To help Peti consistently check on her own understanding and search for and use multiple sources of information when meaning breaks down, her teacher used teaching, prompting, and reinforcing language such as:

- ❑ *It has to make sense, sound right and look right.*
- ❑ *Listen (say whole sentences) It makes sense, sounds right, and looks right.*
- ❑ *Does that make sense and sound right?*
- ❑ *Try that again and make it sound right.*

To help Peti pay more attention to the end of words, she used prompts like:

- ❑ *Look at the end of the word.*
- ❑ *Look at this part of the word* (pointing to the end of the word).

Also, Peti's teacher used language to reinforce effective behaviors when she had to problem-solve. This helped her understand that what she was doing was worth continuing.

Peti's fluency scores on the three texts she read ranged from 1–2. She needed intensive teaching for fluency and phrasing. Teaching Peti to read larger, meaningful phrases or word groups with smooth, expressive interpretation and pausing helped her comprehension and allowed her to interpret the author's message more effectively.

She taught Peti to listen to how her reading sounds with teaching prompts such as these to help her achieve integration.

- *Listen to me read this part. Now you read it just like I did.*
- *Listen to how I put my words together.*

After teaching, prompts such as these supported her effective processing:

- *Are you listening to how your reading sounds?*
- *These words make sense together. Read them together.*

FROM *TEACHING FOR COMPREHENDING AND FLUENCY: THINKING, TALKING, AND WRITING ABOUT READING, K–8*

To deepen Peti's ability to think within, beyond, and about the text, her teacher used specific language to demonstrate that type of thinking and foster those conversations such as this, found on pages 400–402 (for fiction) and on pages 430–432 (for nonfiction):

- *At the beginning of the story _____ was like this _____. But he is going to change. You'll find out that _____.*
- *What was _____ like at the beginning (or end) of the story? Is _____ changing?*
- *Based on what you know about the character, you will want to think about _____.*
- *What do you think will happen to _____?*
- *A very important thing that happens here. [Provide example]*
- *What do you think is important about _____?*
- *_____ seemed real to me because _____.*
- *Did _____ seem like a real person to you? What made you feel that way?*

FROM *WHEN READERS STRUGGLE: TEACHING THAT WORKS*

Since Peti was strengthening her reading in a comprehensive manner, the following prompts were useful:

- *Think about what would sound right.*
- *Try _____. Would that sound right?*
- *Try that again and think about what would make sense.*
- *What do you want to remember about this book?*
- *Did you find yourself reading faster in the exciting parts?*
- *Think about what you know. What do you think will happen?*
- *What do you think the writer will teach you about?*
- *That's what the writer said. What do you think it means?*
- *What did the writer do to make this story funny?*
- *What did the writer say to make you think that?*

Classroom Teaching

Peti was an English Language Learner reading at a level M in fourth grade, which is a more appropriate level for the beginning of third grade. She benefited from many opportunities to read independent texts and discuss what she read with peers. She also benefited from participation in interactive read aloud and reader's theater to hear, understand, and gain familiarity with the syntax of English. She needed small-group instruction at level M with emphasis on reading meaningfully. Instruction included searching for and using multiple sources of information and discussing texts to gain deeper meaning.

▶ Cynthia, Grade 3 Student

Background and Assessment Summary

Cynthia was a Khmer-speaking third grader. She entered U.S. schools in kindergarten.

Cynthia's mid-year benchmark scores showed evidence that she read level M texts independently and level N texts at an instructional level (Figure 5.5). These results suggested Cynthia was reading on grade level for the middle of third grade.

Cynthia's scores on her independent level M reading of the fiction text *Saving Up*, showed that she read with 98% accuracy with 1 self-correction. Her fluency score was 2 and her comprehension score of 9 was in the excellent range. For Cynthia's instructional level N reading of the nonfiction text *Dogs at Work* (Figure 5.6), she scored a 97% for accuracy with no self-corrections, a 1 for fluency and a 10 for comprehension, also in the excellent range. Cynthia reached her hard level with the level O fiction text *The New Girl*, with scores of 92% accuracy, 1 self-correction, a fluency score of 1, and a comprehension score of 8, indicating satisfactory understanding.*

---

*To print full-page versions of all case study reading records go to: *www.fountasandpinnell.com* and click on the link for "Case Study Reading Records."

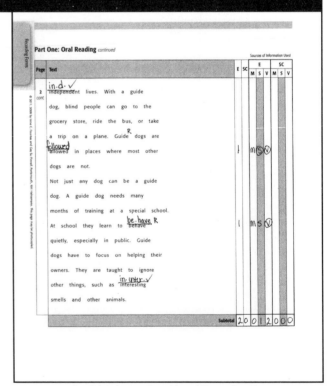

FIGURE 5.5 Cynthia's Assessment Summary Form

Cynthia's Level N Recording Form—Instructional Level

FIGURE 5.6a Cynthia's Instructional Level Recording Form

FIGURE 5.6b Cynthia's Instructional Level Recording Form

Dogs at Work • LEVEL N • NONFICTION   Recording Form

Part One: Oral Reading *continued*

Page	Text	E	SC	Sources of Information Used E / M S V	SC / M S V
3	They also learn to keep still and quiet in busy places, such as shopping malls or offices. Most dogs would have a very hard time doing that! Dogs at Work If you see a guide dog doing its job, remember not to pet or talk to it. Guiding is very hard to do. It requires a dog's full attention.				

Subtotal 3 0 1 1 2 0 0 0
End Time ___ min. ___ sec.   Total 8 0 1 2 6 0 0 0

Have the student finish reading the book silently.

FIGURE 5.6c Cynthia's Instructional Level Recording Form

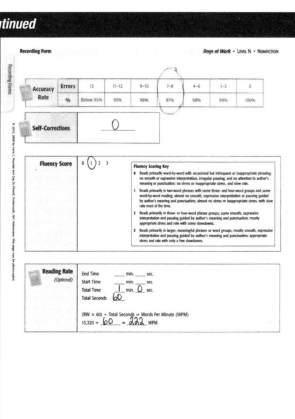

Recording Form   *Dogs at Work* • LEVEL N • NONFICTION

Accuracy Rate	Errors	13	11–12	9–10	7–8	4–6	1–3	0
	%	Below 95%	95%	96%	97%	98%	99%	100%

Self-Corrections   0

Fluency Score 0 (1) 2 3

Fluency Scoring Key

0 Reads primarily word-by-word with occasional but infrequent or inappropriate phrasing; no smooth or expressive interpretation, irregular pausing, and no attention to author's meaning or punctuation; no stress or inappropriate stress, and slow rate.

1 Reads primarily in two-word phrases with some three- and four-word groups and some word-by-word reading; almost no smooth, expressive interpretation or pausing guided by author's meaning and punctuation; almost no stress or inappropriate stress, with slow rate most of the time.

2 Reads primarily in three- or four-word phrase groups; some smooth, expressive interpretation and pausing guided by author's meaning and punctuation; mostly appropriate stress and rate with some slowdowns.

3 Reads primarily in larger, meaningful phrases or word groups; mostly smooth, expressive interpretation and pausing guided by author's meaning and punctuation; appropriate stress and rate with only a few slowdowns.

Reading Rate *(Optional)*

End Time ___ min. ___ sec.
Start Time ___ min. ___ sec.
Total Time 1 min. 0 sec.
Total Seconds 60

(RW × 60) ÷ Total Seconds = Words Per Minute (WPM)
13,320 ÷ 60 = 222 WPM

FIGURE 5.6d Cynthia's Instructional Level Recording Form

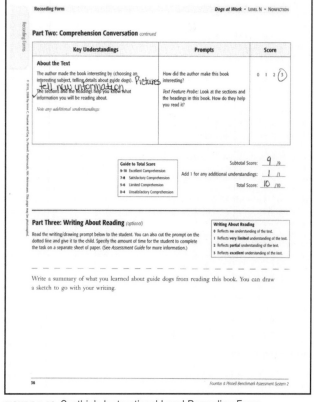

Dogs at Work • LEVEL N • NONFICTION   Recording Form

Part Two: Comprehension Conversation

Have a conversation with the student, noting the key understandings the student expresses. Use prompts as needed to stimulate discussion of understandings the student does not express. It is not necessary to use every prompt for each book. Score for evidence of all understandings expressed—with or without a prompt. Circle the number in the score column that reflects the level of understanding demonstrated.

Teacher: Talk about what you learned in this book.

Comprehension Scoring Key

0 Reflects **unsatisfactory** understanding of the text. Either does not respond or talks off the topic.

1 Reflects **limited** understanding of the text. Mentions a few facts or ideas but does not express the important information or ideas.

2 Reflects **satisfactory** understanding of the text. Includes important information and ideas but neglects other key understandings.

3 Reflects **excellent** understanding of the text. Includes almost all important information and main ideas.

Key Understandings	Prompts	Score
Within the Text Tells 3–4 facts about guide dogs, such as: Guide dogs help blind people; they need special training; they help people go many places (gives an example); you should not pet a guide dog; guide dogs wear special harnesses. The glossary helps you know what some of the words in the story mean. For example, *independent* means needing no help from others. *Best friend to blind people. Help get around. Can go in grocery store. Play at end of day*	Tell what you learned about guide dogs from this book. What else did you learn? Anything else? *Text Feature Probe:* Look at the glossary. How does it help you? Give an example of a word from the glossary.	0 1 2 (3)
Beyond the Text The most important thing about guide dogs is how they help people. Guide dogs do important work because they help blind people be independent. Dogs probably like to help their owners and the owners love their dogs. *Help owner do things, get around. Mentions harness – take off for play. Lead owner around.*	What is the most important thing about guide dogs? Do you think guide dogs do important work? Why (not)? What does the author say that makes you think that? How do you think guide dogs and their owners probably feel about each other?	0 1 2 (3)

Continued on next page.

FIGURE 5.6e Cynthia's Instructional Level Recording Form

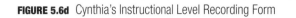

Recording Form   *Dogs at Work* • LEVEL N • NONFICTION

Part Two: Comprehension Conversation *continued*

Key Understandings	Prompts	Score
About the Text The author made the book interesting by (choosing an interesting subject, telling details about guide dogs). *tell new information Pictures* The sections and the headings help you know what information you will be reading about. *Note any additional understandings:*	How did the author make this book interesting? *Text Feature Probe:* Look at the sections and the headings in this book. How do they help you read it?	0 1 2 (3)

Guide to Total Score	
9–10 Excellent Comprehension	
7–8 Satisfactory Comprehension	
5–6 Limited Comprehension	
0–4 Unsatisfactory Comprehension	

Subtotal Score 9 /9
Add 1 for any additional understandings: 1 /1
Total Score: 10 /10

Part Three: Writing About Reading *(optional)*

Read the writing/drawing prompt below to the student. You can also cut the prompt on the dotted line and give it to the child. Specify the amount of time for the student to complete the task on a separate sheet of paper. (See *Assessment Guide* for more information.)

Writing About Reading

0 Reflects **no** understanding of the text.
1 Reflects **very limited** understanding of the text.
2 Reflects **partial** understanding of the text.
3 Reflects **excellent** understanding of the text.

Write a summary of what you learned about guide dogs from reading this book. You can draw a sketch to go with your writing.

FIGURE 5.6f Cynthia's Instructional Level Recording Form

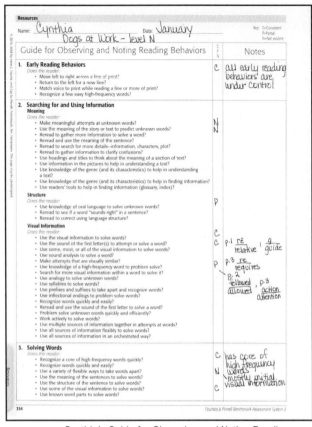

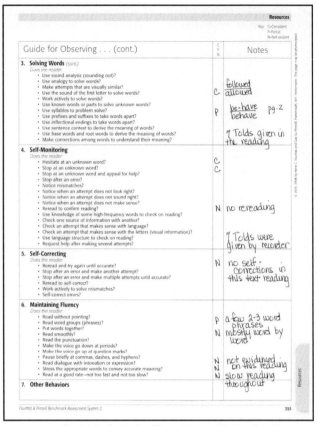

FIGURE 5.7a Cynthia's Guide for Observing and Noting Reading Behaviors

FIGURE 5.7b Cynthia's Guide for Observing and Noting Reading Behaviors

Analysis of Processing Strategies

Using the Guide for Observing and Noting Reading Behaviors (Figure 5.7) along with Cynthia's instructional level reading of *Dogs at Work,* level N, her teacher noticed the following:

Section 1, Early Reading Behaviors: Cynthia's early reading behaviors were under control.

Section 2, Searching for and Using Information: Cynthia used visual information from the beginning of words to attempt word solving.

Section 3, Solving Words: Cynthia recognized a core of high-frequency words. She relied mostly on beginning sound(s) to figure out unknown words. There was some evidence of attempts that were visually similar (*followed* for *allowed*) and using syllables to problem solve (*be-have* for *behave*). On the reading record she made some attempts, but she was "told" a majority of unknown words.

Section 4, Self-Monitoring: Cynthia monitored her reading and stopped at unknown words.

Section 5, Self-Correcting: Cynthia did not self-correct any of her errors in her reading.

Section 6, Maintaining Fluency: Cynthia read primarily word-by-word with occasional but infrequent or inappropriate phrasing, no smooth or expressive interpretation, irregular pausing attention to author's meaning or punctuation, no stress or inappropriate stress, and slow rate.

Overall, Cynthia used some visual information to support her word solving. Her substitutions indicated difficulty with vocabulary, especially words that were multisyllabic and difficult to decode. If these words were not in Cynthia's vocabulary, they were difficult even to attempt. With the help of "tolds," Cynthia was able to access the words and construct meaning from the text, indicating a strength.

Evidence of Comprehension

Cynthia scored high on the comprehension conversation for her instructional level N (Figures 5.6e–f). Her writing provided further evidence of her understanding. She noticed many details about what guide dogs do, and how they help their owners. She noticed how the pictures gave new information to the reader. She was able to think within, beyond, and about the text.

Implications for Instruction

Using *The Continuum of Literacy Learning, Prompting Guide 1, Teaching for Comprehending and Fluency: Thinking, Talking, and Writing about Reading, K-8;* and *When Readers Struggle: Teaching that Works* as resources, the following information was important to consider when instructing Cynthia.

FROM *THE CONTINUUM OF LITERACY LEARNING*

The Guided Reading section for Cynthia's instructional level N contains a description of readers who process texts successfully at that level. Cynthia was capable of much of this with the exception of word solving strategies and fluency.

Specifically, the following goals were identified for Cynthia's instructional program:

- ❑ begin to notice new and interesting words, and add them to speaking and writing vocabulary
- ❑ connect words that mean the same or almost the same to help in acquiring new vocabulary
- ❑ demonstrate knowledge of flexible ways to solve words (noticing word parts, noticing endings and prefixes)
- ❑ use the context of a sentence, paragraph, or whole text to determine the meaning of a word
- ❑ demonstrate phrased, fluent oral reading
- ❑ use multiple sources of information (language structure, meaning, fast word recognition) to support fluency and phrasing
- ❑ through talk or writing, demonstrate learning new content from reading
- ❑ identify important aspects of illustrations.

FROM *PROMPTING GUIDE, PART 1*

To provide Cynthia with strategic ways to problem solve unknown words and improve her fluency, her teacher used prompts like these for the specific behaviors described below.

When Cynthia came to words she didn't know, she tried using the initial sound(s) and then waited for a "told:"

- ❑ *Look carefully and think what you know.*
- ❑ *Think about what you know that might help.*
- ❑ *How can you help yourself?*

To help Cynthia initiate her problem solving, she was taught how to think about approaching the task:

- ❑ *Listen for the first part (next part, last part).*
- ❑ *Do you know a word that starts (ends) like that?*
- ❑ *Is that like a word you know?*

Cynthia noticed some word parts but needed some help developing this strategic action:

- ❑ *Say the first part. Say more. Now, say the ending.*
- ❑ *Look for a part you know.*
- ❑ *What do you know that might help?*

Cynthia's fluency ratings ranged from 1–2 on the three texts she read. She needs intense teaching for fluency and phrasing:

- ❑ *Read these words together.*
- ❑ *These words make sense together. Read them together.*
- ❑ *Make it sound like the characters are talking.*
- ❑ *Read it all smoothly.*

Cynthia monitored her reading and stopped when she didn't know a word. She needed help when problem solving an unknown words:

- ❑ *What's wrong? Why did you stop?*
- ❑ *Do you think it looks like _____?*
- ❑ *Where's the tricky part?*
- ❑ *You're nearly right. Change the middle. (Add the ending.)*
- ❑ *You can try it again and think what would look right.*
- ❑ *Something wasn't quite right. See if you can fix that.*

FROM *TEACHING FOR COMPREHENDING AND FLUENCY: THINKING, TALKING, AND WRITING ABOUT READING, K–8*

To enrich Cynthia's ability to deepen her thinking within, beyond, and about the text, her teacher used specific language to demonstrate that type of thinking and fostered those conversations with prompts such as these found on pages 400–402 (for fiction) and on pages 430–432 (for nonfiction):

❑ *This word is important in understanding this topic.*

❑ *Do you know the meaning of _____?*

❑ *What is this word? Read and think about what you think it means.*

❑ *You know something about this topic already. (Give an example.)*

❑ *What details did you learn from the description?*

❑ *When you read this book, notice how the writer is describing the topic.*

❑ *What did you learn from the kinds of descriptive details the writer provided? Why do you think the writer included these details?*

FROM *WHEN READERS STRUGGLE: TEACHING THAT WORKS*

Since Cynthia used few strategies to figure out unknown words and her English vocabulary was limited, both factors impeded her fluency. The following sample prompts were useful for her:

❑ *Look at the first part of the word. Say more.*

❑ *Think about what that word means in this sentence (in this story).*

❑ *That means the same as (synonym).*

❑ *Try that again and think what would make sense and look right.*

❑ *Put these words together.*

❑ *Think about how to say that.*

❑ *Did you find yourself reading faster in the exciting parts?*

❑ *Think about what you know. What do you think will happen?*

❑ *What do you think the writer will teach you about?*

❑ *That's what the writer said. What do you think it means?*

Classroom Teaching

Cynthia was an English Language Learner reading at level N in the middle of third grade, which was on grade level. She benefited from many opportunities to read independent texts and discuss what she read with peers. She also benefited from opportunities to talk about her reading through interactive read aloud, literature discussion, and guided reading. She needed many opportunities to expand her English vocabulary. In small-group instruction at level N, she needed careful selection of texts and rich conversations around texts, as well as explicit vocabulary instruction.

▶ Francesco, Grade 3 Student

Background and Assessment Summary

Francesco was a third grade student. Figure 5.8 shows the results of his fall Benchmark Assessment.

Although Francesco's prior records indicated he might be reading slightly below grade level, his reading of *Saving Up*, level M fiction, revealed an accuracy rate of 98% with 3 self-corrections. His reading rate of 93 words-per-minute (WPM) was close to the average range for his grade level. He scored a 2 on fluency, indicating he had a lot under control but still needed to be reminded or prompted at times in this area. A comprehension score of 8, was in the satisfactory range, confirming level M as his independent reading level. In his instructional reading of *Dogs at Work* (Figure 5.9), level N nonfiction, Francesco earned a 95% accuracy score with 2 self-corrections. His reading rate of 76 WPM was below the average range and his fluency score was a 2. His comprehension score of 7 was satisfactory. He reached his hard level with the fiction level O text. These results placed Francesco slightly above grade level for the beginning of grade three.*

*To print full-page versions of all case study reading records go to: *www.fountasandpinnell.com* and click on the link for "Case Study Reading Records."

Summary Form

Student Francesco | Grade 3 | Date September
Teacher Wahlberg
School Central

Benchmark Independent Level* M
Benchmark Instructional Level** N
Recommended Placement Level N

Assessment Summary Form *List the titles read by the student from lowest to highest level.*

Title	System 1 or 2	Fiction/Nonfiction	Level	Accuracy	Comprehension	Independent* (check one)	Instructional** (check one)	Hard*** (check one)	Self-Correction	Fluency Levels G–Z	Rate Levels J–Z (optional)	Writing About Reading (optional)
Saving Up	2	F	M	98	8	✓			3	1	93	
Dogs at Work	2	NF	N	95	7		✓		2	1	76	
The New Girl	2	F	O	93	3			✓	1	0	71	

***Independent Level**
Levels A–K: Highest level read with 95–100% accuracy and excellent or satisfactory comprehension.
Levels L–Z: Highest level read with 98–100% accuracy and excellent or satisfactory comprehension.

****Instructional Level**
Levels A–K: Highest level read with 90–94% accuracy and excellent or satisfactory comprehension or 95–100% accuracy and limited comprehension.
Levels L–Z: Highest level read with 95–97% accuracy and excellent or satisfactory comprehension or 98–100% accuracy and limited comprehension.

*****Hard Level**
Levels A–K: Highest level read at which accuracy is below 90% with any level of comprehension.
Levels L–Z: Highest level read at which accuracy is below 95% with any level of comprehension.

Comprehension Levels A–K		Levels L–Z	
6–7	Excellent	9–10	Excellent
5	Satisfactory	7–8	Satisfactory
4	Limited	5–6	Limited
0–3	Unsatisfactory	0–4	Unsatisfactory

Behaviors and Understandings to Notice, Teach, and Support (See *The Continuum of Literacy Learning*)
Some careless monitoring on the part of Francesco: the/their, seventeen/seventy, she is/she's, insertions and omissions at level O.
Comprehending satisfactory at independent & instructional levels.
Fluency is not adequate for the processing required at these levels.
Word solving of unfamiliar multisyllable words needs attention.

Summary Forms

© 2010, 2008 by Irene C. Fountas and Gay Su Pinnell. Portsmouth, NH: Heinemann. This page may be photocopied.

Fountas & Pinnell Benchmark Assessment System 2 167

FIGURE 5.8 Francesco's Assessment Summary Form

Francesco's Level N Recording Form—Instructional Level

Dogs at Work • Level N • Nonfiction — Recording Form

Recording Form

Student Francesco | Grade 3 | Date September
Teacher Wahlberg | School Central

Recording Form
Part One: Oral Reading

Place the book in front of the student. Read the title and introduction.

Introduction: Guide dogs help blind people in many different ways. Read to find out how they are trained and how they do many important jobs.

Summary of Scores:
Accuracy 95%
Self-correction 4
Fluency 2
Comprehension 7/10
Writing

Sources of Information Used

Page	Start Time 0 min. 0 sec. — *Dogs at Work* Level N, RW: 222	E	SC	E: M S V	SC: M S V
1	Who is your best friend? A best				
	friend can be a classmate, a (class-✓)				
	neighbor, or even a relative. But for				
	some people, their best friend				
	walks on four legs, is covered with				
	fur, and takes them anywhere they				
	need to go. It's a dog! But it's not				
	just any dog—their best friend is a (the/their)	1		M S V	
	guide dog. (guard/guide)	1		M S V	
2	What Are Guide Dogs? (guard/Guide)	1		M S V	
	Guide dogs help blind people (guard/Guide)	1		M S V	
	get from place to place and lead				
	Subtotal	4	0	1 4 4	0 0 0

Recording Forms

© 2010, 2008 by Irene C. Fountas and Gay Su Pinnell. Portsmouth, NH: Heinemann. This page may be photocopied.

Fountas & Pinnell Benchmark Assessment System 2 31

FIGURE 5.9a Francesco's Instructional Level Recording Form

Part One: Oral Reading *continued*

Sources of Information Used

Page	Text	E	SC	E: M S V	SC: M S V
2 cont.	independent lives. With a guide (independence/independent; guard/A/T/guide; R)	2		M S V; M S V	
	dog, blind people can go to the				
	grocery store, ride the bus, or take				
	a trip on a plane. Guide dogs are				
	allowed in places where most other (yellow/allowed)	1		M S V	
	dogs are not.				
	Not just any dog can be a guide (g-✓)				
	dog. A guide dog needs many				
	months of training at a special school. (Specie/special)	1		M S V	
	At school they learn to behave (be/behave)	1		M S V	
	quietly, especially in public. Guide (quiet/quietly; specie/sc/especially)	1, 1	1	M S V; M S V	M S V
	dogs have to focus on helping their (focal/focus)	1		M S V	
	owners. They are taught to ignore (teach/sc/taught)		1	M S V	M S V
	other things, such as interesting				
	smells and other animals.				
	Subtotal	7	2	4 4 9	1 2 1

Recording Forms

© 2010, 2008 by Irene C. Fountas and Gay Su Pinnell. Portsmouth, NH: Heinemann. This page may be photocopied.

32 *Fountas & Pinnell Benchmark Assessment System 2*

FIGURE 5.9b Francesco's Instructional Level Recording Form

continues

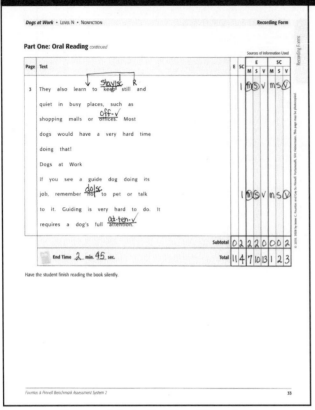

FIGURE 5.9c Francesco's Instructional Level Recording Form

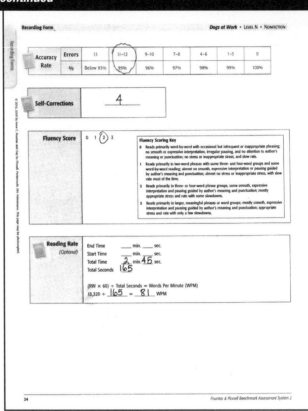

FIGURE 5.9d Francesco's Instructional Level Recording Form

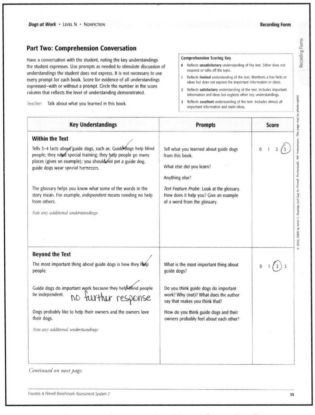

FIGURE 5.9e Francesco's Instructional Level Recording Form

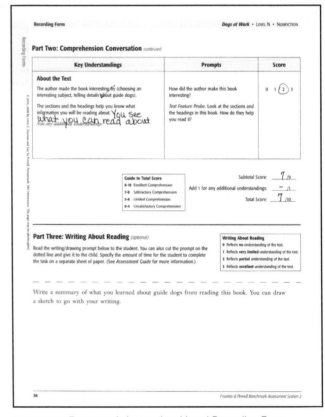

FIGURE 5.9f Francesco's Instructional Level Recording Form

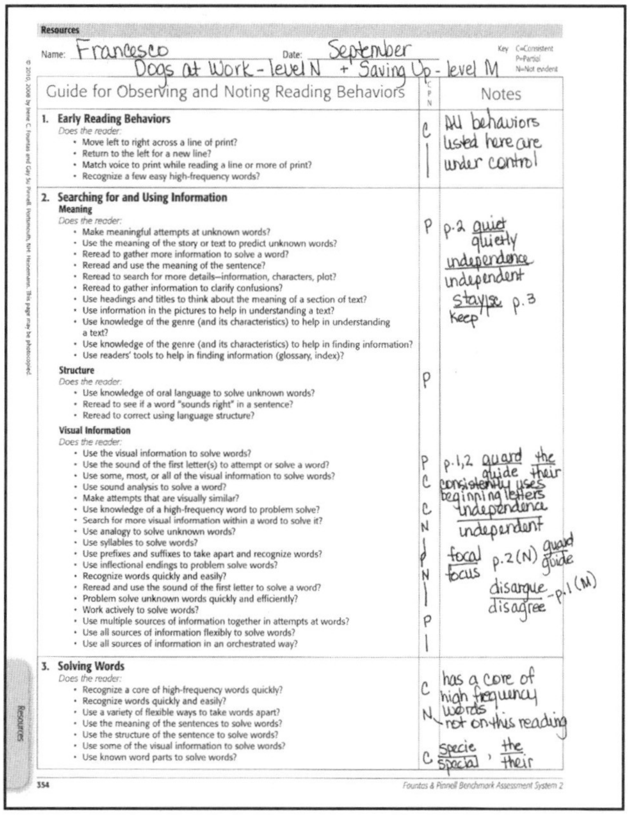

FIGURE 5.10a Francesco's Guide for Observing and Noting Reading Behaviors

FIGURE 5.10b Francesco's Guide for Observing and Noting Reading Behaviors

Analysis of Processing Strategies

Using the Guide for Observing and Noting Behaviors (Figure 5.10), along with Francesco's instructional level N reading of *Dogs at Work* (Figure 5.9), his teacher noticed the following.

Section 1, Early Reading Behaviors: Francesco had the early reading behaviors under control.

Section 2, Searching for and Using Information: Francesco was not consistently searching for and using information in text with efficiency. At his independent and instructional levels, he used visual beginning letter information while neglecting some visual middles and ends. He did not use meaning and/or structure in his attempts at unknown words (*disargue/disagree, guard/guide, focal/focus*). However, some self-corrections demonstrated that he was beginning to notice middle and ends of words (*teach/taught, total/totally* and he successfully took apart two multisyllabic words to solve them (*at-ten/attention, all-allowance*).

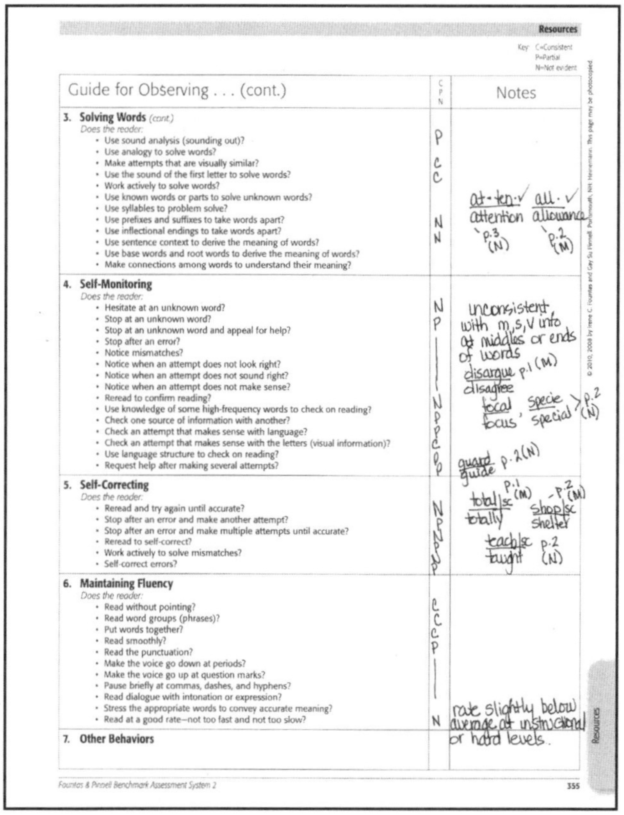

Section 3, Word Solving: Francesco recognized and used a large core of high-frequency words in his reading. He consistently used beginning word parts or letters, including some prefixes, digraphs, and blends in attempts to solve words (*disargue/disagree, independence/independent, specie/special*), but neglected to consistently look at details at the middle or ends of words (*quiet/quietly, seventeen/seventy, guard/guide*).

Section 4, Self-Monitoring: Francesco did not consistently self-monitor for meaning, structure, or visual details at the middle or end of words (*disargue/disagree, focal/focus, specie/special*). He did appeal for help once (*guard/guide*) but read the word incorrectly again and didn't self-monitor.

Section 5, Self-Correcting: Francesco exhibited self-correction behavior at the independent and instructional levels (*total/totally, shop/shelter, teach/taught*). However, he was not consistent in searching for more information.

Section 6, Maintaining Fluency: Francesco scored a 2 on the fluency rubric for both his independent and instructional level readings. He read mostly in smooth phrase groups but wasn't always consistent with expressive interpretation and use of appropriate stress. He had some slow downs causing his reading rate to be below average for his instructional level.

Overall, Francesco was reading on grade level. He used meaning, structure and visual beginning information consistently. He didn't always use visual information from the middle or end of words and didn't use meaning or structure to self-monitor and self-correct these errors. He was beginning to notice some mismatches that didn't sound right or make sense, leading to self-corrections. He was able to take apart and read some multisyllabic words. He used larger phrase groups to read smoothly but didn't consistently use appropriate stress, expressive interpretation, and pausing guided by the author's message. Several slow downs affected his rate, which was slightly below average for his grade level.

Evidence of Comprehension

During the comprehension conversation for his independent and instructional levels, Francesco demonstrated an excellent understanding of information stated within and beyond the text. At his instructional level N, he was able to make inferences about the important work of guide dogs (Figures 5.9e–f). For *Saving Up*, at his independent level M, he was able to clearly interpret the character's feelings. In the about the text area however, Francesco was unable to articulate how nonfiction text features like headings and sections help readers. He had a limited understanding of the techniques that the author used to make a book interesting. Thus, the focus of comprehension work for Francesco was on analyzing and critiquing text as well as explicit teaching about nonfiction text features.

Implications for Instruction

Using *The Continuum of Literacy Learning, Prompting Guide 1*, and *When Readers Struggle: Teaching that Works*, the following information was important to consider when instructing Francesco.

FROM *THE CONTINUUM OF LITERACY LEARNING*

The Guided Reading section for Francesco's instructional level N, contains a description of readers who process texts successfully at that level. Some of this description fit Francesco, but in the areas of efficient word solving of middle and ends of multisyllabic words, self-monitoring errors for meaning and structure, as well as visual details, fluency and rate, Francesco needed explicit teaching. He also needed to learn more about analyzing texts to understand the author's techniques and features of nonfiction texts.

Specifically, the following goals were identified for Francesco's instructional program:

- ❑ demonstrate knowledge of flexible ways to solve words (noticing word parts, noticing endings and prefixes)
- ❑ solve words of two or three syllables, many words with inflectional endings and complex letter-sound relationships
- ❑ continue to monitor accuracy and understanding, self-correcting when errors distract from meaning
- ❑ read dialogue with phrasing and expression that reflects understanding of characters and events
- ❑ demonstrate appropriate stress on words, pausing and phrasing, intonation and use of punctuation
- ❑ use multiple sources of information (language structure, meaning, fast word recognition) to support fluency and phrasing
- ❑ demonstrate the ability to identify how a text is organized
- ❑ notice variety in layout (words in bold or larger font, or italics, variety in layout)
- ❑ notice descriptive language and how it adds to enjoyment or understanding
- ❑ notice specific writing techniques (for example, question and answer format)
- ❑ evaluate aspects of a text that add to enjoyment (for example, humorous characters or situations).

FROM *PROMPTING GUIDE, PART 1*

For some specific help with self-monitoring, his teacher found that teaching, prompting and reinforcing language like the following was helpful:

- ❑ *That didn't make sense. You need to stop when it doesn't make sense.*
- ❑ *You said _____. Does that make sense?*
- ❑ *Check the middle part.*

- ❑ *It has to make sense and go with the letters.*
- ❑ *You thought about what would make sense and look right.*
- ❑ *You made it all fit together.*

For specific teaching, prompting, and reinforcing language for solving words, particularly going beyond the first part of the word to solve new multisyllabic words, his teacher tried the following:

- ❑ *You can look at the next part.*
- ❑ *You can break the word.*
- ❑ *Look at the middle of this word.*
- ❑ *Look at the ending of the word.*
- ❑ *Use your finger to break the word.*
- ❑ *You looked at the ending.*
- ❑ *You used your finger to break the word apart.*

To help with maintaining fluency his teacher used this teaching, prompting and reinforcing language:

- ❑ *Listen to me read fast. Can you read it like that?*
- ❑ *Listen to how I make my voice sound _____. (scared, excited, happy etc.)*
- ❑ *Listen to me read this. Can you hear how I sound like the characters who are talking?*
- ❑ *Listen to me read this. Notice how I make my voice show what the writer means here.*
- ❑ *Read these words quickly. (model)*
- ❑ *In this part, _____ is very excited. How would_____ say that?*
- ❑ *Make your voice show what you think the author meant.*
- ❑ *You read it quickly.*
- ❑ *You sounded excited when you read that part.*
- ❑ *You made that part sound interesting.*

FROM *WHEN READERS STRUGGLE: TEACHING THAT WORKS*

For teaching, prompting and reinforcing language to promote thinking about the text, his teacher tried language like this from page 429:

- ❑ *Notice how the book is divided into different sections.*
- ❑ *Notice how the headings reveal categories of information.*
- ❑ *Notice how the writer uses language to construct meaning.*
- ❑ *Look at this section. What kind of information will you find here? How can you tell?*
- ❑ *Notice how the writer uses language to construct meaning.*
- ❑ *What did the writer do to make the story interesting?*
- ❑ *You chose the right section to find out about that topic.*
- ❑ *You noticed how the author's description made that section interesting.*

Classroom Teaching

Francesco was a beginning third grader whose instructional reading level was N, slightly ahead of grade level. He benefited from many opportunities to read independent level texts in a variety of genres and to participate in book discussion or literature circle groups. He also benefited from interactive read aloud by seeing his teacher model how to analyze texts for author's craft, noticing how the author used language to make the text interesting or exciting. He needed small group, guided reading instruction at Level N with instruction on self-monitoring, taking apart multisyllabic words, fluency, nonfiction text features and author's technique. He benefited from discussing and revisiting the text after reading and some planned word work with multisyllabic words.

▶ Orlando, Grade 5 Student

Background and Assessment Summary

Orlando was born in Puerto Rico and came to the United States at the age of 4. He was placed in a transitional bilingual education class for kindergarten through Grade 2. He moved into an English-only mainstream classroom at the beginning of grade 3 and was now in the fifth grade. Orlando's parents spoke only Spanish. His only experiences speaking English were at school, playing with friends, watching television, and speaking with his younger brother.

Figure 5.11 is a summary of his spring Benchmark Assessment scores. Orlando read *Amazing Animal Adaptations*, the level S nonfiction text, with 99% accuracy and satisfactory comprehension. This indicated that level S was Orlando's independent level. At level T, Orlando read the fiction text *Get a Horse!* (Figure 5.12) with 96% accuracy and satisfactory comprehension making this his instructional level. Finally, Orlando's reading of the level U nonfiction text, *Earthquakes,* proved to be too difficult for him. His accuracy level fell below 95% and he was unable to discuss the meaning of the text.*

---

* To print full-page versions of all case study reading records go to: *www.fountasandpinnell.com* and click on the link for "Case Study Reading Records."

FIGURE 5.11 Orlando's Assessment Summary Form

Orlando's Level T Recording Form—Instructional Level

FIGURE 5.12a Orlando's Instructional Level Recording Form

FIGURE 5.12b Orlando's Instructional Level Recording Form

continues

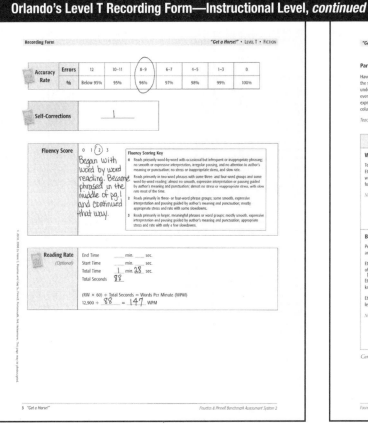

"Get a Horse!" · LEVEL T · FICTION

Accuracy Rate	Errors	12	10–11	8–9	6–7	4–5	1–3	0
	%	Below 95%	95%	96%	97%	98%	99%	100%

(8–9 circled)

Self-Corrections | 1

Fluency Score 0 1 (2) 3

Handwritten: Began with word by word reading. Became phrased in the middle of pg. 1 and continued that way.

Fluency Scoring Key

0 Reads primarily word-by-word with occasional but infrequent or inappropriate phrasing; no smooth or expressive interpretation, irregular pausing, and no attention to author's meaning or punctuation; no stress or inappropriate stress, and slow rate.

1 Reads primarily in two-word phrases with some three- and four-word groups and some word-by-word reading; almost no smooth, expressive interpretation or pausing guided by author's meaning and punctuation; almost no stress or inappropriate stress, with slow rate most of the time.

2 Reads primarily in three- or four-word phrase groups; some smooth, expressive interpretation and pausing guided by author's meaning and punctuation; mostly appropriate stress and rate with some slowdowns.

3 Reads primarily in larger, meaningful phrases or word groups; mostly smooth, expressive interpretation and pausing guided by author's meaning and punctuation; appropriate stress and rate with only a few slowdowns.

Reading Rate *(Optional)*

End Time ___ min. ___ sec.
Start Time ___ min. ___ sec.
Total Time 1 min. 28 sec.
Total Seconds 88

(RW × 60) ÷ Total Seconds = Words Per Minute (WPM)
12,900 ÷ 88 = 147 WPM

3 *"Get a Horse!"* — Fountas & Pinnell Benchmark Assessment System 2

FIGURE 5.12c Orlando's Instructional Level Recording Form

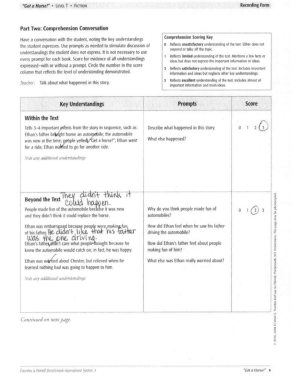

"Get a Horse!" · LEVEL T · FICTION — Recording Form

Part Two: Comprehension Conversation

Have a conversation with the student, noting the key understandings the student expresses. Use prompts as needed to stimulate discussion of understandings the student does not express. It is not necessary to use every prompt for each book. Score for evidence of all understandings expressed—with or without a prompt. Circle the number in the score column that reflects the level of understanding demonstrated.

Teacher: Talk about what happened in this story.

Comprehension Scoring Key

0 Reflects **unsatisfactory** understanding of the text. Either does not respond or talks off the topic.

1 Reflects **limited** understanding of the text. Mentions a few facts or ideas but does not express the important information or ideas.

2 Reflects **satisfactory** understanding of the text. Includes important information and ideas but neglects other key understandings.

3 Reflects **excellent** understanding of the text. Includes almost all important information and main ideas.

Key Understandings	Prompts	Score
Within the Text Tells 3–4 important events from the story in sequence, such as: Ethan's father brought home an automobile; the automobile was new at the time; people yelled "Get a horse!"; Ethan went for a ride; Ethan wanted to go for another ride. *Note any additional understandings:*	Describe what happened in this story. What else happened?	0 1 2 (3)
Beyond the Text *They didn't think it could happen.* People made fun of the automobile because it was new and they didn't think it could replace the horse. Ethan was embarrassed because people were making fun of his father. *He didn't like that his father was the one driving.* Ethan's father didn't care what people thought because he knew the automobile would catch on; in fact, he was happy. Ethan was worried about Chester, but relieved when he learned nothing bad was going to happen to him. *Note any additional understandings:*	Why do you think people made fun of automobiles? How did Ethan feel when he saw his father driving the automobile? How did Ethan's father feel about people making fun of him? What else was Ethan really worried about?	0 1 (2) 3

Continued on next page.

Fountas & Pinnell Benchmark Assessment System 2 — *"Get a Horse!"* 4

FIGURE 5.12d Orlando's Instructional Level Recording Form

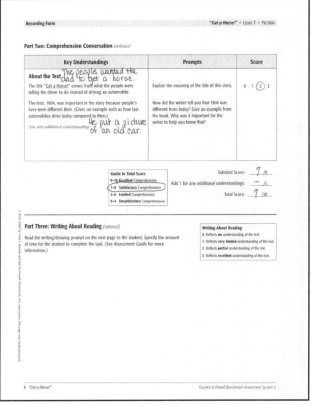

"Get a Horse!" · LEVEL T · FICTION

Part Two: Comprehension Conversation *continued*

Key Understandings	Prompts	Score
About the Text *The people wanted the dad to get a horse.* The title "Get a Horse!" comes from what the people were telling the driver to do instead of driving an automobile. The time, 1904, was important in the story because people's lives were different then. (Gives an example such as how fast automobiles drive today compared to then.) *Note any additional understandings:* *He put a picture of an old car.*	Explain the meaning of the title of this story. How did the writer tell you that 1904 was different from today? Give an example from the book. Why was it important for the writer to help you know that?	0 1 (2) 3

Guide to Total Score
9–10 **Excellent** Comprehension
7–8 **Satisfactory** Comprehension (circled)
5–6 **Limited** Comprehension
0–4 **Unsatisfactory** Comprehension

Subtotal Score: 7 /9
Add 1 for any additional understandings: — /1
Total Score: 7 /10

Part Three: Writing About Reading *(optional)*

Read the writing/drawing prompt on the next page to the student. Specify the amount of time for the student to complete the task. (See *Assessment Guide* for more information.)

Writing About Reading
0 Reflects **no** understanding of the text.
1 Reflects **very limited** understanding of the text.
2 Reflects **partial** understanding of the text.
3 Reflects **excellent** understanding of the text.

5 *"Get a Horse!"* — Fountas & Pinnell Benchmark Assessment System 2

FIGURE 5.12e Orlando's Instructional Level Recording Form

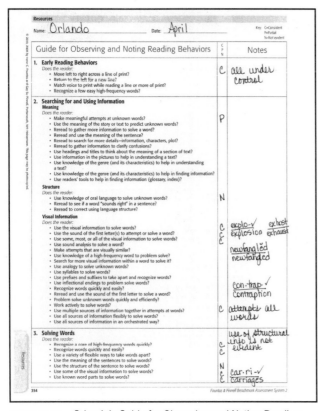

FIGURE 5.13a Orlando's Guide for Observing and Noting Reading Behaviors

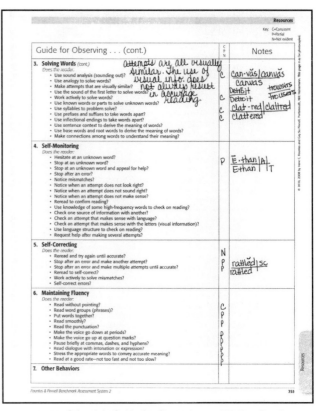

FIGURE 5.13b Orlando's Guide for Observing and Noting Reading Behaviors

Analysis of Processing Strategies

Using the Guide for Observing and Noting Reading Behaviors (Figure 5.13) and his instructional level reading record for level T, Orlando's teacher noticed the following:

Section 1, Early Reading Behaviors: Orlando had all early behaviors under control.

Section 2, Searching for and Using Information: Orlando searched for and used mostly visual information while problem solving words. All of the nine errors that Orlando made were visually similar. It might have been that these words were not part of his oral vocabulary so he was unable to use meaning and structure to cross-check his use of visual information. For example, he said *exhost* for *exhaust*. On several occasions, however, he used parts of the visual information and appeared to cross check it with meaning and structure to solve new words. For example, he read *con-trap-* and then reads *contraption*.

Section 3, Solving Words: Orlando actively attempted to solve each unknown word. At the point of

error, Orlando demonstrated the use of visual information. Again, it might have been that the unknown words were not part of Orlando's oral English vocabulary. For example, he attempted the words *trousers, newfangled, exhaust,* and *Detroit.* At times when word solving, Orlando tried to use syllables to break down words, yet was unsuccessful. For example, he read *clat-red/clattred* for *clattered.* There were several instances where Orlando decoded just the beginning part of a word and then solved it using meaning and structure as supports. For example, on the first page of the text when the author described that *it sounded like the end of the world outside,* he said *ex-plo* and then quickly read *explosion.*

Section 4, Self-Monitoring: Orlando did not reread to check his reading. He did, however, monitor his reading at one point by reading *ratt-led* for *rattled* and then self-corrected. It might have been that his understanding of past tense endings supported him in monitoring and self-correcting right at the point of error. He attempted all words, yet most times when the word did not make sense or sound right to him he didn't appeal for help. He needed to do a better job of self-monitoring so he didn't miss out on words that were critical to his understanding of the text.

Section 5, Self-Correcting: Orlando made only one self-correction out of nine errors. Again, it's important to remember that as an English language learner, he could not self-correct words that weren't a part of his oral vocabulary.

Section 6, Maintaining Fluency: Orlando scored a 2 on the fluency rubric. He read in mostly 3–4 word phrases. He slowed down his reading just to problem solve unknown words. He used the punctuation to support his oral reading, making his voice go down at periods and up at question marks. The passage he read orally contained no dialogue, yet he demonstrated some expression when he read these phrases: *up and down the street* and *terrifying the horses and making people jump out of the way.*

Evidence of Comprehension

For the comprehension conversation portion of his level T instructional text, Orlando received a satisfactory score. He was able to discuss his thinking for within the text more easily than for beyond and about the text. He was able to provide four important events from the story, however when discussing his thinking beyond the text he provided a partial response. For example, when prompted to talk about how the character Ethan felt when he saw his father driving the automobile, Orlando said that Ethan didn't like that his father was the one driving. Yet, he was unable to describe why Ethan didn't want his father to be the driver. In discussing how Ethan and his father felt about Chester, Orlando identified the feelings but was unable to expand on why they felt that way. In terms of thinking about the text, again Orlando was able to provide partial answers, but was unable to provide the details to back up his responses.

Implications for Instruction

Using *The Continuum of Literacy Learning* and *Teaching for Comprehending and Fluency: Thinking, Talking, and Writing About Reading, K–8* as resources,

the following information was important to consider when instructing Orlando.

FROM *THE CONTINUUM OF LITERACY LEARNING*

The Guided Reading section for Orlando's instructional level T contains a description of readers who process texts successfully at that level. Most of this description fits Orlando.

Specifically, the following goals were identified for Orlando's instructional program:

- ❏ notice new and useful words and intentionally record and remember them to expand oral and written vocabulary

- ❏ use the context of a sentence, paragraph, or whole text to determine the meaning of words

- ❏ continue to monitor accuracy and understanding, self-correcting when errors detract from meaning

- ❏ organize important information in summary form in order to remember and use them as background knowledge in reading or for discussion and writing

- ❏ demonstrate appropriate stress on words, pausing and phrasing, intonation, and use of punctuation while reading in a way that reflects understanding

- ❏ integrate existing content knowledge with new information from a text to consciously create new understandings

- ❏ infer character traits, motivations, and changes through examining how the writer describes them, what they do, what they say and think, and what other characters say about them

- ❏ infer big ideas or themes of a text and discuss how they are applicable to people's lives today;

- ❏ notice descriptive language and discuss how it adds to enjoyment or understanding

- ❏ evaluate aspects of a text that add to enjoyment or interest

- ❏ use other sources of information to check the authenticity of a text when questions arise.

Orlando attempted each unknown word—evidence that he was an active word solver. He primarily used visual information to solve unknown words. His teacher theorized that the words that were unfamiliar to Orlando were not part of his oral vocabulary. Level

T texts often have content that goes beyond a reader's personal experiences. Even within fiction stories, the text might require that the reader have some content knowledge to support the reading. The vocabulary demands increase at level T, as well. There are many new words that readers might derive the meaning from context or they might need to use a glossary or dictionary. Orlando's teacher kept these characteristics in mind when introducing new books to him. The text introductions were conversational and included vocabulary that was important for Orlando to know when reading the book.

FROM *TEACHING FOR COMPREHENDING AND FLUENCY: THINKING, TALKING, AND WRITING ABOUT READING, K–8*

Before Orlando's teacher worked with him on solving the meaning of new words she needed to first encourage him to self-monitor when meaning was lost or when he didn't know a word. She then taught for, prompt, and reinforced ways to solve unknown vocabulary words by using language like this from page 400:

- ❑ *When you get to a word you don't know stop and think about how the story helps you understand the meaning of that word.*

- ❑ *Have you seen this word before? What do you think that word means?*

- ❑ *You stopped when you got to a word you didn't understand and tried to figure it out by thinking about the story.*

Orlando's teacher reminded him that if he was unable to understand a word using the context, he should look the word up or discuss it with her during a reading conference, a guided reading group, or write about it in his writer's notebook. Supporting students in identifying and understanding new words helps students in monitoring their own understanding.

To support Orlando in expanding his responses during discussions after the reading of the text, his teacher used prompts during interactive read aloud, guided reading, and reading conferences such as:

- ❑ *Say more about that.*

- ❑ *Talk more about that.*

It was important that Orlando's teacher demonstrated the kind of thinking beyond and about the text she wanted him to do and then probe for it. For example, to support Orlando in inferring causes for character's feelings and providing evidence from the text she used language such as this from page 401:

- ❑ *The author doesn't tell how _____ feels, but readers will know because _____.*

- ❑ *How does _____ feel? How do you know?*

She then chose to use reinforcing language when she observed Orlando taking on this kind of thinking on his own. For example, she said:

- ❑ *You thought about how the character, _____, felt and described how you knew that. That will help you understand the story even more.*

Orlando had some difficulty explaining how the setting is important to understanding the story, *Get a Horse!* Readers needed to think about the relevance of the setting to have a deeper understanding of the story. Orlando's teacher supported him by using language such as this from page 402:

- ❑ *The time (and/or place) of the story is important because _____.*

- ❑ *This book would not be the same in another time (and/or place) because _____.*

- ❑ *How important was the time (and/or place) of the story?*

- ❑ *Could it have happened in the same way in another time or place? Why or why not?*

- ❑ *You thought about the importance of the setting and described how this helped you understand this story.*

Since many of Orlando's errors were attributed to his lack of experience with particular English words, his teacher supported him by integrating vocabulary instruction into his literacy block in these ways:

- ❑ facilitating interactive vocabulary lessons

- ❑ discussing words that are interesting or that they do not understand during interactive read aloud and guided reading

- ❑ teaching students how to use the context of the story to solve vocabulary words
- ❑ supporting students in making connections among words by meaning
- ❑ teaching students to make connections in flexible ways—word part, part of speech, affixes, sounds, meaning.

Orlando's teacher also conferenced with him about books he chose to read independently. She encouraged him to choose books that were just right for him and spend time talking with him about vocabulary that was new (within the context of the conversation about the book) while supporting him in thinking beyond and about the text.

Classroom Instruction

Orlando benefited from daily participation in interactive read aloud and independent reading as well as guided reading lessons and reading conferences at least three times a week. His teacher continued to observe his oral reading behaviors and talked with him about books to support his ongoing learning and her ongoing teaching decisions.

▶ Hannah, Grade 5 Student

Background and Assessment Summary

Hannah was a fifth grade student at Morey School. Identified as a student with a learning disability, she had been on an Individualized Education Plan (IEP) since third grade. She received reading comprehension support from a special education teacher in her regular classroom during the language arts block.

Figure 5.14 is a summary of Hanna's fall Benchmark Assessment scores. In her independent reading of the level N nonfiction text, *Dogs at Work*, Hannah read with 98% accuracy and 2 self-corrections. Her fluency score was 2 and her comprehension score of 7 was in the satisfactory range. Hannah read the level O fiction text, *The New Girl* (Figure 5.15), with 99% accuracy, and 1 self-correction. Her fluency score was 2. Her comprehension score of 6 (limited comprehension) combined with high accuracy (99%) made level O her instructional level. Hannah read the level P nonfiction text *Animal Instincts* with 99% accuracy, 2 self-corrections, and a fluency score of 2. Her comprehension score of 4 was unsatisfactory, making this her hard level. Hannah's instructional level of O fell well below level S, her district's expectation for beginning grade five. *

* To print full-page versions of all case study reading records go to: *www.fountasandpinnell.com* and click on the link for "Case Study Reading Records."

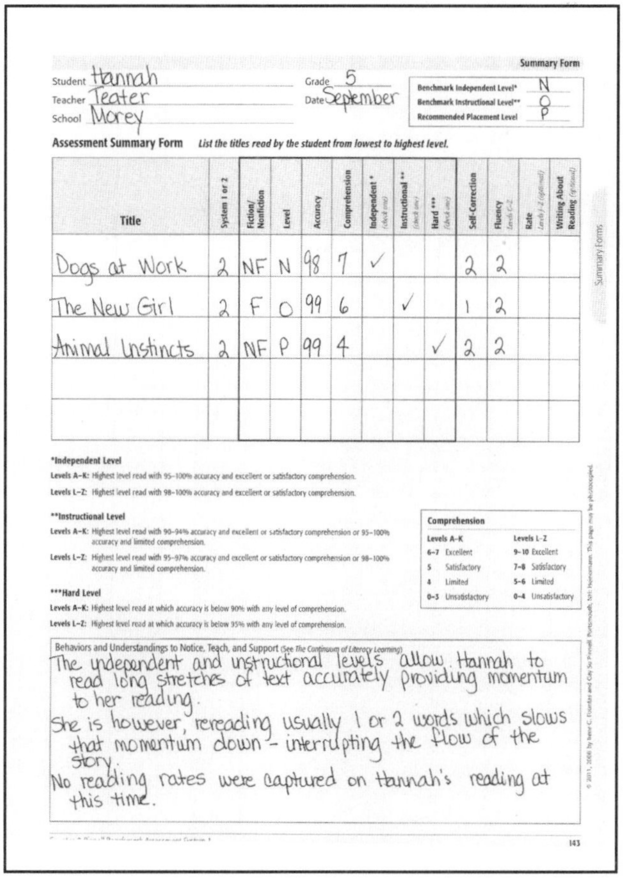

Summary Form

Student Hannah — Grade 5
Teacher Teater — Date September
School Morey

Benchmark Independent Level* N
Benchmark Instructional Level** O
Recommended Placement Level P

Assessment Summary Form *List the titles read by the student from lowest to highest level.*

Title	System 1 or 2	Fiction/Nonfiction	Level	Accuracy	Comprehension	Independent * (check one)	Instructional ** (check one)	Hard *** (check one)	Self-Correction	Fluency Levels C–Z	Rate Levels J–Z (optional)	Writing About Reading (optional)
Dogs at Work	2	NF	N	98	7	✓			2	2		
The New Girl	2	F	O	99	6		✓		1	2		
Animal Instincts	2	NF	P	99	4			✓	2	2		

***Independent Level**
Levels A–K: Highest level read with 95–100% accuracy and excellent or satisfactory comprehension.
Levels L–Z: Highest level read with 98–100% accuracy and excellent or satisfactory comprehension.

****Instructional Level**
Levels A–K: Highest level read with 90–94% accuracy and excellent or satisfactory comprehension or 95–100% accuracy and limited comprehension.
Levels L–Z: Highest level read with 95–97% accuracy and excellent or satisfactory comprehension or 98–100% accuracy and limited comprehension.

*****Hard Level**
Levels A–K: Highest level read at which accuracy is below 90% with any level of comprehension.
Levels L–Z: Highest level read at which accuracy is below 95% with any level of comprehension.

Comprehension Levels A–K		Levels L–Z	
6–7	Excellent	9–10	Excellent
5	Satisfactory	7–8	Satisfactory
4	Limited	5–6	Limited
0–3	Unsatisfactory	0–4	Unsatisfactory

Behaviors and Understandings to Notice, Teach, and Support (See *The Continuum of Literacy Learning*)

The independent and instructional levels allow Hannah to read long stretches of text accurately providing momentum to her reading.
She is however, rereading usually 1 or 2 words which slows that momentum down - interrupting the flow of the story.
No reading rates were captured on Hannah's reading at this time.

143

FIGURE 5.14 Hannah's Assessment Summary Form

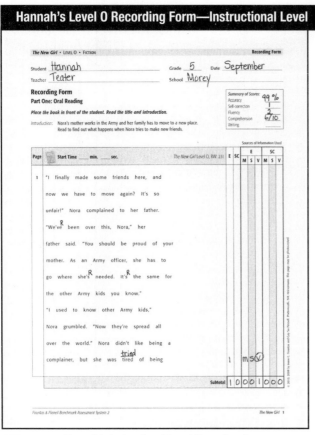

FIGURE 5.15a Hannah's Instructional Level Recording Form

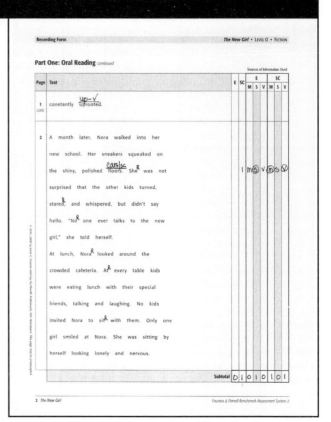

FIGURE 5.15b Hannah's Instructional Level Recording Form

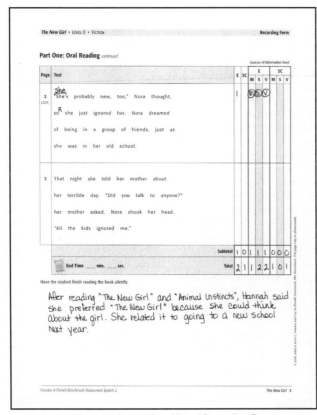

FIGURE 5.15c Hannah's Instructional Level Recording Form

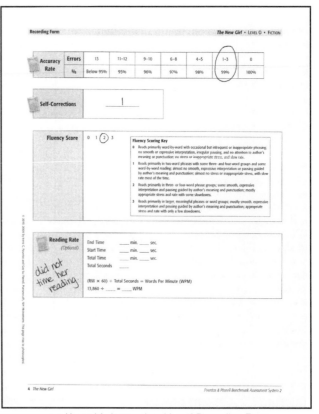

FIGURE 5.15d Hannah's Instructional Level Recording Form

continues

The New Girl · LEVEL O · FICTION — Recording Form

Part Two: Comprehension Conversation

Have a conversation with the student, noting the key understandings the student expresses. Use prompts as needed to stimulate discussion of understandings the student does not express. It is not necessary to use every prompt for each book. Score for evidence of all understandings expressed—with or without a prompt. Circle the number in the score column that reflects the level of understanding demonstrated.

Teacher: Talk about what happened in this story.

Comprehension Scoring Key

0 Reflects **unsatisfactory** understanding of the text. Either does not respond or talks off the topic.

1 Reflects **limited** understanding of the text. Mentions a few facts or ideas but does not express the important information or ideas.

2 Reflects **satisfactory** understanding of the text. Includes important information and ideas but neglects other key understandings.

3 Reflects **excellent** understanding of the text. Includes almost all important information and main ideas.

Key Understandings	Prompts	Score
Within the Text Tells 3–4 important events from the story, such as: Nora had to move to a new school; she doesn't like leaving her school; none of the kids talked to her at the new school; her mom told her to do something herself; she made one new friend. *Note any additional understandings:*	What was Nora's problem in the story? What happened? What else happened? How did Nora solve her problem?	0 1 2 ③
Beyond the Text Nora was very unhappy about moving because her friends were important to her (or other reason consistent with the text). *She would miss her friends.* She acted like the other kids when she wouldn't talk to the other new girl. She learned that she had to make friends if she wanted to be included. *You have to be nice and talk to them to make new friends.*	Why was Nora so unhappy about moving to a new place? How was Nora like the kids she complained about at her new school? *Some were army kids.* How did Nora change in the story? What did she learn?	0 1 ② 3

Continued on next page.

Fountas & Pinnell Benchmark Assessment System 2 — The New Girl **5**

Recording Form — *The New Girl* · LEVEL O · FICTION

Part Two: Comprehension Conversation *continued*

Key Understandings	Prompts	Score
About the Text The title is good because Nora was a new girl in her school. Her friend is also a new girl and the story shows how she treated her. The writer meant that Mom was always teaching her things with short little pieces of advice. You knew Nora had learned a lesson when she smiled at the new girl. *Note any additional understandings:*	What makes the title The New Girl a good one for this book? Any other reason? What did the writer mean when she said "Mom was always coming up with sayings that sounded like 'bumper stickers'"? *no response* Find the part of the story where the writer showed that Nora had learned something.	0 ① 2 3

Guide to Total Score
9–10 **Excellent** Comprehension
7–8 **Satisfactory** Comprehension
5–6 **Limited** Comprehension
0–4 **Unsatisfactory** Comprehension

Subtotal Score: **6** /9
Add 1 for any additional understandings: **—** /1
Total Score: **6** /10

Part Three: Writing About Reading *(optional)*

Read the writing/drawing prompt on the next page to the student. Specify the amount of time for the student to complete the task. (See *Assessment Guide* for more information.)

Writing About Reading
0 Reflects **no** understanding of the text.
1 Reflects **very limited** understanding of the text.
2 Reflects **partial** understanding of the text.
3 Reflects **excellent** understanding of the text.

6 The New Girl — Fountas & Pinnell Benchmark Assessment System 2

FIGURE 5.15e Hannah's Instructional Level Recording Form

FIGURE 5.15f Hannah's Instructional Level Recording Form

Resources

Name: **Hannah** Date: **September**

Key: C=Consistent
P=Partial
N=Not evident

Guide for Observing and Noting Reading Behaviors	C P N	Notes
1. Early Reading Behaviors *Does the reader:* • Move left to right across a line of print? • Return to the left for a new line? • Match voice to print while reading a line or more of print? • Recognize a few easy high-frequency words?	C ↓	*all in place*
2. Searching for and Using Information **Meaning** *Does the reader:* • Make meaningful attempts at unknown words? • Use the meaning of the story or text to predict unknown words? • Reread to gather more information to solve a word? • Reread and use the meaning of the sentence? • Reread to search for more details—information, characters, plot? • Reread to gather information to clarify confusions? • Use headings and titles to think about the meaning of a section of text? • Use information in the pictures to help in understanding a text? • Use knowledge of the genre (and its characteristics) to help in understanding text? • Use knowledge of the genre (and its characteristics) to help in finding information? • Use readers' tools to help in finding information (glossary, index)?	C C N C C P	*Rereading causes a breakdown in comprehension* *rereads to search for (m) info.*
Structure *Does the reader:* • Use knowledge of oral language to solve unknown words? • Reread to see if a word "sounds right" in a sentence? • Reread to correct using language structure?	P ↓	
Visual Information *Does the reader:* • Use the visual information to solve words? • Use the sound of the first letter(s) to attempt or solve a word? • Use some, most, or all of the visual information to solve words? • Use sound analysis to solve a word? • Make attempts that are visually similar? • Use knowledge of a high-frequency word to problem solve? • Search for more visual information within a word to solve it? • Use analogy to solve unknown words? • Use syllables to solve words? • Use prefixes and suffixes to take apart and recognize words? • Use inflectional endings to problem solve words? • Recognize words quickly and easily? • Reread and use the sound of the first letter to solve a word? • Problem solve unknown words quickly and efficiently? • Work actively to solve words? • Use multiple sources of information together in attempts at words? • Use all sources of information flexibly to solve words? • Use all sources of information in an orchestrated way?	C ↓	*tried she* *tired she's*
3. Solving Words *Does the reader:* • Recognize a core of high-frequency words quickly? • Recognize words quickly and easily? • Use a variety of flexible ways to take words apart? • Use the meaning of the sentence to solve words? • Use the structure of the sentence to solve words? • Use the visual information to solve words? • Use known word parts to solve words?	C C C C	*up—✓* *uprooted*

354 — Fountas & Pinnell Benchmark Assessment System 2

FIGURE 5.16a Hannah's Guide for Observing and Noting Reading Behaviors

---

Resources

Key: C=Consistent
P=Partial
N=Not evident

Guide for Observing . . . (cont.)	C P N	Notes
3. Solving Words *(cont.)* • Use sound analysis (sounding out)? • Use analogy to solve words? • Make attempts that are visually similar? • Use the sound of the first letter to solve words? • Work actively to solve words? • Use known words or parts to solve unknown words? • Use syllables to problem solve? • Use prefixes and suffixes to take words apart? • Use inflectional endings to take words apart? • Use sentence context to derive the meaning of words? • Use base words and root words to derive the meaning of words? • Make connections among words to understand their meaning?	C P P P P	*needs to use word parts to solve unknown words*
4. Self-Monitoring *Does the reader:* • Hesitate at an unknown word? • Stop at an unknown word? • Stop at an unknown word and appeal for help? • Stop after an error? • Notice mismatches? • Notice when an attempt does not look right? • Notice when an attempt does not sound right? • Notice when an attempt does not make sense? • Reread to confirm reading? • Use knowledge of some high-frequency words to check on reading? • Check one source of information with another? • Check an attempt that makes sense with language? • Check an attempt that makes sense with the letters (visual information)? • Use language structure to check on reading? • Request help after making several attempts?	P P P C C	*once text is too difficult—attempts are visual* *self-corrects high frequency words* *does appeal for help*
5. Self-Correcting *Does the reader:* • Reread and try again until accurate? • Stop after an error and make another attempt? • Stop after an error and make multiple attempts until accurate? • Reread to self-correct? • Work actively to solve mismatches? • Self-correct errors?	P P	*some of the time*
6. Maintaining Fluency *Does the reader:* • Read without pointing? • Read word groups (phrases)? • Put words together? • Read smoothly? • Read the punctuation? • Make the voice go down at periods? • Make the voice go up at question marks? • Pause briefly at commas, dashes, and hyphens? • Read dialogue with intonation or expression? • Stress the appropriate words to convey accurate meaning? • Read at a good rate—not too fast and not too slow?	C C C C P P ↓	*uses a place marker card to support her*
7. Other Behaviors		

Fountas & Pinnell Benchmark Assessment System 2 355

FIGURE 5.16b Hannah's Guide for Observing and Noting Reading Behaviors, *continued*

Analysis of Processing Strategies

Using the Guide for Observing and Noting Reading Behaviors (Figure 5.16) along with Hannah's instructional reading of level N, *The New Girl* (Figure 5.15), and her independent reading of level M, *Dogs at Work,* her teacher noticed the following:

Section 1, Early Reading Behaviors: Hannah had the early reading behaviors under control.

Section 2, Searching for and Using Information: Hannah showed evidence of searching for and using all sources of information flexibly. Some errors showed use of beginning and ending visual information only, neglecting visual middles as well as meaning and structure (*were/wore, fluted/fluttered, tried/tired*). Hannah repeated ten individual words on different lines of text in her instructional reading but maintained a high degree of accuracy and good fluency. It may be that she used this strategy to give her time to problem solve the next word in her head.

Section 3, Solving Words: Hannah recognized and used a large core of high-frequency words in her reading. Her self-correction of *the/that* at the word level indicated use of analogy to solve words. She used some word parts (*tiptoe/tiptoed, swoop-ed/swooped, up/uprooted*) in attempts to solve words. She used some inflectional endings (*tried/tired, fluted/fluttered*) but was not consistent (*tiptoe/tiptoed, swooped/swooped*).

Section 4, Self-Monitoring: Hannah did not always monitor meaning and structure after attempts to solve words using visual information (*sign/since, were/wore, fluted/fluttered*).

Section 5, Self-Correction: Hannah showed evidence of good self-correction behavior. She was inconsistent however, in making all sources match, leaving several errors uncorrected that did not make sense or sound right.

Section 6, Maintaining Fluency: Hannah's reading was expressive and smooth with primarily 3–4 word phrase groups. She did not always pause appropriately at commas or use the author's syntax appropriately. She had some slow downs and used a place-marker card for support.

Overall, Hannah used all sources of information with flexibility. In problem solving unknown words, she sometimes relied on visual beginnings/ends and did not self-monitor meaning and structure. She frequently neglected the visual details in the middle of words. She read smoothly in three- to four-word phrases with some slow downs, but did not always pause appropriately or use the author's syntax.

Evidence of Comprehension

During the comprehension conversation at her instructional level O, Hannah was able to discuss the important details and main ideas from within the text. She had partial understanding of key understandings for beyond the text. She knew the character Nora was unhappy about moving because she would miss her friends. She also understood an important lesson Nora learned at the end: *You have to be nice and talk to them to make friends.* However, Hannah missed a key understanding by not inferring that Nora acted just like the other kids when she didn't speak to another new student. In the discussion of about the text key understandings, Nora missed the double meaning of the title, *The New Girl.* She had no response to a prompt about what the writer meant when she talked about her mom coming up with sayings that *sound like bumper stickers.* But, Hannah did discuss how the writer showed that Nora learned something. At Hannah's hard level P, she demonstrated unsatisfactory understanding in the beyond and about the text conversations. She did not understand the key understandings about animal instincts or the author's purpose in writing the book.

Implications for Instruction

Using *The Continuum of Literacy Learning, Prompting Guide 1, When Readers Struggle: Teaching That Works,* and *Comprehending and Fluency, Thinking, Talking, and Writing About Reading, K–8,* the following information was important to consider when instructing Hannah.

FROM *THE CONTINUUM OF LITERACY LEARNING*

The Guided Reading section for Hannah's instructional level O contains a description of readers who process texts successfully at that level. Some of this description fit Hannah, but she needed explicit instruction in the areas of word solving multisyllabic words with complex letter/sound relationships; inferential, analytical, and critical comprehension; and fluency.

Specifically, the following goals were identified for Hannah's instructional program:

- solve words of two or three syllables, many words with inflectional endings and complex letter-sound relationships

- use the context of a sentence, paragraph, or whole text to determine the meaning of a word

- continue to monitor accuracy and understanding, self-correcting when errors detract from meaning

- demonstrate appropriate stress on words, pausing, phrasing and intonation, using size of font, bold, and italics as appropriate

- use multiple sources of information (language structure, meaning, fast word recognition) to support fluency and phrasing

- infer the big ideas or themes in a text and discover how they are applicable to people's lives today

- infer causes of problems or of outcomes in fiction and nonfiction texts

- notice specific writing techniques (for example, question and answer format)

- understand when a writer has used underlying organizational structures (description, compare/contrast, temporal sequence, problem/solution, cause/effect)

- hypothesize how characters could have behaved differently.

FROM *PROMPTING GUIDE, PART 1*

The following were some options for teaching, prompting, and reinforcing language Hannah's teacher used to help her self-monitor whether her attempts using visual beginning and ending information made sense or sound right:

- *That didn't make sense. You need to stop when it doesn't make sense.*

- *You said _____. Does that make sense?*

- *Check the middle part.*

- *Try that again and think what would make sense (sound right).*

- *It has to make sense and go with the letters.*

- *You thought about what would make sense and look right.*

- *You made it all fit together.*

To help Hannah with looking at the visual details in the middle of the word to solve new multisyllabic words, her teacher used specific teaching, prompting, and reinforcing language like the following:

- *You can look for a part you know.*

- *You can cover up the last part.*

- *You can look at the middle part.*

- *You can break the word.*

- *If you are not sure how to say a word, you can use the words around it to make meaning.*

- *Look at the middle of this word.*

- *Look at this part* (point to the middle).

- *Where can you break the word apart?*

- *Use your finger to break the word.*

- *Think about what that word means in this sentence (story).*

- *You looked at the middle part.*

- *You used your finger to break the word apart.*

- *You thought about what that word means in this sentence (story).*

To help Hannah with maintaining fluency, her teacher used specific teaching, prompting and reinforcing language like this:

- *Listen to me read this. Can you hear me take a little breath at the comma?*

- *Listen to me read this. Can you hear how I make my voice show what the writer means?*

- *Take a little (or short) pause when you see the comma (or dash).*

- *Make your voice show what the writer means here.*

- *You took a short breath when you saw the comma.*

- *You made the story sound interesting.*

- *You made your voice show what the writer means here.*

FROM *WHEN READERS STRUGGLE: TEACHING THAT WORKS* AND *COMPREHENDING AND FLUENCY, THINKING, TALKING, AND WRITING ABOUT READING, K–8*

For additional prompts for helping Hannah with self-monitoring, word solving, and maintaining fluency, her teacher used pages 426–427 of *When Readers Struggle: Teaching That Works.*

For some specific teaching, prompting, and language for reinforcing effective inferring actions, she tried language like this found on page 401 of *Comprehending and Fluency, Thinking, Talking, and Writing About Reading, K–8,* and on page 429 of *When Readers Struggle: Teaching That Works:*

- ❑ *The author doesn't tell how_____ feels (or what she wants), but readers will know because_____.*

- ❑ *The author doesn't tell us why_____ is doing that, but readers have an idea because_____.*

- ❑ *_____ changed because_____.*

- ❑ *There might be several reasons why _____ changed. For example,_____.*

- ❑ *How does_____ feel?*

- ❑ *Why does _____ behave the way he does?*

- ❑ *Why do you think _____ changed?*

- ❑ *How do you know _____ has changed?*

- ❑ *How would you feel if you were _____?*

- ❑ *You used the information in the story to infer how the character changed.*

- ❑ *You used your background knowledge and evidence from the story to infer why_____ behaved the way he did.*

- ❑ *You told how you would feel if you were _____.*

- ❑ *That's what the writer said. What do you think he means?*

For specific teaching, prompting and reinforcing language for analyzing texts, her teacher referred to page 402 of *Comprehending and Fluency, Thinking, Talking, and Writing About Reading, K–8,* and pages 429–430 of *When Readers Struggle: Teaching That Works:*

- ❑ *Notice how the author showed the difference between _____ and _____ by _____.*

- ❑ *Notice how the author uses headings to organize the information in the book.*

- ❑ *Notice how the author uses language to convey meaning here. This language helped me realize _____.*

- ❑ *The author wrote this book to _____. I learned that_____.*

- ❑ *What did you notice about the author's language?*

- ❑ *What was the author's purpose in writing this book?*

- ❑ *What did the writer do to make the story interesting?*

- ❑ *Look at this section. What kind of information will you find here?*

- ❑ *How was the story organized?*

- ❑ *You noticed how the writer used that language to make the story exciting.*

- ❑ *You used the heading to find the information.*

- ❑ *You noticed how the writer compared and contrasted information to teach us about _____.*

Classroom Teaching

Hannah was a beginning fifth grader whose instructional reading level of O was nearly two years below her school's grade-level expectation. Hannah benefited from many opportunities to read independent texts in a variety of genres and participated in book discussions or literature circle groups. She also benefited from interactive read aloud by seeing her teachers model strategies for inferring meaning and analyzing texts. Hannah needed small group, guided reading instruction at level O with direct instruction in thinking beyond and about the text. She needed specific instruction in self-monitoring for meaning and structure and in visual analysis of the details in the middle of words. She also benefited from fluency instruction on appropriate pausing and used the author's syntax to convey meaning as she read.

▶ Forest, Grade 5 Student

Background and Assessment Summary

Forest was a grade 5 student. Figure 5.17 shows his fall Assessment Summary Form.

In his independent reading of the level T fiction text, *Get a Horse!*, Forest read with 98% accuracy and 4 self-corrections. His fluency score of 3, his reading rate of 167 words per minute (WPM), and his comprehension score of 9 were all excellent. In his instructional reading of the level U nonfiction text, *Earthquakes* (Figure 5.18), Forest had a 96% accuracy score with 3 self-corrections. His reading rate of 170 WPM was excellent, but his fluency score dropped down to a 2. His comprehension score of 7 was satisfactory. Forest reached his hard level with the level V fiction text, *A Call for Change*. His accuracy score was 95% with 2 self-corrections, which was low. His fluency score was 2 and his rate of 146 WPM was in the below average range. His comprehension score of 4 was unsatisfactory, making this his hard level. These results placed Forest above grade level for the middle of Grade 5.*

---

* To print full-page versions of all case study reading records go to: *www.fountasandpinnell.com* and click on the link for "Case Study Reading Records."

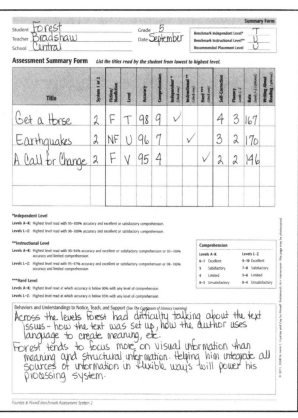

FIGURE 5.17 Forest's Assessment Summary Form

Forest's Level U Recording Form—Instructional Level

FIGURE 5.18a Forest's Instructional Level Recording Form

FIGURE 5.18b Forest's Instructional Level Recording Form

continues

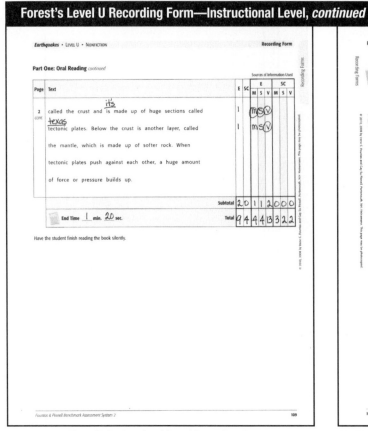

FIGURE 5.18c Forest's Instructional Level Recording Form

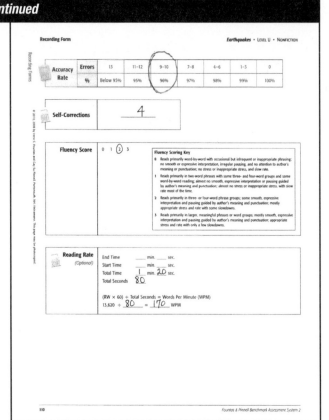
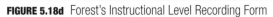

FIGURE 5.18d Forest's Instructional Level Recording Form

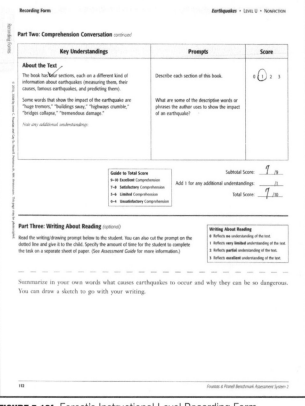

FIGURE 5.18e Forest's Instructional Level Recording Form

FIGURE 5.18f Forest's Instructional Level Recording Form

FIGURE 5.18c content

Earthquakes • LEVEL U • NONFICTION — Recording Form

Part One: Oral Reading *continued*

Page	Text	E	SC	Sources of Information Used E: M S V	SC: M S V
2 cont	it's / called the crust and is made up of huge sections called	I		M S V	
	texas / tectonic plates. Below the crust is another layer, called	I		M S V	
	the mantle, which is made up of softer rock. When				
	tectonic plates push against each other, a huge amount				
	of force or pressure builds up.				

Subtotal: 20 | 1 | 1 | 2 0 0 0
End Time 1 min. 20 sec. Total: 9 4 4 4 13 3 2 2

Have the student finish reading the book silently.

FIGURE 5.18d content

Recording Form — *Earthquakes* • LEVEL U • NONFICTION

Accuracy Rate	Errors	13	11–12	9–10	7–8	4–6	1–3	0
	%	Below 95%	95%	96%	97%	98%	99%	100%

(9–10 / 96% circled)

Self-Corrections 4

Fluency Score 0 1 (2) 3

Fluency Scoring Key

0 Reads primarily word-by-word with occasional but infrequent or inappropriate phrasing; no smooth or expressive interpretation, irregular pausing, and no attention to author's meaning or punctuation; no stress or inappropriate stress, and slow rate.

1 Reads primarily in two-word phrases with some three- and four-word groups and some word-by-word reading; almost no smooth, expressive interpretation or pausing guided by author's meaning and punctuation; almost no stress or inappropriate stress, with slow rate most of the time.

2 Reads primarily in three- or four-word phrase groups; some smooth, expressive interpretation and pausing guided by author's meaning and punctuation; mostly appropriate stress and rate with some slowdowns.

3 Reads primarily in larger, meaningful phrases or word groups; mostly smooth, expressive interpretation and pausing guided by author's meaning and punctuation; appropriate stress and rate with only a few slowdowns.

Reading Rate *(Optional)*

End Time ___ min. ___ sec.
Start Time ___ min. ___ sec.
Total Time 1 min. 20 sec.
Total Seconds 80

(RW × 60) ÷ Total Seconds = Words Per Minute (WPM)
13,620 ÷ 80 = 170 WPM

FIGURE 5.18e content

Earthquakes • LEVEL U • NONFICTION — Recording Form

Part Two: Comprehension Conversation

Have a conversation with the student, noting the key understandings the student expresses. Use prompts as needed to stimulate discussion of understandings the student does not express. It is not necessary to use every prompt for each book. Score for evidence of all understandings expressed—with or without a prompt. Circle the number in the score column that reflects the level of understanding demonstrated.

Teacher: Talk about what you learned in this book.

Comprehension Scoring Key

0 Reflects **unsatisfactory** understanding of the text. Either does not respond or talks off the topic.

1 Reflects **limited** understanding of the text. Mentions a few facts or ideas but does not express the important information or ideas.

2 Reflects **satisfactory** understanding of the text. Includes important information and ideas but neglects other key understandings.

3 Reflects **excellent** understanding of the text. Includes almost all important information and main ideas.

Key Understandings	Prompts	Score
Within the Text Reports 3–4 details from the text, such as: Earthquakes are caused by moving plates; Earth's crust has plates that push against each other; below the crust, there is a soft mantle; the plates push against each other and slide around on top of the mantle; when the plates collide, an earthquake happens; movements also cause cracks. *Note: Earthquakes happen a lot and people don't know it.*	Talk about what you learned from this book. What causes earthquakes?	0 1 2 (3)
Earthquakes are happening all the time all over the world and we can't feel most of them.	Talk about all of the kinds of earthquakes that happen. Do all of them cause destruction?	
The diagram on page 3 shows how rocks below the surface of the earth can shift.	*Text Feature Probe:* Look at the diagram on page 3. Describe what this drawing shows.	
Beyond the Text You are more likely to have earthquakes where there is a track (fault) in Earth's crust.	What is a fault line and why is it important?	0 1 2 (3)
People cannot get away from earthquakes because scientists cannot predict them.	Why is it so hard to help people avoid the danger of earthquakes?	
Scientists need to discover how to predict earthquakes. *Note: Earthquakes are very destructive.*	What do scientists need to discover about earthquakes?	

Continued on next page.

FIGURE 5.18f content

Recording Form — *Earthquakes* • LEVEL U • NONFICTION

Part Two: Comprehension Conversation *continued*

Key Understandings	Prompts	Score
About the Text The book has four sections, each on a different kind of information about earthquakes (measuring them, their causes, famous earthquakes, and predicting them). Some words that show the impact of the earthquake are "huge tremors," "buildings sway," "highways crumble," "bridges collapse," "tremendous damage." *Note any additional understandings.*	Describe each section of this book. What are some of the descriptive words or phrases the author uses to show the impact of an earthquake?	0 (1) 2 3

Guide to Total Score
9–10 Excellent Comprehension
7–8 Satisfactory Comprehension
5–6 Limited Comprehension
0–4 Unsatisfactory Comprehension

Subtotal Score: 7 /9
Add 1 for any additional understandings: /1
Total Score: 7 /10

Part Three: Writing About Reading *(optional)*

Read the writing/drawing prompt below to the student. You can also cut the prompt on the dotted line and give it to the child. Specify the amount of time for the student to complete the task on a separate sheet of paper. (See *Assessment Guide* for more information.)

Writing About Reading
0 Reflects **no** understanding of the text.
1 Reflects **very limited** understanding of the text.
2 Reflects **partial** understanding of the text.
3 Reflects **excellent** understanding of the text.

Summarize in your own words what causes earthquakes to occur and why they can be so dangerous. You can draw a sketch to go with your writing.

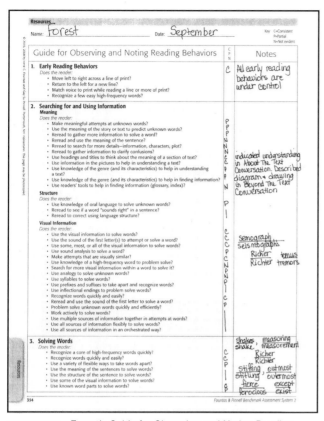

FIGURE 5.19a Forest's Guide for Observing and Noting Reading Behaviors

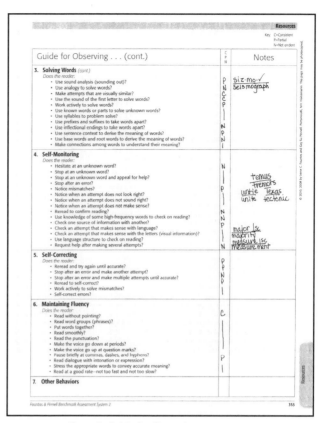

FIGURE 5.19b Forest's Guide for Observing and Noting Reading Behaviors, *continued*

Analysis of Processing Strategies

Using the Guide for Observing and Noting Behaviors (Figure 5.19), along with Forest's instructional level reading of *Earthquakes,* level U (Figure 5.18), his teacher noticed the following:

Section 1, Early Reading Behaviors: It was evident that Forest had the early reading behaviors under control.

Section 2, Searching for and Using Information: For the most part, Forest was searching for and using all sources of information. However at times he made visually similar attempts and neglected meaning and structure, particularly on content specific words (*semograph/seismograph's, Richer/Richter, temus/tremors*).

Section 3, Word Solving: Forest recognized and used a large core of high-frequency words in his reading. He used syllables, word parts, and letter sounds at the beginning, middle and end of words. At times he neglected the visual details in the middle of words (*stiffing/stifling, Richer/Richter, outmost/outermost, fierce/ferocious, except/exist*) or at the ends of words (*shakes/shake, measuring/measurement*).

Section 4, Self-Monitoring: Forest showed evidence of self-monitoring errors. However, he was not always consistent in monitoring for meaning or structure when making errors, relying solely on visual information (*temus/tremors, untie/unite, Texas/tectonic*).

Section 5, Self-Correcting: Forest had a good self-correction score at his independent and instructional levels. At times he left errors that were visually similar and did not make sense or sound right (*temus/tremors, untie/unite, Texas/tectonic*). At the hard level, his self-correction rate was low, which may have affected his comprehension score.

Section 6, Maintaining Fluency: Forest had an excellent fluency score of 3 at his independent level but at his instructional and hard levels his fluency score was 2. He read mostly in smooth phrase groups but was not always consistent with expressive interpretation and pausing guided by the author's meaning. He also did not always use appropriate stress. Forest's quick attempts at words, while not always working to self-correct them when they didn't make sense, may have affected his fluency.

Overall, Forest used all sources of information (meaning, structure, visual) flexibly to read with high accuracy. At times, he did not notice the visual details in the middle or end of words and neglected to use meaning or structure to self-monitor and self-correct such errors. He read at a good rate, primarily in larger phrase groups, but was not always consistent in using expressive interpretation and pausing guided by the author's meaning.

Evidence of Comprehension

At Forest's instructional level U, the comprehension conversation revealed a satisfactory level of understanding for within and beyond the text (Figures 5.18e–f). He demonstrated excellent understanding of the destructiveness of earthquakes and their unpredictability. For the key understandings in about the text, however, Forest showed very limited understanding of the author's use of language to demonstrate the impact of earthquakes.

At his hard level V, Forest's comprehension broke down and he received an unsatisfactory score of 2.

Implications for Instruction

Using *The Continuum of Literacy Learning, Prompting Guide 1*, and *When Readers Struggle: Teaching that Works* as resources, the following information was important to consider when instructing Forest.

FROM *THE CONTINUUM OF LITERACY LEARNING*

The Guided Reading section for Forest's instructional level U, contains a description of readers who process texts successfully at that level. Some of this description currently fit Forest, but he needed some explicit teaching in the areas of self-monitoring errors for meaning, structure and visual details, use of expressive interpretation and pausing guided by the author's meaning and use of appropriate stress. He also needed to learn more about analyzing texts to understand the author's techniques and use of language.

Specifically, the following goals were identified for Forest's instructional program:

❑ continue to monitor accuracy and understanding, self-correcting when errors detract from meaning

❑ read dialogue with phrasing and expression that reflects understanding of characters and events

❑ demonstrate appropriate stress on words, pausing and phrasing, intonation, and use of punctuation while reading in a way that reflects understanding

❑ notice descriptive language and how it adds to enjoyment or understanding

❑ notice aspects of writer's craft (style, language, perspective, themes) after reading several texts by the same author

❑ notice and discuss aspects of genres-realistic and historical fiction, fantasy, myths and legends, biography, autobiography, memoir, and diaries and other nonfiction hybrids

❑ discuss the selection of a genre in relation to inferred writer's purpose for a range of text

❑ evaluate aspects of a text that add to enjoyment (e.g., a humorous character) or interest (plot or information).

FROM *PROMPTING GUIDE, PART 1*

The following were some options for teaching Forest how to self-monitor whether his attempts using visually similar words made sense or sounded right:

❑ *That didn't make sense.*

❑ *You need to stop when it doesn't make sense.*

❑ *That didn't sound right.*

❑ *You need to stop when it doesn't sound right.*

To follow up when Forest made an error and continues reading, his teacher tried prompts such as:

❑ *You said_____. Does that make sense?*

❑ *You said_____. Does that sound right?*

❑ *Check the middle part.*

❑ *Check the end part.*

❑ *Try that again and think what would make sense.*

❑ *Try that again and think what would sound right.*

❑ *It has to make sense and go with the letters.*

❑ *It has to sound right and go with the letters.*

After prompting, he used reinforcing language like this to support Forest's understanding:

❑ *You thought about what would make sense and look right.*

- ❑ *You thought about what would sound right and look right.*
- ❑ *You checked the middle (end) of the word.*
- ❑ *You made it all fit together.*

For teaching, prompting and reinforcing language for maintaining fluency, his teacher tried this language:

- ❑ *Listen to how I make my voice sound _____ (scared, excited, happy etc.).*
- ❑ *Listen to me read this. Can you hear how I sound like the characters who are talking?*
- ❑ *Listen to me read this. Notice how I make my voice show what the writer means here.*
- ❑ *In this part, _____ is very excited. How would _____ say that?*
- ❑ *Make your voice show what the author means there.*
- ❑ *Think about how to say that.*
- ❑ *Did you find you were stopping to think more during this part of the text?*
- ❑ *You sounded excited when you read that part.*
- ❑ *You made that part sound interesting.*
- ❑ *You stopped to think more during this part of the text.*
- ❑ *Your voice really showed what the author meant there.*

FROM *WHEN READERS STRUGGLE: TEACHING THAT WORKS*

For specific teaching, prompting and reinforcing language to strengthen Forest's ability to think about the text, his teacher used examples like these found on page 429:

- ❑ *Notice how the writer uses language to construct meaning.*
- ❑ *I noticed this language (read). What did the writer mean by that? (figurative language, metaphor, idiom).*
- ❑ *Notice the writer's style…*

- ❑ *Notice the characteristics of this genre.*
- ❑ *What did the writer do to make the story interesting (funny, sad)?*
- ❑ *How did the writer start the story? What did you think about that?*
- ❑ *I noticed this language (metaphor, simile, idiom etc.) What did the writer mean by that?*
- ❑ *What did you notice about how the writer did that?*
- ❑ *What was the writer's purpose in writing this book?*
- ❑ *What did the writer say to make you think that?*
- ❑ *What makes a good_____? (e.g. biography, fantasy)*
- ❑ *You noticed how the writer started the story.*
- ❑ *You noticed how the author used language to make the story interesting.*
- ❑ *You noticed how the author's description made that section interesting.*
- ❑ *You used the information from the text to form an opinion.*

Classroom Teaching

Forest was a fifth grader whose instructional reading level was U, above grade level for the beginning of grade 5. He benefited from many opportunities to read independent level texts in a variety of genres and participated in book discussion or literature circle groups. He also benefited from interactive read aloud by seeing his teacher model how to analyze texts for author's craft, noticing how the author used language to make the text interesting or exciting. He needed small group, guided reading instruction at level U with some instruction on self-monitoring and fluency (expressive interpretation and pausing guided by the author's meaning and use of appropriate stress). In discussing and revisiting text after reading, he benefited from a focus on the author's craft and techniques and characteristics of genre.

► Tanicia, Grade 7 Student

Background and Assessment Summary

Tanicia was a seventh grader at Eagle Middle School. Her fall scores on the independent reading of the level X, fiction text, *A Weighty Decision*, showed that she read with 98% accuracy, with 3 self-corrections. Her fluency score was 3 and her comprehension score of 10 was in the excellent range. For Tanicia's instructional level reading of the level Y non-fiction text, *The International Space Station* (Figure 5.21), she scored a 96% for accuracy, with 1 self-correction, a 3 for fluency, and 8 out of 10 for comprehension, which was in the satisfactory range. These results placed Tanicia on grade level for the beginning of seventh grade.*

---

* To print full-page versions of all case study reading records go to: *www.fountasandpinnell.com* and click on the link for "Case Study Reading Records."

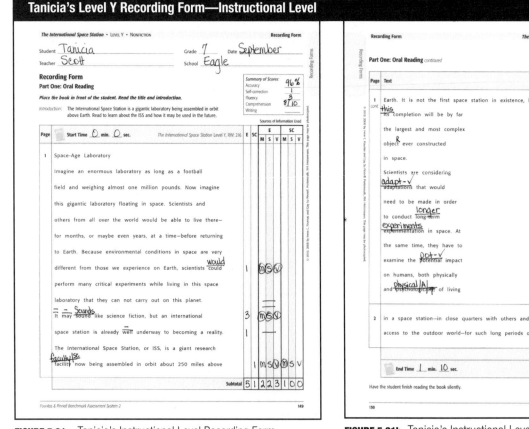

FIGURE 5.20 Tanicia's Assessment Summary Form

Tanicia's Level Y Recording Form—Instructional Level

FIGURE 5.21a Tanicia's Instructional Level Recording Form

FIGURE 5.21b Tanicia's Instructional Level Recording Form

continues

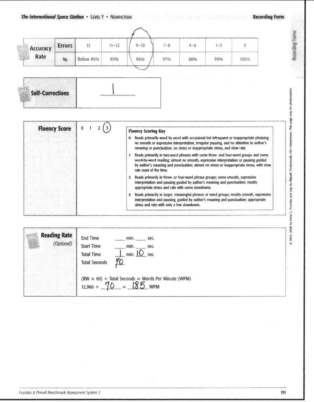

The International Space Station • LEVEL Y • NONFICTION   **Recording Form**

	Errors	13	11–12	9–10	7–8	4–6	1–3	0
Accuracy Rate	%	Below 95%	95%	96%	97%	98%	99%	100%

(9–10 column circled)

Self-Corrections   1

Fluency Score   0   1   2   (3)

Fluency Scoring Key

0 Reads primarily word by word with occasional but infrequent or inappropriate phrasing; no smooth or expressive interpretation, irregular pausing, and no attention to author's meaning or punctuation; no stress or inappropriate stress, and slow rate.

1 Reads primarily in two-word phrases with some three- and four-word groups and some word-by-word reading; almost no smooth, expressive interpretation or pausing guided by author's meaning and punctuation; almost no stress or inappropriate stress, with slow rate most of the time.

2 Reads primarily in three- or four-word phrase groups; some smooth, expressive interpretation and pausing guided by author's meaning and punctuation; mostly appropriate stress and rate with some slowdowns.

3 Reads primarily in larger, meaningful phrases or word groups; mostly smooth, expressive interpretation and pausing, guided by author's meaning and punctuation; appropriate stress and rate with only a few slowdowns.

Reading Rate *(Optional)*

End Time   ____ min. ____ sec.
Start Time   ____ min. ____ sec.
Total Time   1 min. 10 sec.
Total Seconds   70

(RW × 60) ÷ Total Seconds = Words Per Minute (WPM)
12,960 ÷ 70 = 185 WPM

Fountas & Pinnell Benchmark Assessment System 2   151

FIGURE 5.21c Tanicia's Instructional Level Recording Form

Recording Form   *The International Space Station* • LEVEL Y • NONFICTION

Part Two: Comprehension Conversation

Have a conversation with the student, noting the key understandings the student expresses. Use prompts as needed to stimulate discussion of understandings the student does not express. It is not necessary to use every prompt for each book. Score for evidence of all understandings expressed—with or without a prompt. Circle the number in the score column that reflects the level of understanding demonstrated.

Teacher: Talk about what you learned in this book.

Comprehension Scoring Key

0 Reflects **unsatisfactory** understanding of the text. Either does not respond or talks off the topic.

1 Reflects **limited** understanding of the text. Mentions a few facts or ideas but does not express the important information or ideas.

2 Reflects **satisfactory** understanding of the text. Includes important information and ideas but neglects other key understandings.

3 Reflects **excellent** understanding of the text. Includes almost all important information and main ideas.

Key Understandings	Prompts	Score
Within the Text Tells 3–4 facts from the book, such as: The International Space Station is a giant laboratory in space; it is being built in orbit above Earth; the space station will help us learn more about living in space; three crew members can live on the ISS; scientists will perform experiments (creating better medicines, light metals, and robots; studying weightlessness and human cells) *They need to see if there is other life.* The ISS will help astronauts learn to live in space. *People can learn to live in space. How to get food and water.* We have to learn how the ISS can make its own oxygen and electricity. The drawing on page 2 shows how 16 countries are helping to build different parts of the space station. *It's really big — weighs almost 4 million pounds.* *Note any additional understanding:*	What did you learn about the International Space Station? What else did you learn? *Text Feature Probe:* Look at the drawing on page 2. What information do you learn from this drawing?	0 1 2 (3)
Beyond the Text The International Space Station is important because it provides research in many different areas. (Gives examples such as engineering, medicine, space exploration.) *Have more explorers in space.* It would be hard to live for a long time in space because (weightlessness, unable to go outside, close quarters with others) *being weightless. Getting food and water.* To go on long voyages, scientists will need to make the ISS self-sufficient by making its own oxygen. *Note any additional understanding:*	Why is the International Space Station important? What kinds of problems need to be overcome before people can take long voyages in space?	0 1 2 (3)

Continued on next page.

152   *Fountas & Pinnell Benchmark Assessment System 2*

FIGURE 5.21d Tanicia's Instructional Level Recording Form

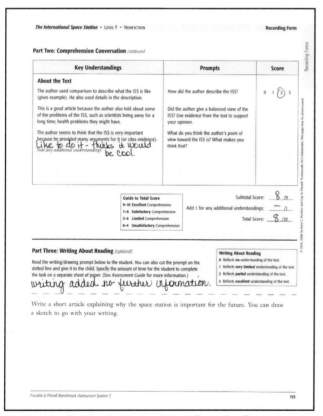

The International Space Station • LEVEL Y • NONFICTION   **Recording Form**

Part Two: Comprehension Conversation *continued*

Key Understandings	Prompts	Score
About the Text The author used comparison to describe what the ISS is like (gives example). He also used details in the description. This is a good article because the author also told about some of the problems of the ISS, such as scientists being away for a long time; health problems they might have. The author seems to think that the ISS is very important because he provided many arguments for it (or cites evidence). *Like to do it – thinks it would be cool.* *Note any additional understanding:*	How did the author describe the ISS? Did the author give a balanced view of the ISS? Use evidence from the text to support your opinion. What do you think the author's point of view toward the ISS is? What makes you think that?	0 1 (2) 3

Guide to Total Score
9–10 **Excellent** Comprehension
7–8 **Satisfactory** Comprehension
5–6 **Limited** Comprehension
0–4 **Unsatisfactory** Comprehension

Subtotal Score: 8 /9
Add 1 for any additional understandings: — /1
Total Score: 8 /10

Part Three: Writing About Reading *(optional)*

Read the writing/drawing prompt below to the student. You can also cut the prompt on the dotted line and give it to the child. Specify the amount of time for the student to complete the task on a separate sheet of paper. (*See Assessment Guide for more information.*)

writing added no further information.

Write a short article explaining why the space station is important for the future. You can draw a sketch to go with your writing.

Writing About Reading

0 Reflects **no** understanding of the text.
1 Reflects **very limited** understanding of the text.
2 Reflects **partial** understanding of the text.
3 Reflects **excellent** understanding of the text.

Fountas & Pinnell Benchmark Assessment System 2   153

FIGURE 5.21e Tanicia's Instructional Level Recording Form

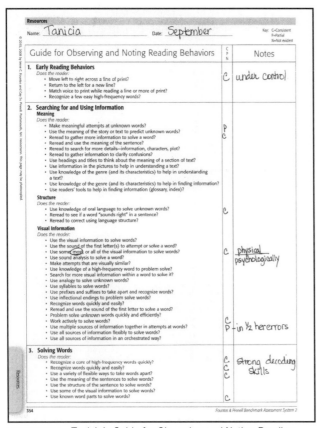

FIGURE 5.22a Tanicia's Guide for Observing and Noting Reading Behaviors

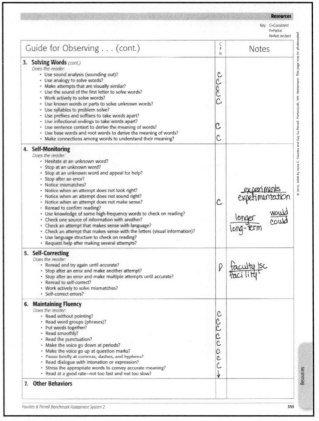

FIGURE 5.22b Tanicia's Guide for Observing and Noting Reading Behaviors

Analysis of Processing Strategies

Using the Guide for Observing and Noting Reading Behaviors (Figure 5.22) along with Tanicia's instructional reading of *The International Space Station*, level Y (Figure 5.21), her teacher noticed the following:

Section 1, Early Reading Behaviors: Tanicia's early reading behaviors were under control.

Section 2, Searching for and Using Information: Tanicia recognized words quickly and easily. She consistently searched for and used most of the visual information in her attempts of unknown words (*physical/ psychologically*). She searched for multiple sources of information in half of her errors. She gained important information from texts that had new and unfamiliar concepts and ideas.

Section 3, Solving Words: Tanicia was an excellent decoder of words. She automatically (and flexibly) used a wide range of word solving strategies (e.g., using word parts and connecting words to known words). She anticipated words through the meaning of the sentence.

Section 4, Self-Monitoring: Tanicia noticed when an attempt did not make sense. She didn't fix minor word errors if meaning and syntax held the piece together.

Section 5, Self-Correcting: Tanicia read with a high level of accuracy. Her self-correction rate was low. Many of her errors were attributed to reading quickly and not noticing unimportant errors (*would/could*). Many of her errors didn't interfere with meaning or syntax.

Section 6, Maintaining Fluency: Tanicia read primarily in larger, meaningful phrases or word groups; mostly smooth, expressive interpretation and pausing guided by author's meaning and punctuation; appropriate stress and rate with only a few slow downs.

Overall, Tanicia read fluently and monitored her own reading using all sources of information to gain understanding. Her error and self-correction behavior suggested that she was processing text as language, using meaning and language structure, as well as visual information. Most of her errors made sense and supported her comprehension of the text.

Evidence of Comprehension

In the independent level X fiction text, *A Weighty Decision,* the comprehension conversation showed that Tanicia understood the idea of athletic competition and the temptation to take over-the-counter diet pills. She also understood the descriptive language of the text.

In the comprehension conversation for the instructional level Y nonfiction text *The International Space Station* (Figures 5.21d–e), Tanicia discussed the importance of the space station and some of the problems that needed to be overcome before people can take long voyages in space—for example, finding ways to get water and food and ways to exercise. She did not pick up on the idea that people who stay in space a long time can have psychological difficulties and her written response was at a fairly superficial level, yet she demonstrated adequate comprehension overall.

Implications for Instruction

Using *The Continuum of Literacy Learning, Teaching for Comprehending and Fluency: Thinking, Talking, and Writing about Reading, K–8,* and *When Readers Struggle: Teaching that Works* as resources, the following information was important to consider when instructing Tanicia.

FROM *THE CONTINUUM OF LITERACY LEARNING*

The Guided Reading section for Tanicia's instructional level Y, contains a description of readers who process texts successfully at this level. Tanicia was capable of much of this, but to deeply understand these more complex texts, she needed specific teaching on how writer's craft supported the author's purpose.

Specifically, the following goals were identified for Tanicia's instructional program:

❑ recognize and interpret a writer's use of language to convey a point of view or bias

❑ recognize the use of figurative or descriptive language (or special types of language such as irony) and talk about how it adds to the quality (enjoyment and understanding) of a text

❑ notice how an author uses words in a connotative way (to imply something beyond the literal meaning)

❑ infer the meaning of symbols (objects, events, motifs, characters) that the writer uses to convey and enhance meaning

❑ critique the impact of the writer's style in supporting meaning and purpose.

FROM *TEACHING FOR COMPREHENDING AND FLUENCY: THINKING, TALKING, AND WRITING ABOUT READING, K–8*

To enrich Tanicia's ability to think beyond and about the text, her teacher used specific language to demonstrate that type of thinking and foster those conversations such as the examples below from pages 400–402 (for fiction) and pages 430–432 (for nonfiction):

❑ _____ *makes me think that the writer is really trying to say* _____.

❑ *What do you think the writer is really trying to say?*

❑ *This language helped me realize* _____.

❑ *What are some examples of language that helped you understand* _____?

❑ *When you read this book, think about* _____.

❑ *What did you already know about this topic? Did you change any of your ideas after reading?*

❑ *When you read this book, notice how the writer is describing the topic.*

❑ *What did you learn from the kinds of descriptive details the writer provided?*

❑ *Why do you think the writer included these details?*

FROM *WHEN READERS STRUGGLE: TEACHING THAT WORKS*

Since Tanicia was an accomplished reader, pointing out the literary techniques a writer uses when crafting a text helped her develop a deeper understanding of the writer's intent. In addition, more complex texts made greater demands on her knowledge about how texts work. The following prompts from pages 426–430 supported Tanicia in thinking more fully within, beyond and about texts she read.

Searching for and finding specific facts (ideas) and other information in a text:

❑ *Look back to find where the writer tells about* _____.

- *How did the writer make his point effectively?*
- *What other information did you learn about from this (graphic)?*

Summarizing to determine the important pieces of information:
- *What were some of the most important things this writer had to say?*

Making connections to think about how the text content relates what you know about the world:
- *Think about what you already know about _____.*
- *What do you think the writer will teach you about _____.*

Synthesizing to use information from the text to create new understandings:
- *What was the writer teaching you about _____.*
- *What was new information?*
- *How did your thinking change?*

Inferring to grasp the big ideas or messages of a text:
- *That's what the writer said. What do you think he means?*
- *What was the writer trying to say?*
- *How did you know _____ has changed?*

Analyzing the text to understand how the text is constructed or notice how the writer uses language to construct meaning:
- *What did you notice about the writer's language?*
- *What did the writer do to make that point powerful? (funny, sad, interesting?)*
- *What kind of information will you find in this section? How can you tell?*

Critiquing the text to evaluate it:
- *What did the writer say to make you think that?*
- *Do you think this book sounds real (or true)? What makes you think that?*

Classroom Teaching

Tanicia was a strong reader who needed more opportunity to experience texts that included a wide range of challenging themes requiring her to take on diverse perspectives and new content. She also required more experience with highly literary texts to acquire new content and understandings of how authors imply something beyond the literal meaning. She participated in literature discussion groups, had regular individual conferences, and some small group lessons at level Y. These conversations provided opportunities for Tanicia to articulate her thinking, consider new ideas, and reflect on the text to support new understandings.

▶ Looking at One Reader at Three Points in Time

As one example of change over time in a school year, let's look at Henry's reading at five points in time, with assessment taking place twice a year.* First, take a look at the Assessment Summary Form recorded in the fall of grade 3 (Figure 5.23). You'll notice that Henry read *City Hawks*, level M nonfiction, at an independent level with high comprehension. He was generally fluent, with a rating of 2. He then read *Vanessa's Butterfly*, level N fiction, with 95% accuracy, satisfactory comprehension, and good fluency, which indicated that N would be a good instructional level for him (Figure 5.24).

Overall, Henry's reading of the level N text indicated that he was monitoring his reading, self-correcting some errors, and using all sources of information. He made a few careless errors that he appeared not to notice (*thing* for *chore*); and occasionally he lost meaning but did not stop to search for information. He was able to demonstrate good retention of the important information in the text and to hypothesize as to why and how the character Vanessa changed.

In the spring of third grade, Henry's assessment indicated that he could read level N at an independent level and that his new instructional level was O (Figure 5.25). Henry started the year slightly above grade level, but was ending the year just on grade level. A look at rate and fluency indicated, however, that he could now read faster and that his phrasing and

---

* To print full-page versions of all case study reading records go to: *www.fountasandpinnell.com* and click on the link for "Case Study Reading Records."

expression had improved. He read *The New Girl*, level O fiction with 97% accuracy—almost at an independent level—with satisfactory comprehension. Figure 5.25 (the Bi-annual Assessment Summary Form) shows Henry's progress over the year. He achieved only one measured level of growth; however, when he began instruction in September, level N was slightly challenging for him, and at the end of the year, level O was almost in the easy category. His teacher expected him to move quickly to level P in fourth grade.

Henry's assessment in the fall of grade 4 indicated that he had made progress over the summer. His independent reading level was P and his instructional level was Q, although it was slightly challenging for him in terms of comprehension. In Figure 5.26, you see his Assessment Summary Form and in Figure 5.27, his instructional level reading record for *Not Too Cold for a Polar Bear,* level Q nonfiction.

Henry read at a faster pace; however, his fluency rating did not increase, largely because he was reading a little too fast for his processing system. An examination of the errors on *Not Too Cold for a Polar Bear* indicated that while he read with 96% accuracy, he did make careless mistakes and was not monitoring closely. He did, however, show excellent word-solving strategies. He was able to break words apart by saying the first part of an unfamiliar word, and he sometimes reread to search for meaning. He used all sources of information in a smooth, orchestrated way. His comprehension was satisfactory; however, he might have been be relying on background knowledge of bears. For example, he stated that polar bears sleep in dens in the winter when the text clearly stated that they stay awake. This was a relatively minor fact and did not mean his comprehension was poor; however, the teacher was concerned because Henry encountered the information during the silent part of his reading. This evidence might have meant that he was not monitoring closely while reading silently.

Figure 5.28 shows Henry's Assessment Summary Form for spring of grade 4, and Figure 5.29 shows his reading record for the instructional level. He read level Q fiction, *A Secret Home,* with 100% accuracy, at a very fast pace with satisfactory comprehension. His fluency rating, however, was only 1, mostly because his reading sounded robotic and he was not noticing punctuation. In his instructional level reading of the level R fiction text, *The Election,* he achieved satisfactory comprehension but was again showing evidence of sliding over words rather than noticing errors, even when meaning was lost. His understanding of the text was just barely satisfactory. On the next level, his reading of *Amazing Animal Adaptations,* level S nonfiction, was fairly accurate but he had low comprehension and fluency.

Figure 5.30 shows Henry's Grade 4 Bi-annual Assessment Summary Form. In spring of grade 4, he began participation in daily small group guided reading, which continued until the second week of June. He also participated in a summer reading program in which he selected books of interest, and he resumed small-group instruction in September of fifth grade.

By the time his reading was assessed in the fall of fifth grade, Henry was reading level T independently and level U instructionally (Figures 5.31, 5.32). Systems seem to be coming together for Henry. He was again reading right on grade level; he had slowed down a bit and was paying more attention to punctuation. His fluency rating was excellent again, as well as his comprehension. He was developing a real preference for informational texts!

In Figure 5.33, you see Henry's graph of reading progress for grades K–5. Like all other readers, Henry's path of progress was individual. Looking at it overall, he had made steady progress along a continuum of development. Sometimes the progress was very rapid, and at other times it seemed to slow while, perhaps, some systems of strategies where being consolidated. The important thing was that he had continued to make progress and at the same time to enjoy texts of his own choosing for independent reading, as well as to participate in reading instruction at an appropriate level to support efficient processing.

FIGURE 5.23 Henry's Assessment Summary Form, Grade 3, September

FIGURE 5.24a Henry's Instructional Level Recording Form, Grade 3, September

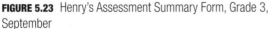

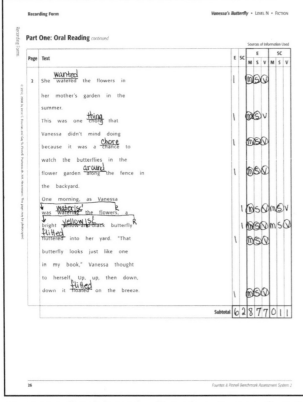

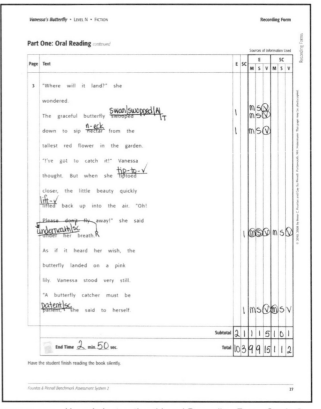

FIGURE 5.24b Henry's Instructional Level Recording Form, Grade 3, September

FIGURE 5.24c Henry's Instructional Level Recording Form, Grade 3, September

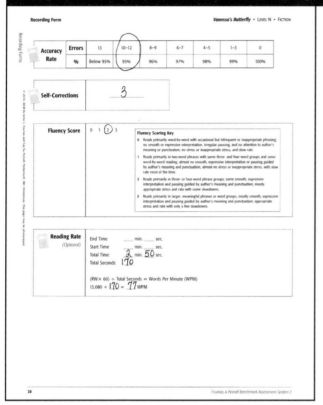

Recording Form — Vanessa's Butterfly • LEVEL N • FICTION

Accuracy Rate	Errors	13	10–12	8–9	6–7	4–5	1–3	0
	%	Below 95%	95%	96%	97%	98%	99%	100%

(10–12 / 95% circled)

Self-Corrections 3

Fluency Score 0 1 ②(2) 3

Fluency Scoring Key
0 Reads primarily word-by-word with occasional but infrequent or inappropriate phrasing; no smooth or expressive interpretation, irregular pausing, and no attention to author's meaning or punctuation; no stress or inappropriate stress, and slow rate.
1 Reads primarily in two-word phrases with some three- and four-word groups and some word-by-word reading; almost no smooth, expressive interpretation or pausing guided by author's meaning and punctuation; almost no stress or inappropriate stress, with slow rate most of the time.
2 Reads primarily in three- or four-word phrase groups, some smooth, expressive interpretation and pausing guided by author's meaning and punctuation; mostly appropriate stress and rate with some slowdowns.
3 Reads primarily in larger, meaningful phrases or word groups, mostly smooth, expressive interpretation and pausing guided by author's meaning and punctuation; appropriate stress and rate with only a few slowdowns.

Reading Rate *(Optional)*
End Time ___ min. ___ sec.
Start Time ___ min. ___ sec.
Total Time 2 min. 50 sec.
Total Seconds 170

(RW × 60) ÷ Total Seconds = Words Per Minute (WPM)
13,080 ÷ 170 = 77 WPM

FIGURE 5.24d Henry's Instructional Level Recording Form, Grade 3, September

---

Recording Form — Vanessa's Butterfly • LEVEL N • FICTION

Part Two: Comprehension Conversation

Have a conversation with the student, noting the key understandings the student expresses. Use prompts as needed to stimulate discussion of understandings the student does not express. It is not necessary to use every prompt for each book. Score for evidence of all understandings expressed—with or without a prompt. Circle the number in the score column that reflects the level of understanding demonstrated.

Teacher: Talk about what happened in this story.

Comprehension Scoring Key
0 Reflects **unsatisfactory** understanding of the text. Either does not respond or talks off the topic.
1 Reflects **limited** understanding of the text. Mentions a few facts or ideas but does not express the important information or ideas.
2 Reflects **satisfactory** understanding of the text. Includes important information and ideas but neglects other key understandings.
3 Reflects **excellent** understanding of the text. Includes almost all important information and main ideas.

Key Understandings	Prompts	Score
Within the Text Tells 3–4 events in sequence, such as: Vanessa wanted to catch a butterfly; she was helping in the garden she saw a beautiful butterfly; Vanessa decided not to catch the butterfly but just to watch it. *Complete recount of events*	What happened in this story? What else happened?	0 1 2 ③
Beyond the Text Vanessa always loved butterflies because that was the special meaning of her name. *Remember the name and book.* Vanessa changed her mind because she saw how beautiful the butterfly was. *and that it should be free.* Vanessa felt that the butterfly should be free. *because it was yellow*	How did Vanessa feel about butterflies? Why did she feel that way? Vanessa changed during the story. Tell how she changed and why. In the end, how do you think Vanessa felt about the butterfly?	0 1 2 ③

Continued on next page.

FIGURE 5.24e Henry's Instructional Level Recording Form, Grade 3, September

---

Recording Form — Vanessa's Butterfly • LEVEL N • FICTION

Part Two: Comprehension Conversation *continued*

Key Understandings	Prompts	Score
About the Text Gives an example of words the author used to describe the butterfly, such as: "graceful"; "swooped down to sip nectar"; "little beauty"; "stripes like a zebra." *Said it lifted and was pretty* The most important part of the story was when Vanessa looked closely at the beautiful butterfly and wanted it to be free. *Noticed when she changed her mind.*	Give an example of a description the author used to show what the butterfly was like. Why did the author use this description? What was the most important part of the story? Why was that part important?	0 1 ②(2) 3

Guide to Total Score
9–10 Excellent Comprehension
7–8 Satisfactory Comprehension
5–6 Limited Comprehension
0–4 Unsatisfactory Comprehension

Subtotal Score: 8 /9
Add 1 for any additional understandings: — /1
Total Score: 8 /10

Part Three: Writing About Reading *(optional)*

Read the writing/drawing prompt below to the student. You can also cut the prompt on the dotted line and give it to the child. Specify the amount of time for the student to complete the task on a separate sheet of paper. (See *Assessment Guide* for more information.)

Writing About Reading
0 Reflects **no** understanding of the text.
1 Reflects **very limited** understanding of the text.
2 Reflects **partial** understanding of the text.
3 Reflects **excellent** understanding of the text.

Explain what Vanessa meant when she thought to herself, "I don't need to be a butterfly catcher. I can be a butterfly watcher." You can draw a sketch to go with your writing.

FIGURE 5.24f Henry's Instructional Level Recording Form, Grade 3, September

---

Summary Form

Student: Henry   Grade: 3   Year: ___
Teacher: Bennett   School: Mountainview

Bi-Annual Assessment Summary

	Date September	Date May
Independent Level	Level M – NF	Level N – NF
Accuracy	98 %	99 %
Comprehension	10 / 10	9 / 10
Self-Correction	3	1
Fluency	0 1 ②(2) 3	0 1 2 ③
Rate *(optional)*	85 WPM	115 WPM
Writing About Reading *(optional)*	0 1 2 3	0 1 2 3
Instructional Level	Level N – F	Level O – F
Accuracy	95 %	97 %
Comprehension	8 / 10	7 / 10
Self-Correction	5	5
Fluency	0 1 ②(2) 3	0 1 2 ③
Rate *(optional)*	77 WPM	103 WPM
Writing About Reading *(optional)*	0 1 2 3	0 1 2 3

Behaviors and Understandings to Notice, Teach, and Support

Level N (across the year) - all scores increase at the level except SC - which might be appropriate as more words are self-corrected in the head before being spoken.

Instructional text comparisons show increases as well; accuracy and fluency up and rate improves significantly. Comprehension scores remain satisfactory across time.

FIGURE 5.25 Henry's Bi-annual Assessment Summary, Grade 3

FIGURE 5.26 Henry's Assessment Summary Form, Grade 4, September

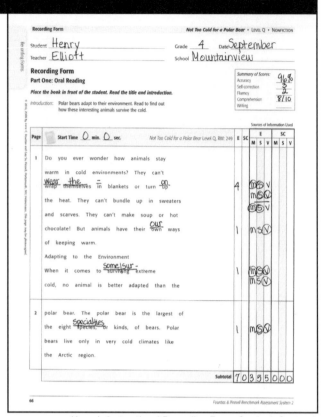

FIGURE 5.27a Henry's Instructional Recording Form, Grade 4, September

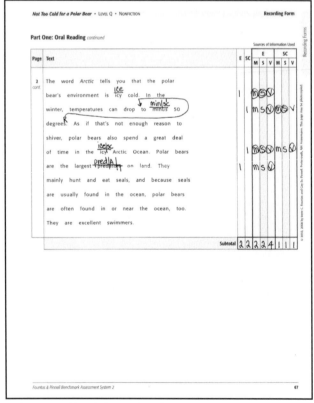

FIGURE 5.27b Henry's Instructional Recording Form, Grade 4, September, *continued*

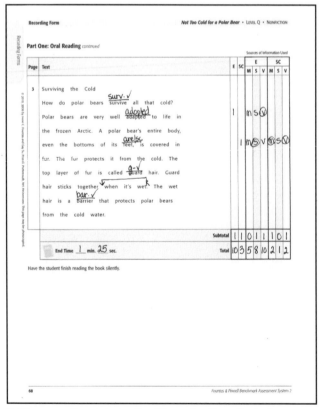

FIGURE 5.27c Henry's Instructional Recording Form, Grade 4, September, *continued*

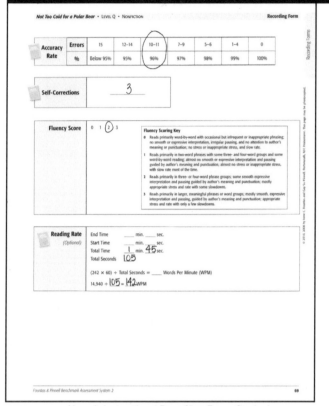

FIGURE 5.27d Henry's Instructional Recording Form, Grade 4, September

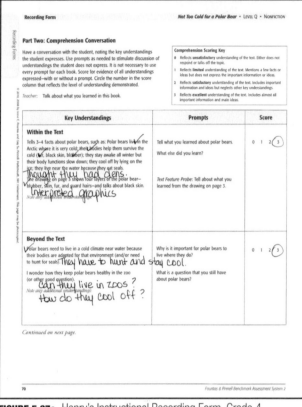

FIGURE 5.27e Henry's Instructional Recording Form, Grade 4, September, *continued*

FIGURE 5.27f Henry's Instructional Recording Form, Grade 4, September, *continued*

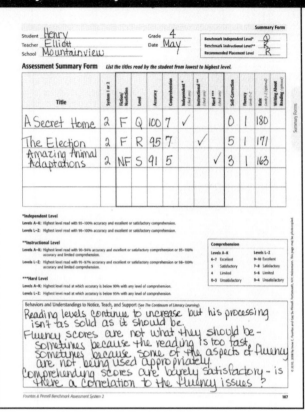

FIGURE 5.28 Henry's Assessment Summary Form, Grade 4, May

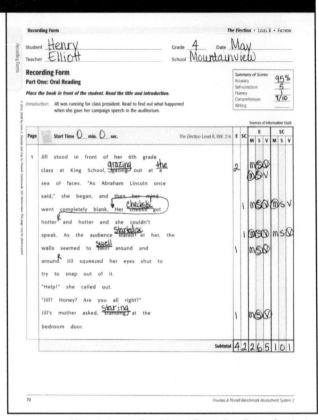

FIGURE 5.29a Henry's Instructional Level Recording Form, Grade 4, May

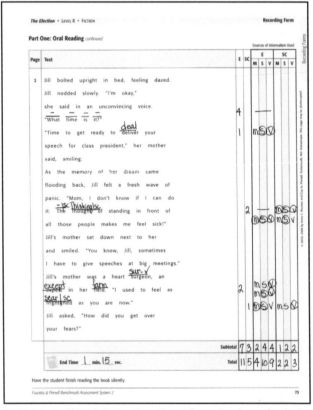

FIGURE 5.29b Henry's Instructional Level Recording Form, Grade 4, May, *continued*

Henry's Grade 4 May Assessment Conference *(continued)* and Bi-Annual Assessment summary

The Election • Level R • Fiction — Recording Form

Part One: Oral Reading *continued*

Sources of Information Used

Page	Text	E	SC	E M	E S	E V	SC M	SC S	SC V
2	Jill bolted upright in bed, feeling dazed.								
	Jill nodded slowly. "I'm okay,"								
	she said in an unconvincing voice.								
	"What time is it?"	4		—					
	"Time to get ready to deliver (deal) your	1		m	Ⓢ	Ⓥ			
	speech for class president," her mother								
	said, smiling.								
	As the memory of her dream came								
	flooding back, Jill felt a fresh wave of								
	panic. "Mom, I don't know if I can do								
	it. The (– | sc) thought (Thinking | sc) of standing in front of		2	—			Ⓜ	Ⓢ	Ⓥ
	all those people makes me feel sick!"			Ⓜ	Ⓢ	Ⓥ	m	Ⓢ	v
	Jill's mother sat down next to her								
	and smiled. "You know, Jill, sometimes								
	I have to give speeches at big meetings."								
	Jill's mother was a heart surgeon (sur- ✓), an								
	expert (except) in her field (farm). "I used to feel as	2		m / m	s / Ⓢ	Ⓥ / Ⓥ			
	frightened (scar | sc) as you are now."		1	Ⓜ	Ⓢ	v	m	s	Ⓥ
	Jill asked, "How did you get over								
	your fears?"								
	Subtotal	7	3	2	4	4	1	2	2
	End Time 1 min. 15 sec. — Total	11	5	4	10	9	2	2	3

Have the student finish reading the book silently.

Fountas & Pinnell Benchmark Assessment System 2 — 73

© 2010, 2008 by Irene C. Fountas and Gay Su Pinnell. Portsmouth, NH: Heinemann. This page may be photocopied.

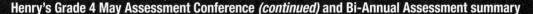

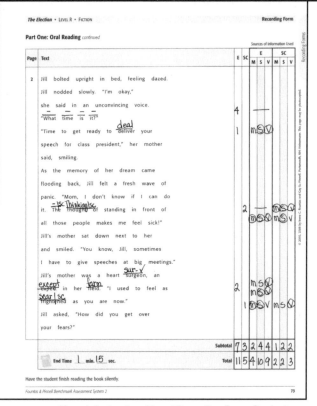

FIGURE 5.29c Henry's Instructional Level Recording Form, Grade 4, May, *continued*

The Election • Level R • Fiction — Recording Form

Part Two: Comprehension Conversation

Have a conversation with the student, noting the key understandings the student expresses. Use prompts as needed to stimulate discussion of understandings the student does not express. It is not necessary to use every prompt for each book. Score for evidence of all understandings expressed—with or without a prompt. Circle the number in the score column that reflects the level of understanding demonstrated.

Teacher: Talk about what happened in this story.

Comprehension Scoring Key
- 0 Reflects **unsatisfactory** understanding of the text. Either does not respond or talks off the topic.
- 1 Reflects **limited** understanding of the text. Mentions a few facts or ideas but does not express the important information or ideas.
- 2 Reflects **satisfactory** understanding of the text. Includes important information and ideas but neglects other key understandings.
- 3 Reflects **excellent** understanding of the text. Includes almost all important information and main ideas.

Key Understandings	Prompts	Score
Within the Text Tells 3–4 important events from the story, such as: Jill was very nervous about her speech; her mom gave her the suggestion of looking at a friendly face; Jill imagined herself talking to her friend Eduardo; she got over being scared and gave a good speech. She was afraid but she got over it. *Note any additional understandings:*	What was Jill's problem in the story? How did she solve her problem? What else happened in the story?	0 1 (2) 3
Beyond the Text She was having nightmares because she was so scared of standing up in front of all of those people. Had some trouble knowing it was a dream. Her mom could help because she had to learn to give speeches herself. Jill gave a good speech because she looked at friendly faces and also got excited about her ideas. *Note any additional understandings:*	Tell why Jill was scared. Why was her mom able to help her? What helped Jill give a good speech?	0 1 (2) 3

Continued on next page.

Fountas & Pinnell Benchmark Assessment System 2 — 75

© 2010, 2008 by Irene C. Fountas and Gay Su Pinnell. Portsmouth, NH: Heinemann. This page may be photocopied.

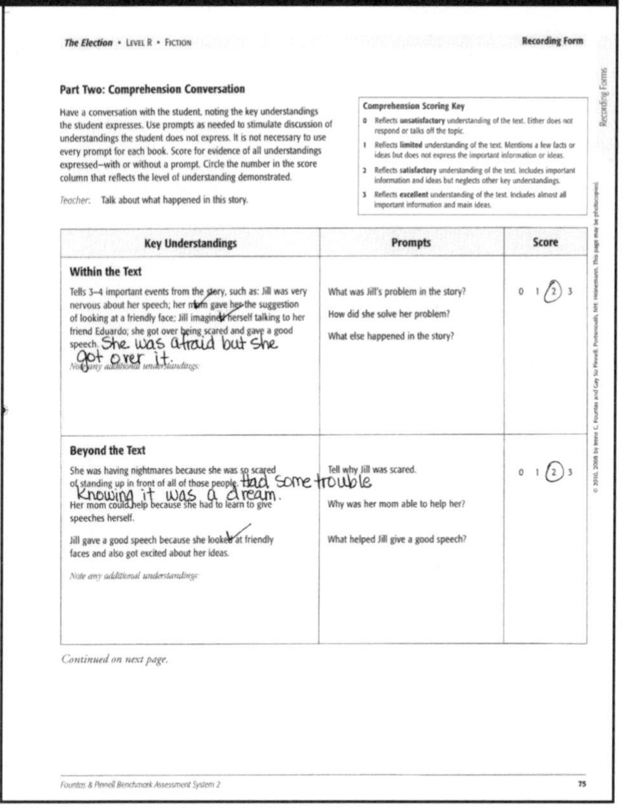

FIGURE 5.29d Henry's Instructional Level Recording Form, Grade 4, May, *continued*

Recording Form — *The Election* • Level R • Fiction

Part Two: Comprehension Conversation *continued*

Key Understandings	Prompts	Score
About the Text The story started with Jill having a dream and then she woke up. It wasn't real. Points out language like "her cheeks got hotter and hotter," or "a fresh wave of panic" to show how scared Jill was. Able to identify words showing feelings. The author showed that Jill would be a good class president by giving details about her ideas for improvement. *Note any additional understandings:* Said it was a good ending because Jill deserved to get elected. She had good ideas.	Look at the beginning. What was happening in the first paragraph? Show a place in the book where the author showed you how scared Jill was. How did this help you? How did the author show you that Jill would be a good class president?	0 1 (2) 3

Guide to Total Score
- 9–10 **Excellent** Comprehension
- 7–8 **Satisfactory** Comprehension
- 5–6 **Limited** Comprehension
- 0–4 **Unsatisfactory** Comprehension

Subtotal Score: 6 /9
Add 1 for any additional understandings: 1 /1
Total Score: 7 /10

Part Three: Writing About Reading *(optional)*

Read the writing/drawing prompt below to the student. You can also cut the prompt on the dotted line and give it to the child. Specify the amount of time for the student to complete the task on a separate sheet of paper. (See *Assessment Guide* for more information.)

Writing About Reading
- 0 Reflects **no** understanding of the text.
- 1 Reflects **very limited** understanding of the text.
- 2 Reflects **partial** understanding of the text.
- 3 Reflects **excellent** understanding of the text.

Describe how Jill felt and tell what advice you would give her to get through her speech. You can draw a sketch to go with your writing.

76 — Fountas & Pinnell Benchmark Assessment System 2

© 2010, 2008 by Irene C. Fountas and Gay Su Pinnell. Portsmouth, NH: Heinemann. This page may be photocopied.

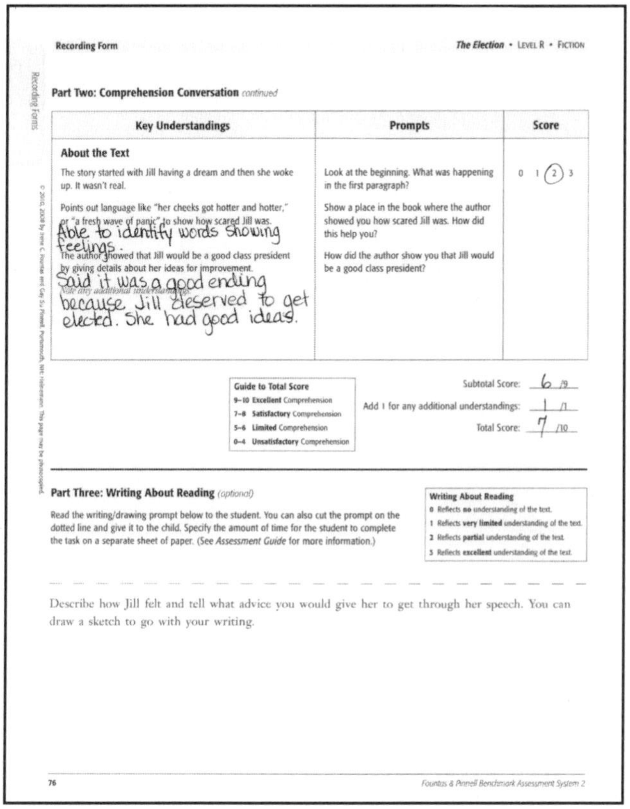

FIGURE 5.29e Henry's Instructional Level Recording Form, Grade 4, May, *continued*

Summary Form

Student: Henry — Grade: 4 — Year:
Teacher: Elliott — School: Mountainview

Bi-Annual Assessment Summary

	Date: September	Date: May
Independent Level	Level P – F	Level Q – F
Accuracy	98 %	100 %
Comprehension	7 / 10	7 / 10
Self-Correction	4	0
Fluency	0 1 (2) 3	0 (1) 2 3
Rate *(optional)*	150 WPM	180 WPM
Writing About Reading *(optional)*	0 1 2 3	0 1 2 3
Instructional Level	Level Q – NF	Level R – F
Accuracy	96 %	95 %
Comprehension	8 / 10	7 / 10
Self-Correction	3	5
Fluency	0 1 (2) 3	0 (1) 2 3
Rate *(optional)*	142 WPM	171 WPM
Writing About Reading *(optional)*	0 1 2 3	0 1 2 3

Behaviors and Understandings to Notice, Teach, and Support

May scores highlight fluency concerns. Although rate seems to be appropriate, other aspects are not being attended to by the reader.
Comprehending is barely satisfactory on both independent and instructional levels.
Small group, more intensive teaching seems appropriate to get all parts of the processing system working effectively for Henry.
If possible summer work might continue to support his progress.

168 — Fountas & Pinnell Benchmark Assessment System 2

© 2010, 2008 by Irene C. Fountas and Gay Su Pinnell. Portsmouth, NH: Heinemann. This page may be photocopied.

FIGURE 5.30 Henry's Bi-annual Assessment Summary, Grade 4

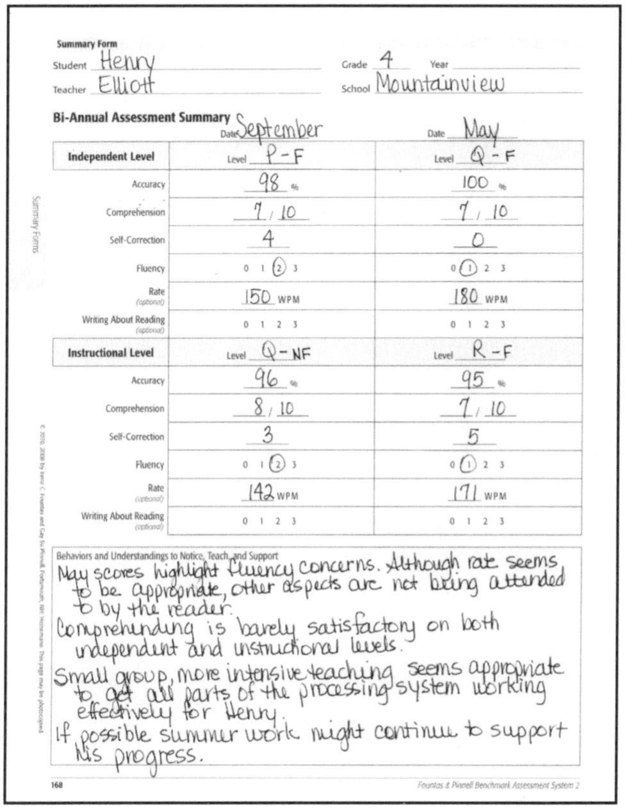

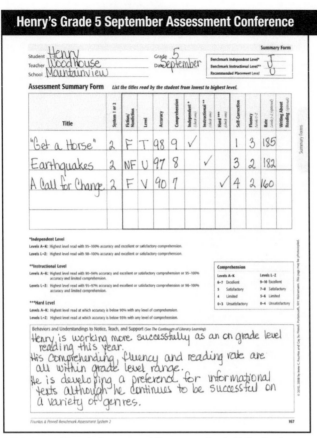

FIGURE 5.31 Henry's Assessment Summary, Grade 5, September

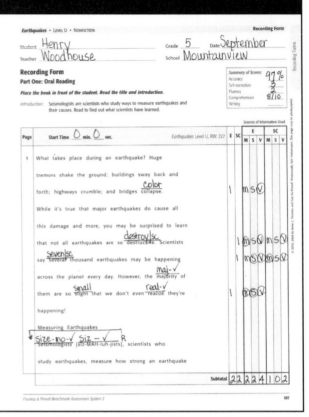

FIGURE 5.32a Henry's Instructional Level Recording Record, Grade 5, September

FIGURE 5.32b Henry's Instructional Level Recording Record, Grade 5, September, *continued*

FIGURE 5.32c Henry's Instructional Level Recording Record, Grade 5, September, *continued*

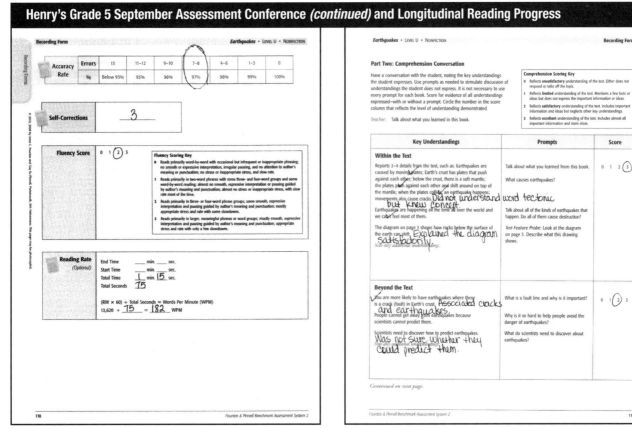

Accuracy	Errors	13	11–12	9–10	7–8	4–6	1–3	0
Rate	%	Below 95%	95%	96%	97%	98%	99%	100%

(7–8 / 97% circled)

Self-Corrections __3__

Fluency Score 0 1 (2) 3

Fluency Scoring Key

0 Reads primarily word-by-word with occasional but infrequent or inappropriate phrasing; no smooth or expressive interpretation, irregular pausing, and no attention to author's meaning or expressive stress, and slow rate.

1 Reads primarily in two-word phrases with some three- and four-word groups and some word-by-word reading; almost no smooth, expressive interpretation or pausing guided by author's meaning and punctuation; almost no stress or inappropriate stress, with slow rate most of the time.

2 Reads primarily in three- or four-word phrase groups; some smooth, expressive interpretation and pausing guided by author's meaning and punctuation; mostly appropriate stress and rate with some slowdowns.

3 Reads primarily in larger, meaningful phrases or word groups; mostly smooth, expressive interpretation and pausing guided by author's meaning and punctuation; appropriate stress and rate with only a few slowdowns.

Reading Rate *(Optional)*

End Time ____ min. ____ sec.
Start Time ____ min. ____ sec.
Total Time __1__ min. __15__ sec.
Total Seconds __75__

(RW × 60) ÷ Total Seconds = Words Per Minute (WPM)
13,620 ÷ __75__ = __182__ WPM

FIGURE 5.32d Henry's Instructional Level Recording Record, Grade 5, September, *continued*

Earthquakes • LEVEL U • NONFICTION   Recording Form

Part Two: Comprehension Conversation

Have a conversation with the student, noting the key understandings the student expresses. Use prompts as needed to stimulate discussion of understandings the student does not express. It is not necessary to use every prompt for each book. Score for evidence of all understandings expressed—with or without a prompt. Circle the number in the score column that reflects the level of understanding demonstrated.

Teacher: Talk about what you learned in this book.

Comprehension Scoring Key

0 Reflects **unsatisfactory** understanding of the text. Either does not respond or talks off the topic.

1 Reflects **limited** understanding of the text. Mentions a few facts or ideas but does not express the important information or ideas.

2 Reflects **satisfactory** understanding of the text. Includes important information and ideas but neglects other key understandings.

3 Reflects **excellent** understanding of the text. Includes almost all important information and main ideas.

Key Understandings	Prompts	Score
Within the Text Reports 3–4 details from the text, such as: Earthquakes are caused by moving plates; Earth's crust has plates that push against each other; below the crust, there is a soft mantle; the plates push against each other and shift around on top of the mantle; when the plates collide, an earthquake happens; movements also cause cracks. *Did not understand word tectonic but knew concept* Earthquakes are happening all the time all over the world and we can't feel most of them. The diagram on page 3 shows how rocks below the surface of the earth can shift. *Explained the diagram satisfactorily*	Talk about what you learned from this book. What causes earthquakes? Talk about all of the kinds of earthquakes that happen. Do all of them cause destruction? *Text Feature Probe:* Look at the diagram on page 3. Describe what this drawing shows.	0 1 2 (3)
Beyond the Text You are more likely to have earthquakes where there is a crack (fault) in Earth's crust. *Associated cracks and earthquakes.* People cannot get away from earthquakes because scientists cannot predict them. Scientists need to discover how to predict earthquakes. *Was not sure whether they could predict them.*	What is a fault line and why is it important? Why is it so hard to help people avoid the danger of earthquakes? What do scientists need to discover about earthquakes?	0 1 (2) 3

Continued on next page.

FIGURE 5.32e Henry's Instructional Level Recording Record, Grade 5, September, *continued*

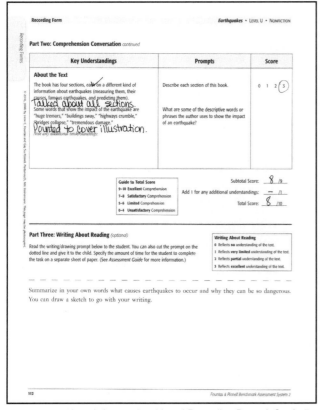

Recording Form   *Earthquakes* • LEVEL U • NONFICTION

Part Two: Comprehension Conversation *continued*

Key Understandings	Prompts	Score
About the Text The book has four sections, each on a different kind of information about earthquakes (measuring them, their causes, famous earthquakes, and predicting them). *Talked about all sections.* Some words that show the impact of the earthquake are "huge tremors," "buildings sway," "highways crumble," "bridges collapse," "tremendous damage." *Pointed to cover illustration.*	Describe each section of this book. What are some of the descriptive words or phrases the author uses to show the impact of an earthquake?	0 1 2 (3)

Guide to Total Score

9–10 **Excellent** Comprehension
7–8 **Satisfactory** Comprehension
5–6 **Limited** Comprehension
0–4 **Unsatisfactory** Comprehension

Subtotal Score: __8__ /9
Add 1 for any additional understandings: __–__ /1
Total Score: __8__ /10

Part Three: Writing About Reading *(optional)*

Read the writing/drawing prompt below to the student. You can also cut the prompt on the dotted line and give it to the child. Specify the amount of time for the student to complete the task on a separate sheet of paper. (See *Assessment Guide* for more information.)

Writing About Reading

0 Reflects **no** understanding of the text.
1 Reflects **very limited** understanding of the text.
2 Reflects **partial** understanding of the text.
3 Reflects **excellent** understanding of the text.

Summarize in your own words what causes earthquakes to occur and why they can be so dangerous. You can draw a sketch to go with your writing.

FIGURE 5.32f Henry's Instructional Level Recording Record, Grade 5, September, *continued*

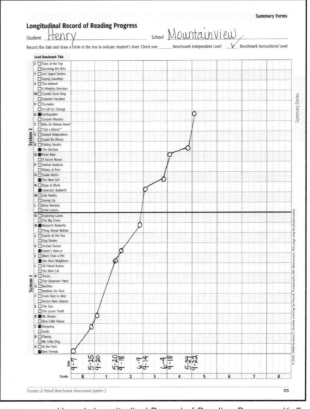

Summary Forms

Longitudinal Record of Reading Progress

Student __Henry__   School __Mountainview__

Record the date and draw a circle in the box to indicate student's level. Check one: ____ Benchmark Independent Level   __✓__ Benchmark Instructional Level

FIGURE 5.33 Henry's Longitudinal Record of Reading Progress, K–5

section 6

Using Results to Group and Inform Instruction

In our view, the most important use of assessment is to inform instruction. Even while administering and analyzing a benchmark assessment, you will find yourself thinking about what the student needs in terms of instruction. When you have completed the assessment, you will have valuable categories of information that will allow you to link your findings directly with instruction.

In this section, we discuss and provide models for using assessment results to place students in groups; to plan for individual, small-group, and whole-class instruction; and to use *The Continuum of Literacy Learning* (Fountas & Pinnell, Heinemann, 2011, 2008) to connect assessment and instruction.

Grouping Children for Instruction

The three levels (independent, instructional, and recommended placement) you determined will help you form groups for reading instruction. List your students on the Class Record Form (Figure 6.1) from lowest to highest instructional level to help you cluster students appropriately. **Note:** The *Online Data Management System* will enable you to sort your students by level (or another variable), which can assist with instructional groupings. For more information on the *Online Data Management System,* see Section 7 of this guide.

With the wide range of students in every classroom, it is a challenge to form reading groups that work efficiently. Figures 6.1 and 6.2 show a class list and reading groups from Mr. Mason's fifth grade class. Ideally, there would be a group for each level, but for this class, that would mean too many groups. It would take so much time to teach the groups that students would not get reading instruction often enough. Also, there are slight differences in students' processing systems even if they are reading at about the same text level.

As you look at the class record form, you can see that the teacher has recommended a placement level of P for Diana even though her instructional level was Q. Diana was not fluent at level Q, and the teacher thought she could benefit from more reading at P. Beth's scores did not show her reading at an instructional level V, but the teacher's assessment was that Beth was a more advanced reader than this assessment showed. The teacher planned to do further assessment but was not worried about Beth's ability to read and understand texts at V.

Mr. Mason used all the data to make his grouping decisions. Sometimes he clustered students who were at slightly different levels together in the same group. You can see that he grouped Sarah, Diana, Troy, and Farah together. Mr. Mason knew that these students needed a great deal of help, so he worked with them daily in a small group, starting at P.

Because Farah's comprehension and fluency were strong, Mr. Mason predicted that she would move to the group with Lisa, Jonathon, David, Kara, Julian, Jennifer, Auggie, Jack, and Jordan before long. He started this group at R, and his agenda included deep discussion of the texts they are reading as well as some readers' theater to help with fluency.

Carrie, Elias, Mary, Ernie, Patrick, Donna, Luke, and Beth form a group with a starting point of level U. Luke was not fluent at level V and it seemed difficult for him. The group with Robert, Jerry, Helen, Vera, and Michael start at W. These six students compose a high-progress group. They read well above grade level but the teacher takes care in selecting texts for them. They need interesting, age-appropriate material. Technically, each can read adult-level literature, but the mature themes and issues could be difficult for them to understand. They need to read widely across genres so that they are engaged in reading interesting texts.

Dynamic Grouping

Benchmark assessment and ongoing assessment allow you to group dynamically as students develop differently from one another. Dynamic grouping

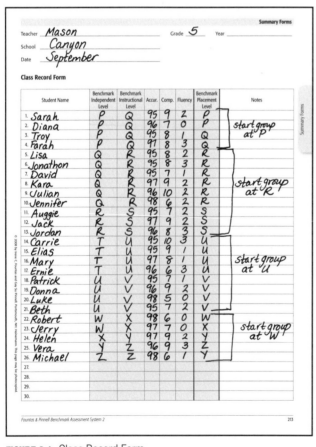

FIGURE 6.1 Class Record Form

Group	Sarah Diana Troy Farah	Lisa Jonathon David Kara Julian Jennifer Auggie Jack Jordan	Carrie Elias Mary Ernie Patrick Donna Luke Beth	Robert Jerry Helen Vera Michael
Comments	Need daily intensive instruction because they are well below grade level. Observe Farah for possible shift to R.	Give extra challenge to Jack and Jordan.	Give more support to Carrie. Work on fluency.	Search for texts that will challenge the group but be age-appropriate. Avoid texts with issues that are too mature.
Starting Level	Start at P.	Start at R and move quickly to S.	Start at U and move quickly to V.	Read age-appropriate texts of interest at W and move to X.

FIGURE 6.2 Sample grouping

means that you move students from group to group as they progress at different rates. You can adjust your groupings as needed. Small, homogeneous groups enable you to choose appropriate texts and teach closely to the needs of the individual students.

We do not recommend naming the groups so they have permanent status. Just call the group by the students' names or by the book they read last and invite them to come to the reading table. Also, have students work in other kinds of groups (e.g., literacy work groups or heterogeneous literature discussion groups) that are not arranged by reading level. In addition to targeted small-group reading instruction, they will need many other group opportunities for age- and grade-appropriate instruction in interactive read-aloud or shared reading contexts. Students who are below-grade level may need a temporary supplemental intervention to help them reach grade level performance. See *www.fountasandpinnell.com* for information on *Leveled Literacy Intervention* (Fountas and Pinnell, Heinemann, 2009).

▶ Planning Individual, Small-Group, and Whole-Class Instruction

Now let's think about how to use the rich information you collect as you begin working with your students in three instructional contexts: the teaching you do with individuals, small groups, and your entire class.

Individual Instruction

Identifying a student's independent level helps you guide her book choices for productive, independent reading. The data you gather in the assessment becomes the foundation for providing students "just right" books for small-group instruction. These levels will also help you think about forming groups of students who, while individual and unique in many ways, are alike enough to teach effectively together. Students learn to read better by reading many texts they can read each day. Easy reading has many benefits.

You can gather evidence of processing through analyzing the errors and self-correction behaviors of the student. Use this information to help you as you interact with him individually during guided reading and reading conferences. It will also help you make teaching points in guided reading lessons.

Fluency scores and observation of oral reading will help you know what a student needs in terms of fluency support. It can inform your interactions with her during guided reading and individual reading conferences.

The comprehension subscore will help the student know whether you need to intervene to help him think more actively before, during, and after reading. Looking at her responses in categories (within, beyond, and about texts) will also inform your interactions with him during guided reading and individual conferences.

Figure 6.3 summarizes some of the ways you can use the data to plan individual instruction.

Small-Group Instruction

The instructional and recommended placement levels of your class will help you form groups and select texts for them to read. Examining the demands of texts at that level will be helpful in constructing introductions to texts before students read them. You can look at the evidence of processing in the Guide for Observing and Noting Reading Behaviors from the *Assessment Forms Book* and *CD-ROM* for each student, searching for similar needs. Use this information to inform your teaching points after reading as well as your information interactions while reading. (See *Prompting Guide, Part 1* [Fountas & Pinnell, Heinemann, 2009]).

The fluency scores of individuals in the group help you decide whether to do some intensive teaching or prompt for fluency and phrasing as students read the text. You may want to incorporate readers' theater into your small-group work to help them become more conscious of how their reading sounds.

Planning Individual Instruction

Data from Benchmark Assessment	How the Information Helps in Making Teaching Decisions in Literacy Contexts
• Benchmark independent level • Benchmark instructional level • Recommended placement level	• Guiding students' book choices for independent reading • Placing the student in a small group for instruction • Reconsidering grouping decisions regarding the individual • Informing individual reading conferences
• Evidence of processing (strategic actions and MSV analysis)	• Interacting with individuals in guided reading lessons • Interacting with individuals in conferences
• Fluency score	• Interacting with individuals in guided reading or small-group lessons • Interacting in individual conferences during reading workshop
• Comprehension subscores and total score	• Interacting with individuals during guided reading or small-group lessons • Interacting with individuals in reading conferences • Responding to writing about reading in the reader's notebook

FIGURE 6.3 Planning individual instruction

The comprehension scores will help you know how much you need to support students' active thinking. Of course, you will always be teaching for comprehension because that is one of the main goals of instruction. But you may find that you need to adjust the text level to one that is very accessible and work intensively to get students to express their thinking. Looking at the patterns of performance within categories (within, beyond, and about the text) will help you plan teaching points and design activities for writing about reading that will also extend students' thinking about texts.

Figure 6.4 summarizes some of the ways you can use data to help you plan small-group instruction.

Whole-Class Instruction

Individual assessments can inform your teaching of the whole class as well. Use your Class Record Form to evaluate your classroom library. Make sure that you have a quantity of high-quality books at levels your students can read independently. Also, as you give book talks,

present a range of levels. It is extremely important for students to process a large quantity of text independently every day. You are helping them take on more difficult texts through guided reading instruction, but they also need to be building stamina and skill on their own.

Look across the assessment data for information on processing and comprehension. It's especially important to look at the extent to which students can express their thinking beyond and about texts. This information will be invaluable as you plan mini-lessons for reading workshop and for intentional conversation during interactive read-aloud. We use the term "intentional conversation" to remind ourselves that we need to simultaneously engage in a real conversation with students and have in mind things that we want to teach them during read-aloud sessions. (See *Teaching for Comprehending and Fluency, K–8* [Heinemann, 2006], Chapters 15–17, for a detailed description.) Finally, you can use the information to help you extend students' thinking through writing

Planning Small-Group Instruction	
Data from Benchmark Assessment	**How the Information Helps in Making Teaching Decisions in Literacy Contexts**
• Benchmark independent level • Benchmark instructional level • Recommended placement level	• Making decisions about grouping • Selecting texts for guided reading or small-group lessons
• Evidence of processing (strategic actions and MSV analysis)	• Preparing an introduction to the text for a guided reading lesson • Making teaching points in guided reading lessons • Planning word work for the end of the guided reading lesson
• Fluency scores	• Selecting texts for guided reading or small-group lessons • Making teaching points in guided reading lessons • Selecting ways to reread the text (readers' theater, shared reading)
• Comprehension subscores and total score	• Introducing texts to students in guided reading lessons • Supporting the student's reading of the text • Discussing the meaning of the text after reading • Making teaching points in guided reading lessons • Extending meaning of a text through writing and drawing about reading

FIGURE 6.4 Planning small-group instruction

and/or drawing about reading as part of interactive read-aloud and literature discussion.

Figure 6.5 summarizes some of the ways you can use data to help you plan whole-class instruction.

▶ Connecting Assessment to Instruction with *The Continuum of Literacy Learning*

As you think about individual, small-group, and whole-class instruction, you will find it helpful to consult *The Continuum of Literacy Learning, Grades 3–8: A Guide to Teaching* (Fountas and Pinnell, Heinemann, 2011, 2008) which is included in your *Fountas & Pinnell Benchmark Assessment System 2* box. This volume contains seven continua (Figure 6.6). Each continuum focuses on an area of the language arts curriculum. Six continua—Interactive Read-Aloud and Literature Discussion; Shared and Performance Reading; Writing About Reading; Writing; Oral, Visual, and Technological Communication; and Phonics and Word Analysis—provide grade-level expectations and are designed for planning whole-group and small-group instruction. The seventh, the Guided Reading continuum, is organized by Fountas and Pinnell levels from L to Z and correlates directly with the benchmark levels you arrived at using the Assessment. Once you have determined a student's benchmark and recommended placement levels, turn directly to the Guided Reading continuum and find the direct link from the assessment to instruction.

(**Note:** There is also a PreK–8, level A–Z version known as *The Continuum of Literacy Learning, Grades PreK–8,* 2011, which will be of interest to administrators, curriculum developers, staff developers, and literacy coaches.)

The continua provide specific descriptions of the texts that students read, listen to, write, and perform. In addition, each continuum lists specific behaviors and understandings that are required at each level for

Planning Whole-Class Instruction	
Data from Benchmark Assessment	**How the Information Helps in Making Teaching Decisions in Literacy Contexts**
• Benchmark independent levels • Benchmark instructional levels	• Stocking the classroom library with books for self-selected independent reading • Giving book talks to students in reading workshop • Providing audio-recorded books for rereading and for literature discussion
• Evidence of processing (strategic actions and MSV analysis)	• Designing minilessons for reading workshop (strategies and skills) • Engaging students in intentional conversation in interactive read-aloud • Planning word study minilessons • Engaging students in literature discussion
• Fluency scores	• Engaging students in shared and performance reading • Providing effective models of oral reading through interactive read-aloud
• Comprehension subscores and total score	• Engaging students in intentional conversation during interactive read-aloud • Engaging students in literature discussion • Providing minilessons (strategies and skills; craft)

FIGURE 6.5 Planning whole-class instruction

students to demonstrate thinking within, beyond, and about the text. Taken together, these behaviors and understandings represent the demands of the text. They form what students will be expected to do in order to effectively read and understand the text. The behaviors and understandings are cumulative across the levels. In other words, the reader is taking on new demands as the texts grow more challenging. A student reading level M and successfully meeting the demands of the text is also able to meet the demands of texts on levels A–L.

▶ Connecting Assessment to Guided Reading, Interactive Read-Aloud, and Whole-Group Minilessons

Figures 6.7–6.9 provide step-by-step examples for connecting Benchmark Assessment to guided reading, interactive read-aloud, and whole-group reading minilessons in a reading workshop.

The Seven Continua from *The Continuum of Literacy Learning, 3–8*

Continuum	Description
Guided Reading Levels L–Z	The teacher works with a small group of students who are similar in their development of a reading process. The teacher introduces the text and the students read it with teaching support.
Interactive Read-Aloud and Literature Discussion Grades 3–8	The teacher reads aloud to students and engages them in intentional conversation. Students discuss their thinking in the whole group or in small groups. This continuum also refers to "book clubs," in which students independently read (or listen to) books and then discuss them in small groups. The books are usually organized by the teacher, and students have a limited choice, although they also may be books read aloud.
Shared and Performance Reading Grades 3–8	Students read together (or in parts) a text that they know well. They show with their voices what the text means.
Writing About Reading Grades 3–8	Students respond to reading by writing and sometimes drawing.
Writing Grades 3–8	Students engage in the writing process and produce pieces of their own writing in many genres.
Oral, Visual, and Technological Communication Grades 3–8	Oral language is used across the curriculum and is embedded in all contexts in the continuum. In this continuum, specific expectations are listed and extended to interactive media for communication.
Phonics, Spelling, and Word Study Grades 3–8	A phonics and word study continuum includes expectations related to six areas of learning: letter-sound relationships, high-frequency words, word meaning/vocabulary, spelling patterns, word structure, and word-solving actions. The K–8 continuum includes nine areas of learning to cover early understandings such as phonemic awareness.

FIGURE 6.6 Seven continua

Step 1. Assess all students in the class and find Benchmark independent, instructional, and recommended placement levels.

Step 2. Form temporary groups according to their placement levels.

Step 3. Go to the Guided Reading section of *The Continuum* and look at the characteristics of the texts at the level. Keep these characteristics in mind when selecting books for the group.

Step 4. Select several possible books for each group so that you will have alternatives across a few days or a week of instruction.

Step 5. Select the text that you will introduce to the group first.

Step 6. Read the text carefully with the characteristics in mind.

Step 7. Look at your student data on strategic actions and sources of information as well as fluency and comprehension. Think about what students need to learn how to do as readers. Reports from the *Data Management System* can be helpful in identifying and analyzing patterns.

Step 8. Look at the behaviors and understandings for the level. These represent what students need to be able to do to read successfully at the level.

Step 9. Think about what your students can do and then find behaviors and understandings that they partially control or do not yet control.

Step 10. Plan your introduction to the text and teaching points for the lesson, keeping in mind the processing needs of your students.

Step 11. Plan for word work at the end of the lesson. You will find specific suggestions for each level in *The Continuum*. If you have students who need basic work because they are reading well below grade level, you may want to consult the *PreK–2* or *PreK–8 Continuum*.

Step 12. Plan for writing about reading (optional element). Here, think about the specific demands of text on the Guided Reading continuum. Then, look at the Writing About Reading continuum for the grade level. Look at the genres that are appropriate and the thinking that students are expected to do.

Step 13. As students grow more proficient and reading becomes easy at a particular level, look at the behaviors and understandings for the next highest level. You'll find many of the same strategies you've been teaching because the reading process is built by applying the same set of complex strategies to increasingly more difficult texts. You may find new understandings or more complex versions of the same understandings. Start to look toward this next level.

Step 15. Select texts from the next level and look at the text characteristics and behaviors and understandings to notice, teach, and support.

Step 15. Continue to introduce texts and teach lessons based on the spiraling of text demands.

FIGURE 6.7 Connecting assessment to Guided Reading Lessons

Connecting Assessment to Interactive Read-Aloud

Step 1. Assess the class and find Benchmark independent, instructional, and recommended placement levels.

Step 2. Look at the total scores for comprehension and subscores within each category (within, beyond, and about the text). Reports from the *Data Management System* can be helpful in identifying and analyzing patterns.

Step 3. Look for patterns across the entire group. Even though students are reading at different levels, there may be some similar needs in terms of comprehending and processing.

Step 4. Go to the Interactive Read-Aloud continuum for the grade level.

Step 5. Look at the characteristics of texts and keep them in mind as you select books to read aloud to students.

Step 6. Select and sequence texts so that students will make connections between them and build on previous understandings.

Step 7. Look at the behaviors and understandings and think about your students' needs in terms of active thinking within, beyond, and about texts.

Step 8. Select goals to accomplish in your interactive read-aloud program.

Step 9. Plan an "opening" to each text that will help your students think more deeply about the text or notice important information and characteristics. The opening should be brief, just a few words to set readers up for successful understanding (see *Teaching for Comprehending and Fluency, K–8* [Heinemann, 2006], Chapter 15).

Step 10. Plan intentional conversation and "turn and talk" routines (see *Teaching for Comprehending and Fluency, K–8,* [Heinemann, 2006] Chapter 18) to support your students' thinking as you think through the text together.

Step 11. Plan for writing about reading (optional). Here, think about the specific demands of the texts on the Interactive Read-Aloud continuum. Then, look at the Writing About Reading continuum for the grade level. Look at the genres that are appropriate and the thinking that students are expected to do.

Step 12. Keep a class record of books read aloud so that you and the class can easily remember connections and make new ones.

FIGURE 6.8 Connecting assessment to interactive read-aloud

Linking Assessment Information to Whole-Group Minilessons in a Reading Workshop

Step 1. Assess the class and find Benchmark independent, instructional, and recommended placement levels.

Step 2. Look at the total scores on comprehension and scores within each category (within, beyond, and about the text).

Step 3. Look at the evidence of processing—strategic actions and analysis of sources of information (MSV).

Step 4. Look for patterns across the entire group. Even though students are reading at different levels, there may be some similar needs in terms of comprehending and processing.

Step 5. Go to the Interactive Read-Aloud section of *The Continuum*. Look at the behaviors and understandings to notice, teach, and support.

Step 6. Think about your students' needs in terms of active thinking within, beyond, and about texts.

Step 7. Select goals and understandings that lend themselves to effective teaching in minilessons.

Step 8. Plan a minilesson (or short series of lessons) to address the goals.

Step 9. Plan for writing about reading (optional element). Here, think about the specific demands of the texts on the Interactive Read-Aloud continuum. Then, look at the Writing About Reading continuum for the grade level. Look at the genres that are appropriate and the thinking that students are expected to do.

Step 10. Students write about reading during their independent work time. They write about the books they have chosen for independent reading.

Step 11. Use the list of behaviors and understandings to guide them in their writing.

Step 12. In grade 2 and up, you may be using a reader's notebook for various forms of writing including dialogue and letters. Prompt and look for evidence of behaviors and understandings in students' writing. (See *Teaching for Comprehending and Fluency, K–8* for specific lessons on using a reader's notebook.)

FIGURE 6.9 Connecting Assessment to whole-group minilessons

▶ Connecting the Assessment to a Core or Basal Reading Program

The correlation between information gained from Benchmark Assessment and a leveled-book reading program is clear. Identification of the independent and instructional levels will allow you to guide the selection of independent reading books and choose books for instruction that are at the optimal level for supporting young readers. You can read detailed descriptions of the levels with sample texts in *Leveled Books K–8: Matching Texts to Readers for Effective Teaching* (Heinemann, 2006) and find over 33,000 leveled book titles in *The Fountas and Pinnell Leveled Book List, K–8+* (Heinemann, 2009) and at *www.fountasandpinnell.com*.

Benchmark Assessment results can inform more than leveled-reading programs. You may be using a set of materials that is usually referred to as a "basal" or "core" system. Most systems consist of anthologies of written material. The anthology may include stories written especially for reading instruction or drawn from various works of literature. Selections are usually sequenced in the anthologies.

With a core or basal system, you still need to think about readability. Understanding the demands of the texts will help you support and teach your students more effectively. Many core programs involve students in small-group reading instruction in addition to whole-group reading in the core anthology. The whole-group reading is usually in the form of read-aloud or shared reading. The basal system ideally includes sets of leveled books to differentiate instruction. Figure 6.10 will help you make a connection between the Fountas & Pinnell A–Z levels and a basal system if you are using the anthology for small-group teaching. You can also use the benchmark books and their text characteristics to help you "level" the materials in your basal system.

Level Correspondence—Core or Basal Reading Programs		
Fountas and Pinnell Benchmark Instructional Level	Guided Reading Level (for instruction)	Basal System Level
A	A	Kindergarten
B	B	Kindergarten
C	C	Preprimer
D	D	Preprimer
E	E	Preprimer
F	F	Primer
G	G	Primer
H	H	Grade 1 (middle)
I	I	Grade 1 (late)
J	J	Grade 2 (early)
K	K	Grade 2 (early)
L	L	Grade 2 (late)
M	M	Grade 2 (late)
N	N	Grade 3 (early)
O	O	Grade 3 (early)
P	P	Grade 3 (late)
Q	Q	Grade 4 (early)
R	R	Grade 4 (early)
S	S	Grade 4 (late)
T	T	Grade 5 (early)
U	U	Grade 5 (early)
V	V	Grade 5 (late)
W	W	Grade 6 (early)
X	X	Grade 6 (early)
Y	Y	Grade 6 (late)
Z	Z	Grades 7 and 8

FIGURE 6.10 Fountas and Pinnell levels correlated to guided reading and core basal levels

Online Data Management System and Professional Development DVD

Assessment data is information about learners that informs your teaching day to day and across time. When you use data along with your observations, you are able to quantify the precise strengths and needs of each of your students.

The Benchmark Assessment *Online Data Management System* will provide you with support to help you teach systematically and effectively. It helps you appreciate the uniqueness of each child's literacy journey. It allows you to capture the data and document change in individuals or groups over time. It becomes a visual record that can be placed in students' literacy files as a record of their development. Your administrators can also benefit from viewing the data from your class or from several classes to gain insights into the achievement of the students in relation to grade level expectations. A description of this powerful system follows.

The Benchmark Assessment *Professional Development DVD*, included in your *Technology Package*, includes many features to help you learn how to administer the assessment from beginning to end. A detailed description of the DVD also follows.

▶ Benchmark Online Data Management System (ODMS)

The *Online Data Management System (ODMS)* is designed to facilitate the sharing of *Benchmark Assessment System* data among teachers and administrators to monitor student progress. This password-protected, web-based system provides robust support for schools and districts interested in collecting and analyzing data on student achievement and progress over time. A one-year subscription to the *ODMS* is included with the purchase of *BAS*. (To sign up for access see the back of your Technology Package.) Access is available for three different levels of users: teachers, school administrators, and district administrators. For a product tour and downloadable user manual, go to: *www.fountasand-pinnell.com* and and scroll down to "Online Data Management System." There are two types of user manuals available on the website: the *Quick Start Guide,* and the complete *User Guide.* The *User Guide* is available in two versions: Teacher and Administrator.

OVERVIEW OF TEACHER SUBSCRIPTION

The information that follows is an overview of the *ODMS* for a teacher subscription. For detailed information about a school or district administrator subscription, see the *Quick Start Guide* or the *User Guide* at the same link as above.

Registration, Log-in, and Navigation   First-time users of the online system go through a simple registration process. Once registered, the log-in process involves just a username and password.

To facilitate navigation through the online system, several features remain consistent including the welcome area where you can log out or access account information and help. Most screens also include a directions box and, in the lower right corner, a print button that enables you to print hard copies of screens. A question mark icon (?) appears wherever additional help is embedded.

ODMS is organized by three main tabs, or sections: Classes, Assessments, and Reports.

Classes   In the Classes section (Figure 7.3), you can set up a class list and edit information on your classes. The columns in the class list table are customizable. You can choose up to eight columns including: first/last name, student ID, gender, date of birth, race/ethnicity, primary language, free/reduced lunch, ELL, Special Education Services, and Additional Reading Services, Benchmark Independent Level, Benchmark Instructional Level, Recommended Placement Level, and Other. (**Note:** If this student information resides elsewhere, it can be directly imported by using the import template.) Student information can also be sorted by clicking on any column header in the table. At any point in the school

FIGURE 7.1 Benchmark Assessment Technology Package

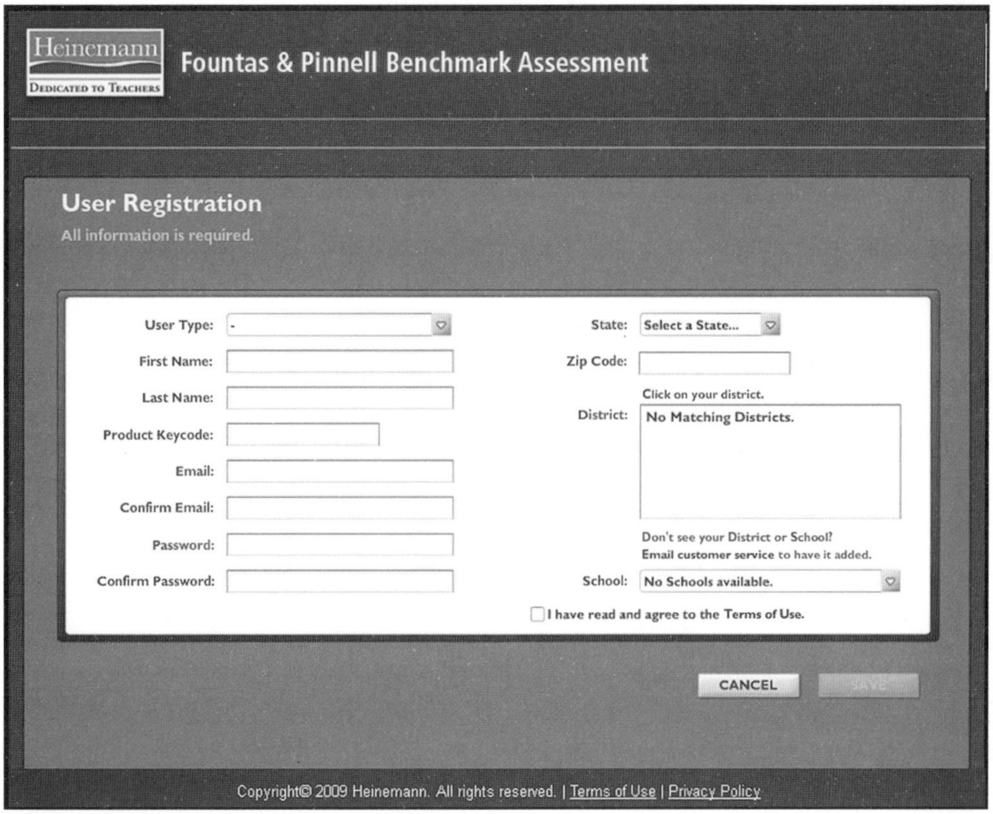

FIGURE 7.2 Registration screen

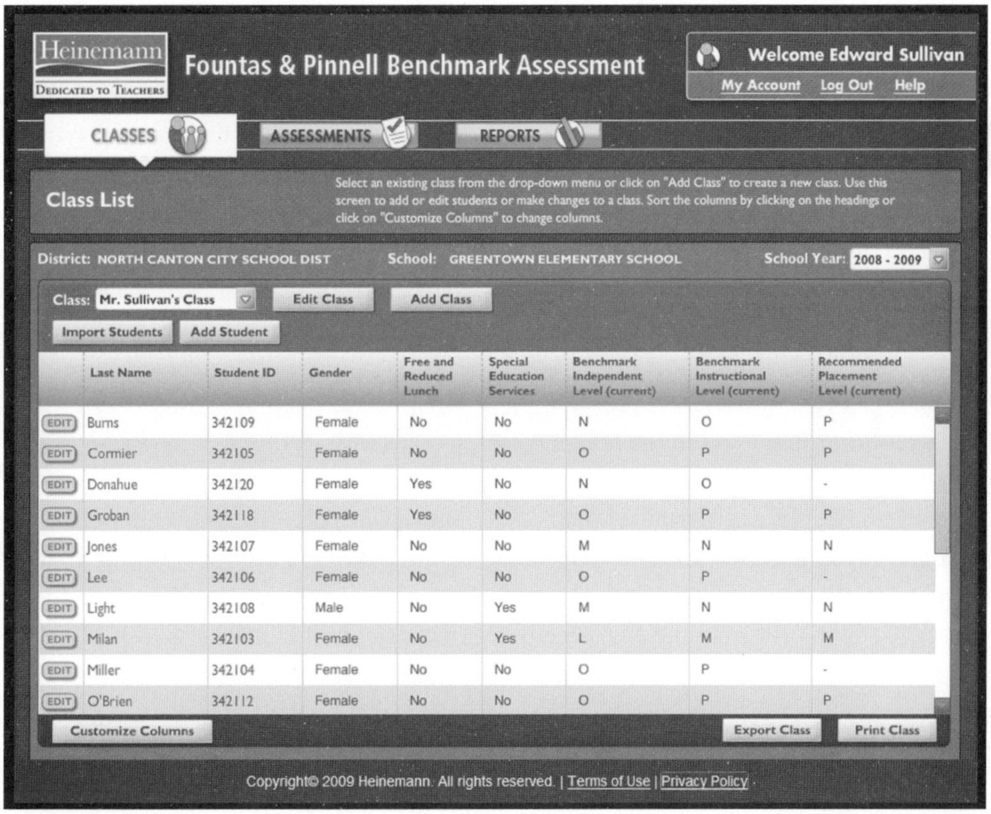

FIGURE 7.3 Class List

year, students can be added or deleted from the class list and student information can be updated.

First, set up a Class Profile (Figures 7.4a, 7.4b), which includes grade level information, start and end dates of the school year, and the text level goals, which can now be set by an administrator before a teacher sets up the class. By establishing text level goals, you will be able to see how your students are performing against those goals at any given time in the school year. (**Note:** At any point in the school year, you can change this information.) If your school or district has not already established its own text level goals by grade level, click on the help icon (?) for a chart of recommended goals.

Assessments The Assessments section is where you enter and view assessment scores. The Class Assessment Summary screen (Figure 7.5) shows the cumulative data for a class of students, and the Student Assessment Summary (Figure 7.6) shows the cumulative data for an individual student.

Once you have completed an assessment conference, enter the scores manually using the information you recorded on the Assessment Summary Form from the *Assessment Forms Book* or *CD-ROM*. Start by clicking on the "Add Text Reading" button (bottom left of screen in Figure 7.6), then proceed step by step through the process. If you choose to conduct some of the Optional Assessments and wish to track the scores, you may do so by clicking on the "Optional Assessments" link. Any additional comments you may want to make about the student's performance can be added in the "Comments" field.

Figures 7.7a–7.7c show the simple steps involved in entering the data in the Assessment Data Profile. The process of entering Benchmark Assessment data here would take place 1–4 times per year, depending on your school/district's requirements. Interval data for progress monitoring using leveled books can be collected and entered at any time throughout the school year. (**Note:** The first prompt in the Assessment Data Profile asks if you are entering *Fountas & Pinnell Benchmark Assessment* data or data from another reading record. If you are using leveled books for interval assessments, choose "Other Reading Record" before inputting data.)

If you are entering *Fountas & Pinnell Benchmark Assessment* data, the book title will automatically appear once you enter the level and genre. Likewise, once the accuracy and comprehension score are entered, the reading level (independent, instructional, or hard) will be calculated automatically. The items with an asterisk are required; those without an asterisk are optional.

REPORTS

The Reports section provides a variety of options for viewing student and class progress throughout the year. There are two main types of reports: Assessment Levels and Comprehension. Data can be viewed as either tables or graphs at the student and class level by toggling between the table and graph icons in the upper right corner.

Student Reports The Student Assessment Levels graph (Figure 7.8) shows the progress of one student over the course of a school year. On the left side, you can opt to see independent or instructional level scores, and you can isolate a time period by selecting start and end dates. The key indicates which scores represent *Fountas & Pinnell Benchmark Assessment* scores and which represent other reading records. By rolling your mouse over each point on the graph, you will see the detail for that particular assessment including: date administered; book title; genre; and accuracy, comprehension, and fluency scores. The gray band on the graph indicates the text level goals that were set at the beginning of the year. This gives you a snapshot of how a student is performing relative to those goals. The same data described above is shown here in table form in Figure 7.9.

The Student Comprehension graph in Figure 7.10 shows the progress of one student over the course of a school year. Again, tabs along the bottom of the graph enable you to compare data across school years. Data can be displayed for independent and instructional levels as well as for total comprehension within, beyond, and about the text scores. Again, rolling your mouse over the bars on the graph reveals the details of the individual assessments. The same data described above is shown in table form in Figure 7.11.

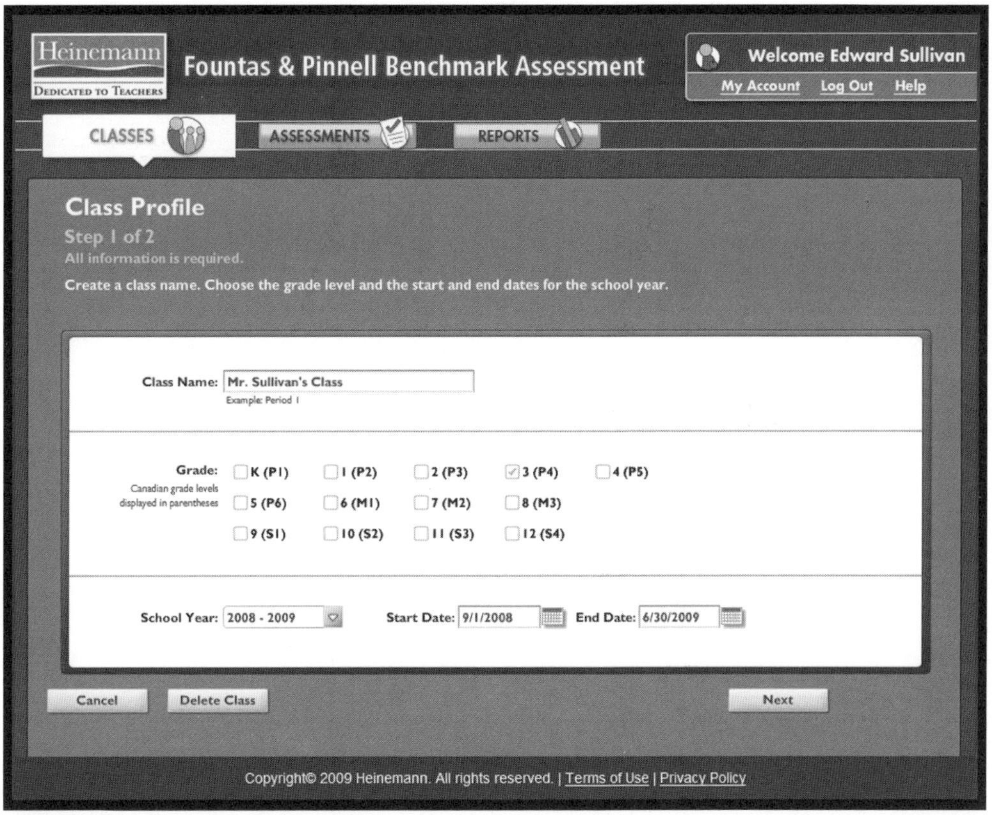

FIGURE 7.4a Class Profile screen 1 of 2

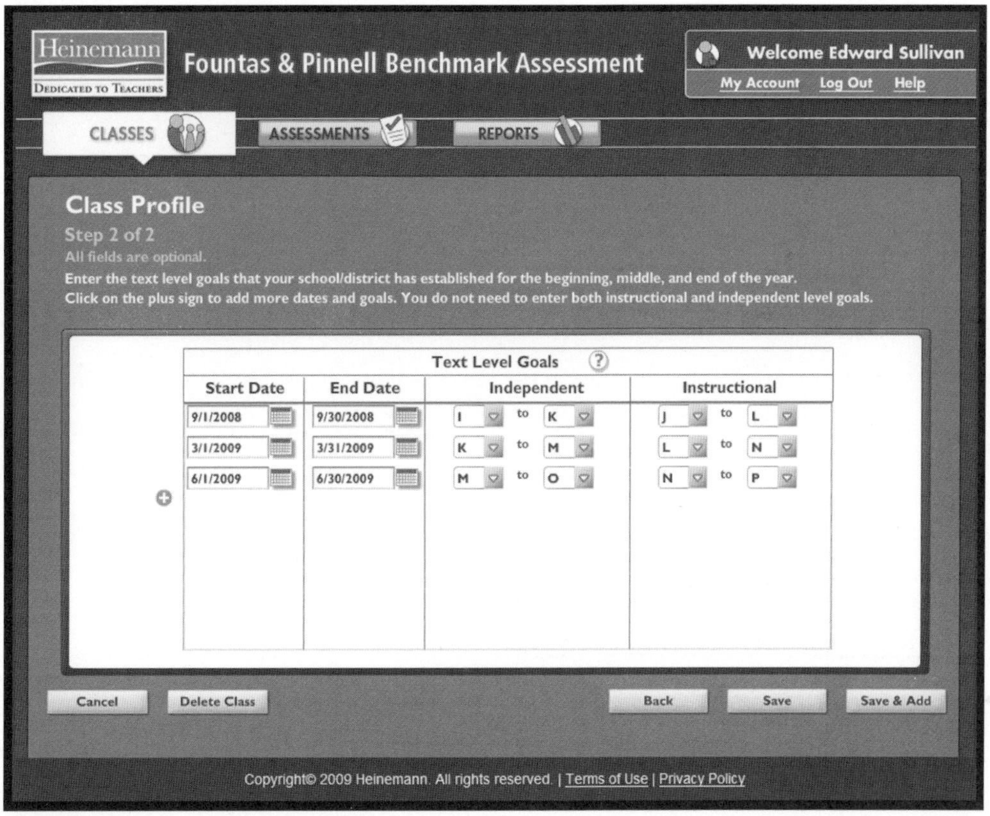

FIGURE 7.4b Class Profile screen 2 of 2

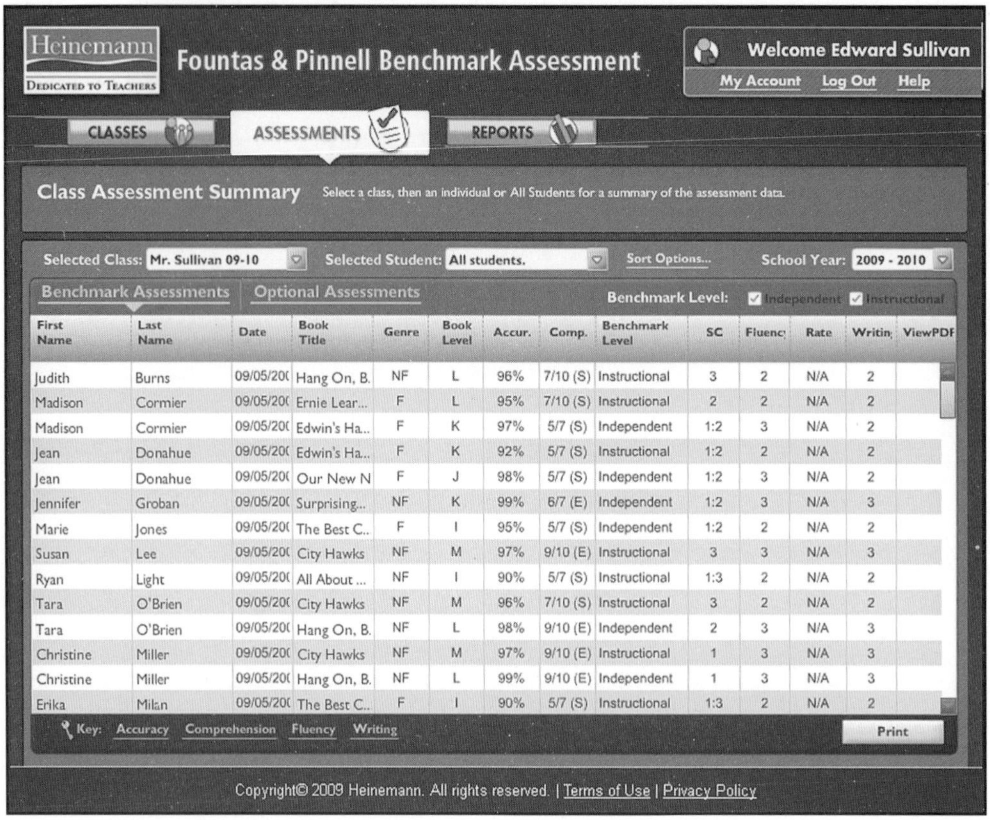
Heinemann
Dedicated to Teachers
Fountas & Pinnell Benchmark Assessment
Welcome Edward Sullivan
My Account Log Out Help
CLASSES
ASSESSMENTS
REPORTS
Class Assessment Summary
Select a class, then an individual or All Students for a summary of the assessment data.
Selected Class: Mr. Sullivan 09-10
Selected Student: All students.
Sort Options...
School Year: 2009 - 2010
Benchmark Assessments
Optional Assessments
Benchmark Level: Independent Instructional
First Name | Last Name | Date | Book Title | Genre | Book Level | Accur. | Comp. | Benchmark Level | SC | Fluency | Rate | Writing | ViewPDF
Judith | Burns | 09/05/200 | Hang On, B. | NF | L | 96% | 7/10 (S) | Instructional | 3 | 2 | N/A | 2
Madison | Cormier | 09/05/200 | Ernie Lear... | F | L | 95% | 7/10 (S) | Instructional | 2 | 2 | N/A | 2
Madison | Cormier | 09/05/200 | Edwin's Ha... | F | K | 97% | 5/7 (S) | Independent | 1:2 | 3 | N/A | 2
Jean | Donahue | 09/05/200 | Edwin's Ha... | F | K | 92% | 5/7 (S) | Instructional | 1:2 | 2 | N/A | 2
Jean | Donahue | 09/05/200 | Our New N | F | J | 98% | 5/7 (S) | Independent | 1:2 | 3 | N/A | 2
Jennifer | Groban | 09/05/200 | Surprising... | NF | K | 99% | 6/7 (E) | Independent | 1:2 | 3 | N/A | 3
Marie | Jones | 09/05/200 | The Best C.. | F | I | 95% | 5/7 (S) | Independent | 1:2 | 2 | N/A | 2
Susan | Lee | 09/05/200 | City Hawks | NF | M | 97% | 9/10 (E) | Instructional | 3 | 3 | N/A | 3
Ryan | Light | 09/05/200 | All About ... | NF | I | 90% | 5/7 (S) | Instructional | 1:3 | 2 | N/A | 2
Tara | O'Brien | 09/05/200 | City Hawks | NF | M | 96% | 7/10 (S) | Instructional | 3 | 2 | N/A | 2
Tara | O'Brien | 09/05/200 | Hang On, B. | NF | L | 98% | 9/10 (E) | Independent | 2 | 3 | N/A | 3
Christine | Miller | 09/05/200 | City Hawks | NF | M | 97% | 9/10 (E) | Instructional | 1 | 3 | N/A | 3
Christine | Miller | 09/05/200 | Hang On, B. | NF | L | 99% | 9/10 (E) | Independent | 1 | 3 | N/A | 3
Erika | Milan | 09/05/200 | The Best C.. | F | I | 90% | 5/7 (S) | Instructional | 1:3 | 2 | N/A | 2
Key: Accuracy Comprehension Fluency Writing
Print
Copyright© 2009 Heinemann. All rights reserved. | Terms of Use | Privacy Policy

FIGURE 7.5 Class Assessment Summary screen

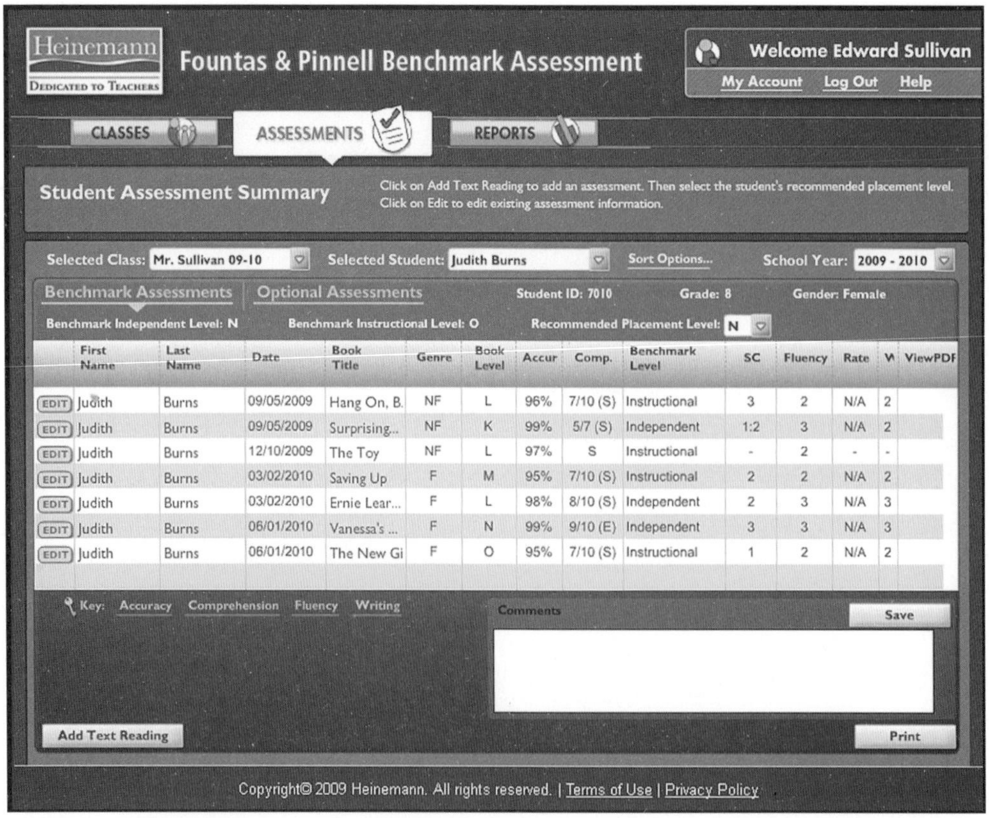
Heinemann
Dedicated to Teachers
Fountas & Pinnell Benchmark Assessment
Welcome Edward Sullivan
My Account Log Out Help
CLASSES
ASSESSMENTS
REPORTS
Student Assessment Summary
Click on Add Text Reading to add an assessment. Then select the student's recommended placement level.
Click on Edit to edit existing assessment information.
Selected Class: Mr. Sullivan 09-10
Selected Student: Judith Burns
Sort Options...
School Year: 2009 - 2010
Benchmark Assessments
Optional Assessments
Student ID: 7010
Grade: 8
Gender: Female
Benchmark Independent Level: N
Benchmark Instructional Level: O
Recommended Placement Level: N
First Name | Last Name | Date | Book Title | Genre | Book Level | Accur | Comp. | Benchmark Level | SC | Fluency | Rate | W | ViewPDF
EDIT Judith | Burns | 09/05/2009 | Hang On, B. | NF | L | 96% | 7/10 (S) | Instructional | 3 | 2 | N/A | 2
EDIT Judith | Burns | 09/05/2009 | Surprising... | NF | K | 99% | 5/7 (S) | Independent | 1:2 | 3 | N/A | 2
EDIT Judith | Burns | 12/10/2009 | The Toy | NF | L | 97% | S | Instructional | - | 2 | - | -
EDIT Judith | Burns | 03/02/2010 | Saving Up | F | M | 95% | 7/10 (S) | Instructional | 2 | 2 | N/A | 2
EDIT Judith | Burns | 03/02/2010 | Ernie Lear... | F | L | 98% | 8/10 (S) | Independent | 2 | 3 | N/A | 3
EDIT Judith | Burns | 06/01/2010 | Vanessa's ... | F | N | 99% | 9/10 (E) | Independent | 3 | 3 | N/A | 3
EDIT Judith | Burns | 06/01/2010 | The New Gi | F | O | 95% | 7/10 (S) | Instructional | 1 | 2 | N/A | 2
Key: Accuracy Comprehension Fluency Writing
Comments
Save
Add Text Reading
Print
Copyright© 2009 Heinemann. All rights reserved. | Terms of Use | Privacy Policy

FIGURE 7.6 Student Assessment Summary screen

Assessment Data Profile

Step 1 of 3

All information is required

Choose the type of assessment you are conducting, the date administered, the genre and text level of the book used for the assessment.

Assessment Type:	◉ F & P Benchmark
	○ Other Reading Record

Note: Assessment Type cannot be altered once the Assessment Data Profile has been saved.

Date Administered: [-] 📅

Genre: ○ Fiction
◉ Nonfiction

Text Level: [- ▽]

Cancel | Delete Text Reading

FIGURE 7.7a Assessment Data Profile, step 1 of 3

Assessment Data Profile: 05/05/2009

Step 2 of 3

All information is required

Accuracy: [0]

Accuracy	Benchmark level
95 - 100%	Independent
90 - 94%	Instructional
Below 90%	Hard

(?) Comprehension:

Within the Text
○0 ○1 ○2 ○3

Beyond the Text
○0 ○1 ○2 ○3

☐ Additional Understanding

Total: -

Comprehension Scoring Guide	
6 - 7	Excellent Comprehension
5	Satisfactory Comprehension
4	Limited Comprehension
0 - 3	Unsatisfactory Comprehension

Benchmark Level: -

Cancel | Delete Text Reading | Back | Next

FIGURE 7.7b Assessment Data Profile, step 2 of 3

Assessment Data Profile: 05/05/2009

Step 3 of 3

Fields marked with an asterisk(*) are required.

(?) Self-Corrections:* [-]

(?) Fluency: * ○0 ○1 ○2 ○3

Rate: [-] WPM (Recommended for Level J and above)

(?) Writing: ○0 ○1 ○2 ○3

Cancel | Delete Text Reading | Back | Save | Save & Add

FIGURE 7.7c Assessment Data Profile, step 3 of 3

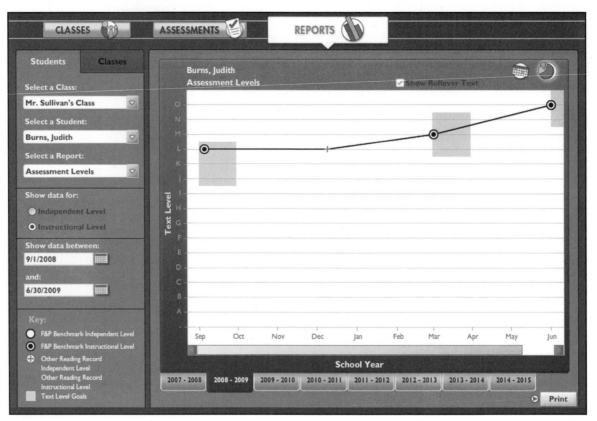

FIGURE 7.8 Student Assessment Levels Graph

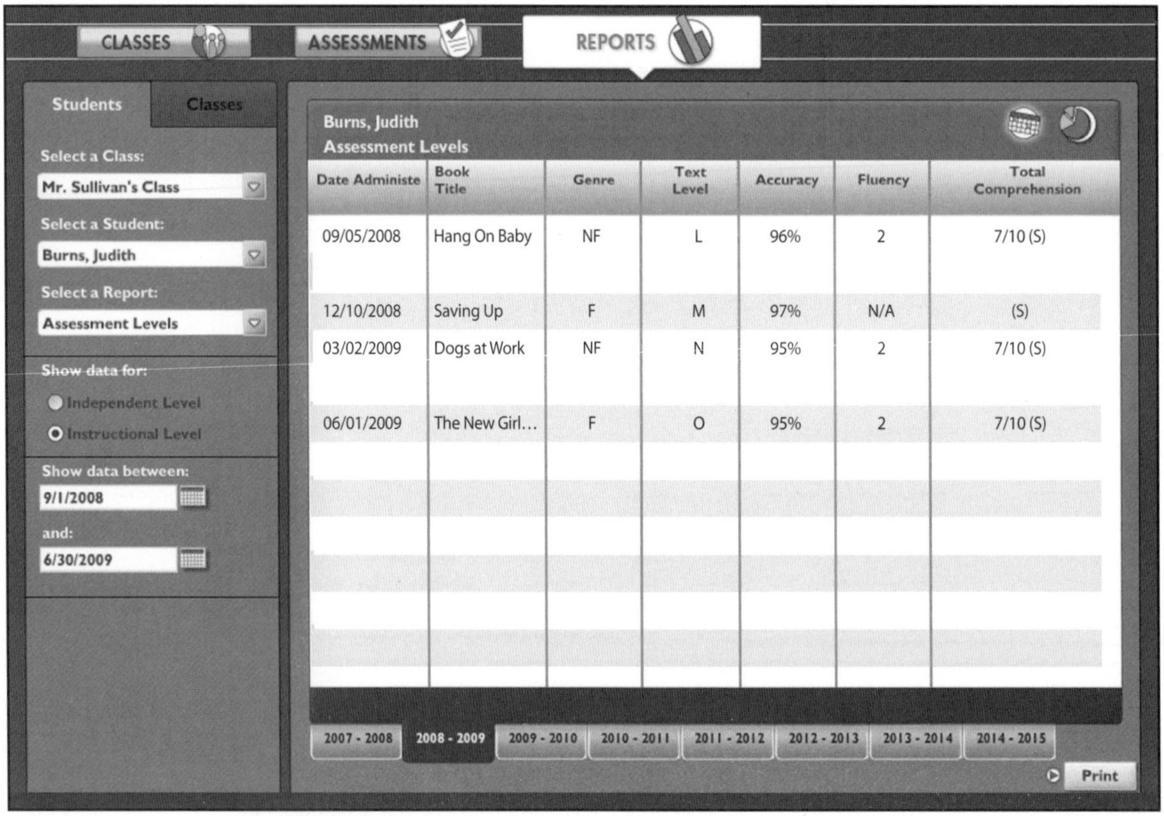

Date Administe	Book Title	Genre	Text Level	Accuracy	Fluency	Total Comprehension
09/05/2008	Hang On Baby	NF	L	96%	2	7/10 (S)
12/10/2008	Saving Up	F	M	97%	N/A	(S)
03/02/2009	Dogs at Work	NF	N	95%	2	7/10 (S)
06/01/2009	The New Girl...	F	O	95%	2	7/10 (S)

FIGURE 7.9 Student Assessment Levels table

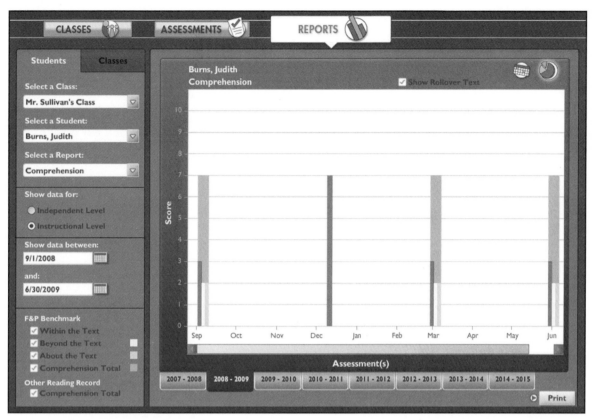

FIGURE 7.10 Student Comprehension graph

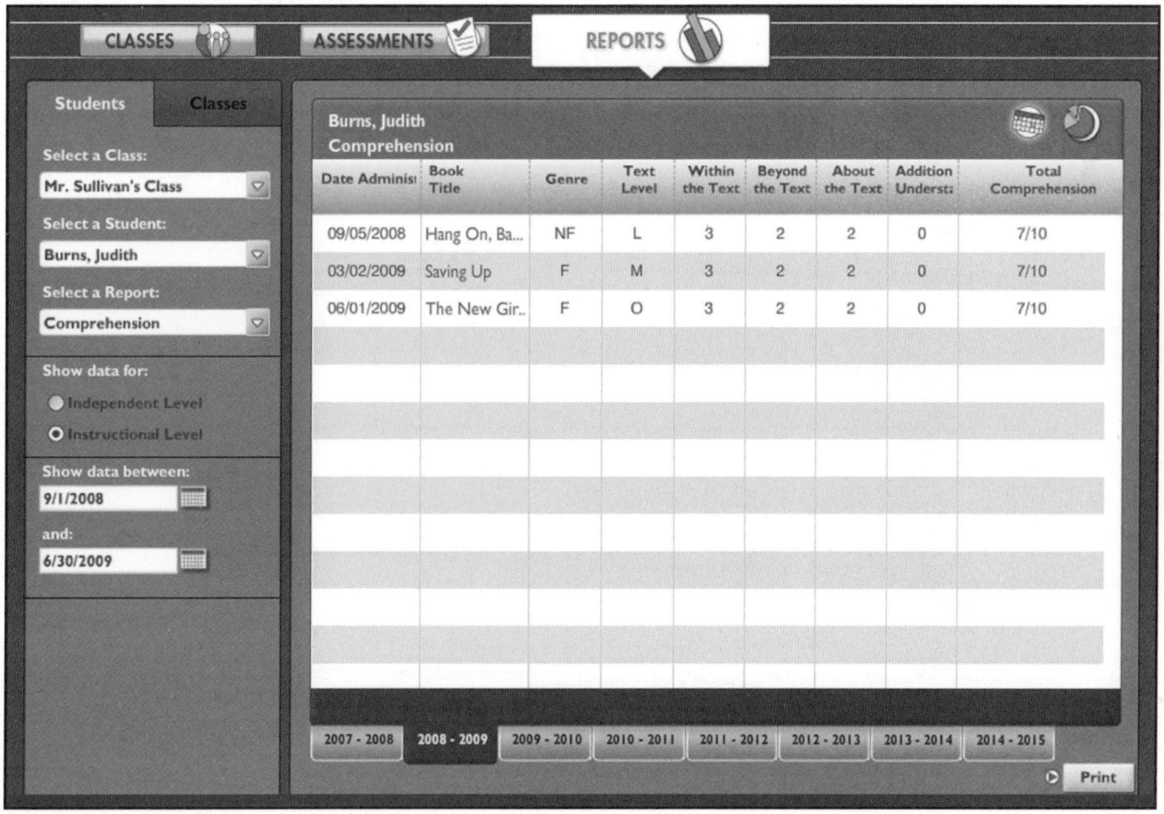

Date Administ	Book Title	Genre	Text Level	Within the Text	Beyond the Text	About the Text	Addition Underst:	Total Comprehension
09/05/2008	Hang On, Ba...	NF	L	3	2	2	0	7/10
03/02/2009	Saving Up	F	M	3	2	2	0	7/10
06/01/2009	The New Gir...	F	O	3	2	2	0	7/10

FIGURE 7.11 Student Comprehension table

Class Reports The Class Assessment Levels graph (Figure 7.12) shows the progress of one class over the course of a school year. As with the student graph, on the left side, you can choose to see either independent or instructional levels. You can also select a time period for viewing data by selecting start and end dates. The data for the class graph appear as a series of "+" icons. By clicking "Show Rollover Text" box, you can roll over the icons with your mouse to view the details of each student represented on the graph. The gray band indicates the text level goals that were set at the beginning of the year. This gives you a snapshot of how your class is performing relative to those goals. To switch to a tabular view of the data, click on the table icon in the upper right corner of the graph. The same data described above is shown here in table form in Figure 7.13.

The Class Assessment Levels log (Figure 7.14) gives you a quick synopsis of students' independent or instructional levels by week. Again, start and end dates can be adjusted for viewing data from a specific time period.

The Class Comprehension graph (Figure 7.15) shows the progress of an entire class for up to four assessment periods. On the left side of the graph, you can choose to view total comprehension scores or you can view separate scores for within, beyond, and about the text. The rollover feature allows you to see summary detail for each bar on the graph. The same data described above is shown here in table form (Figure 7.16).

The Class Profile graph (Figure 7.17) shows the assessment level progress of an entire class for up to four Assessment periods. Data can be displayed for independent and instructional levels. The rollover feature allows you to see the number of students that scored at each level. The gray band indicates your text level goals; thus with this graph you get a snapshot of the number of students performing on, below, or above level. The same data described above is shown in table form in Figure 7.18.

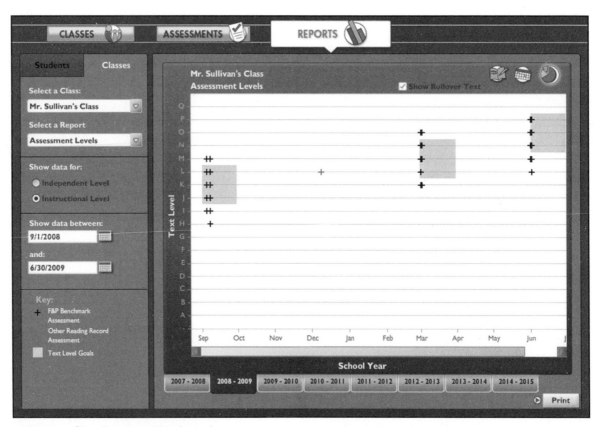

FIGURE 7.12 Class Assessment Levels graph

Date Administered	Student Name	Book Title	Genre	Text Level
09/05/2008	Miller, Christine	City Hawks	NF	M
09/05/2008	Cormier, Madison	Ernie Learns	F	L
09/05/2008	Donahue, Jean	Edwin's Haircut	F	K
09/05/2008	Groban, Jennifer	Hang On, Baby Monkey	NF	L
09/05/2008	Jones, Marie	Our New Neighbors	F	J
09/05/2008	Lee, Susan	City Hawks	NF	M
09/05/2008	Light, Ryan	All About Koalas	NF	I
09/05/2008	Milan, Erika	The Best Cat	F	I
09/05/2008	O'Brien, Tara	City Hawks	NF	M
09/05/2008	Burns, Judith	Hang On, Baby Monkey	NF	L
09/08/2008	Oliveria, Gary	Edwin's Haircut	F	K
09/08/2008	Palmer, Matthew	Saving Up	F	M
09/08/2008	Smith, John	Surprising Animal Sen...	NF	K

FIGURE 7.13   Class Assessment Levels table

Name	09/05/2008	09/08/2008	12/10/2008	03/02/2009	03/03/2009	06/01/2009	06/02/2009
Miller, Christine	M			O		P	
Cormier, Madison	L			N		P	
Donahue, Jean	K			N		O	
Groban, Jennifer	L			N		P	
Jones, Marie	J			L		N	
Lee, Susan	M			O		P	
Light, Ryan	I			K		N	
Milan, Erika	I			K		M	
O'Brien, Tara	M			O		P	
Burns, Judith	L			M		O	
Oliveria, Gary		K			M		O
Palmer, Matthew		M			N		P

FIGURE 7.14   Class Assessment Levels log

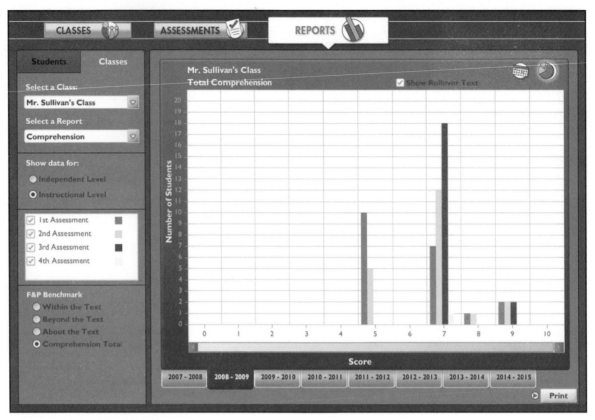

FIGURE 7.15 Class Comprehension graph

Mr. Sullivan's Class
Comprehension

Date Administered	Student Name	Book Title	Genre	Text Level	Within the Text	Beyond the Text	About the Text	Additional Understan	Total Comprehen:
09/05/2008	Miller, Chris	City Hawks	NF	M	3	3	3	0	9/10
09/05/2008	Cormier, M	Ernie Lear...	F	L	3	2	2	0	7/10
09/05/2008	Donahue, .	Edwin's Ha...	F	K	3	2	N/A	0	5/7
09/05/2008	Groban, Je	Hang On, B..	NF	L	3	3	2	0	8/10
09/05/2008	Jones, Mar	Our New N	F	J	3	2	N/A	0	5/7
09/05/2008	Lee, Susan	City Hawks	NF	M	3	3	3	0	9/10
09/05/2008	Light, Ryan	All About ...	NF	I	3	2	N/A	0	5/7
09/05/2008	Milan, Erika	The Best C..	F	I	3	2	N/A	0	5/7
09/05/2008	O'Brien, Ta	City Hawks	NF	M	3	2	2	0	7/10
09/05/2008	Burns, Judi	Hang On, B..	NF	L	3	2	2	0	7/10
09/08/2008	Oliveria, Ga	Edwin's Ha...	F	K	3	2	N/A	0	5/7
09/08/2008	Palmer, Ma	Saving Up	F	M	3	2	2	0	7/10
09/08/2008	Smith, John	Surprising...	NF	K	3	2	N/A	0	5/7

2007 - 2008 | 2008 - 2009 | 2009 - 2010 | 2010 - 2011 | 2011 - 2012 | 2012 - 2013 | 2013 - 2014 | 2014 - 2015

Print

FIGURE 7.16 Class Comprehension table

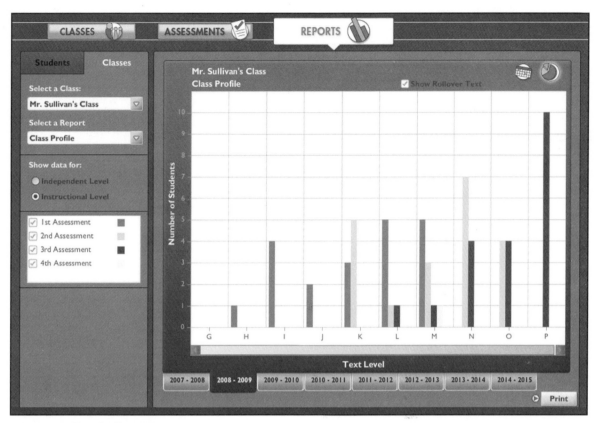

FIGURE 7.17 Class Profile graph

FIGURE 7.18 Class Profile table

► Benchmark Assessment Professional Development DVD

The *Professional Development DVD* in your *Technology Package* was developed to provide you with step-by-step guidance as you are learning to administer the *Fountas & Pinnell Benchmark Assessment System 2*. Teachers learning to use the system will have varying levels of experience and needs. Although the segments have been ordered so they can be viewed sequentially, you will be able to choose from the menu options to meet your specific needs.

It is important to have the complete system available while you view the DVD. It can be played in a standard DVD player or on a computer. Some segments call for blank forms, which are found in the *Assessment Forms Book* and *CD-ROM*.

After inserting the disc, the software will automatically launch. When you see the main menu (Figure 7.19), navigate to the segment you wish to view, using the mouse on your computer or the controls on your DVD player. To choose from the main menu, click on one of the following segments:

- ❏ Overview
- ❏ Assessment Procedures
- ❏ Tutorials
- ❏ Instructional Implications
- ❏ Sample Assessment Conference

When you choose the "Overview" option (Figure 7.20) from the main menu, you will have three segment options to view.

System Components In this segment you will become familiar with the components that come with the *Fountas & Pinnell Benchmark Assessment System 2* and how they are used. The authors introduce the fiction and nonfiction texts, explaining the gradient of text difficulty. They introduce the *Assessment Forms Book* and *CD-ROM*, the *Online Data Management System*, the *Professional Development DVD*, the *F & P Calculator/Stopwatch*, the Optional Assessments, student folders, and the *Assessment Guide*.

Benchmark Assessment at a Glance In this segment you will watch one teacher administering the assessment to a student while the authors explain the assessment procedures: how to determine a starting level, materials to gather, how to use the *F & P Calculator/Stopwatch*, and step-by-step directions for administering the assessment. Viewing this segment will be a helpful overview not only for teachers who are learning to administer the assessment for the first time but for all teachers just before they begin their assessments each fall.

How to Use this DVD In this segment the authors explain the contents of each section of the *Professional Development DVD*.

When you have viewed any or all of the segments from the "Overview," click on "Main Menu" at the bottom of the screen.

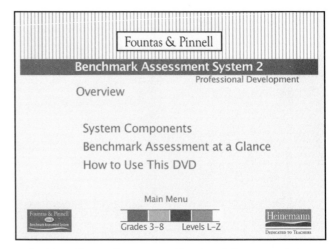

FIGURE 7.19 Main Menu Overview

FIGURE 7.20 System Components, Benchmark Assessment at a Glance, How to Use this DVD

Assessment Procedures

The next option on the main menu screen is "Assessment Procedures" (Figure 7.21) which includes the following four segment options:

Preparation This segment explains how to organize and manage your time efficiently for assessing students at the beginning of the school year and how to prepare your work space for optimal results.

Administering the Benchmark Assessment In this segment, we provide a general overview of one complete assessment. The overview explains the importance of giving a standardized introduction, and how to use the Recording Form. You will also receive a brief description of the three assessment components: recording oral reading behavior, fluency, and comprehension. More detailed tutorials of these three assessment components are available in the "Tutorials" option in the main menu.

Scoring, Analyzing, and Interpreting Reading Records This segment explains in a clear and concise manner how to calculate reading rate using the *F & P Calculator/Stopwatch*. You will learn how to determine a score for fluency and comprehension within, beyond, and about the text, using the holistic scoring rubric and how to determine the benchmark independent and instructional level. The factors and rationales for determining the student's placement level are also explained.

Optional Assessments There are many optional assessments available in the *Fountas & Pinnell*

Benchmark Assessment System. These optional assessments will provide you with more information about your students, especially those students you find most challenging in particular areas. For example, the vocabulary assessments may give you helpful information about your ELL students. This segment on the DVD explains some of the optional assessments and the additional information they provide.

When you have finished viewing the segments in "Assessment Procedures," click on "Main Menu" at the bottom of your screen. The next option from the main menu is "Tutorials" (Figure 7.22).

Tutorials

This option offers you the following six segments:

Introduction This is simply a written narrative of the segments to follow.

Coding Oral Reading This option on the "Tutorials" menu gives you ten segments from which to choose. Each gives you a clear explanation, accompanied by examples, of the conventions for coding oral reading behavior. These conventions are: Accurate Reading, Substitutions, Repetitions, Self-Corrections, Omissions, Insertions, Appeals, and Tolds. You will be able to practice each of these conventions separately and then consolidate your learning by taking a reading record using several conventions in one reading. This is a very helpful tutorial for teachers who are unfamiliar with recording students' oral reading behavior. If you

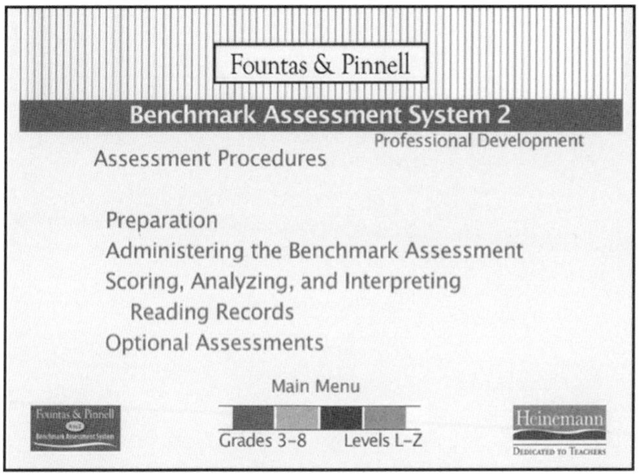

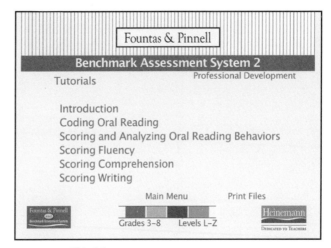

FIGURE 7.21 Assessment Procedures

FIGURE 7.22 Tutorials

are already familiar with taking reading records you may want to choose only the consolidation segments for a quick review. It may be helpful to review these conventions as a school staff before you begin to assess students in the fall as it is important that all teachers in a school use the conventions in a standardized way.

When you have completed the "Coding Oral Reading" tutorial, click on "Previous" at the bottom of the screen. This will bring you back to the "Tutorials" menu.

Scoring and Analyzing Oral Reading Behaviors
This portion on the tutorial is divided into four parts: Scoring, Analysis, and Practice (with commentary) (Figure 7.23).

"Scoring" gives very clear descriptions of what is considered an error and a self-correction, and what is not. Many examples are given to clarify the process. You may find it helpful for all the teachers in your school to view this part of the tutorial together so that you can ensure consistency in scoring.

You will learn how to use the Recording Form to tally errors and calculate an accuracy rate using the calculator. You will also learn how to calculate self-correction and what self-correcting behavior indicates about how students are processing.

The "Analysis" segment provides you with a detailed explanation of how to analyze reading records to determine what kinds of information students are attending to and what information they are neglecting. You will learn to use shorthand: *M* for meaning, *S* for

structure, and *V* for visual information. This tutorial takes you step-by-step through one complete reading record, describing how to think about each error and self-correction. When analysis of both errors and self-corrections are complete, you will tally up the sources of information used and neglected and look for patterns of responding that will help you determine the next steps in instructing the reader. The *Fountas & Pinnell Benchmark Assessment System* can be a valuable formative assessment to measure progress over time, but the information that you gather from analyzing the reading behaviors of your students will be invaluable to you as you plan instruction.

In the "Practice" segment, you will have the opportunity to listen to a student read one book while you practice coding, scoring, and analyzing the reading record on your own. After the reading, you can check your work against the completed reading record on the screen.

In the "commentary" segment we provide a verbal summary of the students' observable behaviors.

When you have viewed the segments in this section, click on "Previous" at the bottom of the screen and it will return you to the "Tutorials" menu.

Scoring Fluency This option on the tutorial provides you with eight segments from which to choose (Figure 7.24). Each one will help you learn how to evaluate the fluency of oral reading. Evaluating fluency will help you determine how consistently the readers are interpreting the meaning of the text.

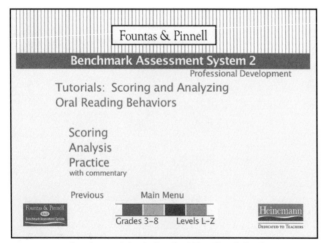

FIGURE 7.23 Scoring and Analyzing Oral Reading Behaviors

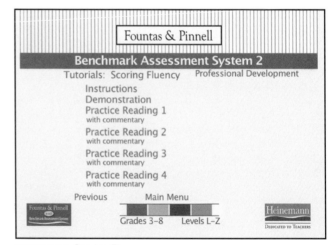

FIGURE 7.24 Scoring Fluency

In the "Instructions" segment you will learn how to use the 0–3 point rubric for scoring fluency. Emphasis is placed on the implications for teaching about fluency.

The "Demonstration" segment will show you examples of students reading and will provide specific explanations of how to use the rubric.

Next, there are three "Practice Readings" followed by "commentary" options. You may want to try your hand at evaluating the fluency of each student. When you have finished, listen to the commentary to check your thinking against the authors'.

When you have finished with these segments of the tutorial, click on "Previous" at the bottom of the screen to return to the "Tutorials" menu and then go to the "Scoring Comprehension" menu.

Scoring Comprehension

This option on the tutorial also has eight segments from which to choose (Figure 7.25). Each will help you learn how to score the comprehension conversation.

The "Instructions" segment explains how to score comprehension with the rubric you use to evaluate the student's thinking within, beyond, and about the text. It explains how the score may also reflect any additional understandings he exhibits that are not listed in the key understandings on the Recording Form.

In the "Demonstrations" segment, you will have the opportunity to listen to two demonstration comprehension conversations and an analysis of the conversations with rationales for the score.

Next there are three "Practice Readings" in which you can try your hand at evaluating the comprehension conversation with each child and then click on "with commentary" to compare your thinking with ours.

When you have finished viewing the comprehension scoring segments of the tutorial, click on "Previous" at the bottom of the menu screen to access "Scoring Writing."

Scoring Writing

This segment explains how to use the rubric to score the optional writing about reading part of the assessment. Three writing samples are shown and evaluated, using the rubric. This will help you use the rubric to score this optional assessment.

You have now finished viewing the "Tutorials" options on the DVD. Click on "Main Menu" at the bottom of the screen.

Instructional Implications

The next option on the main menu is "Instructional Implications." There are two segments available for your viewing:

Using Assessment to Inform Instruction After you have completed the assessments, you will have a rich body of information that you can use to inform your instruction (Figure 7.26). This segment explains some of the ways you can use the assessment information. You will also be introduced to *The Continuum of Literacy Learning, 3–8* (Heinemann, 2011, 2008), a

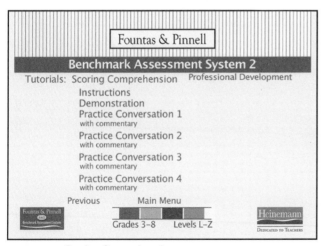

FIGURE 7.25 Scoring Comprehension

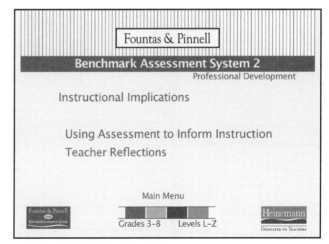

FIGURE 7.26 Instructional Implications

valuable resource that will help you plan for the literacy needs of your students.

Teacher Reflections In this segment you will hear two teachers reflect upon what they learned about their students from the assessments and how they will use that information to inform their teaching.

When you have viewed the segments in "Teaching Implications," return to the "Main Menu."

Sample Assessment

Choose the last menu option, "Sample Assessment Conference" (Figure 7.27) on the DVD to practice an entire assessment with one child. There are three segments included:

Instructions This segment tells you what you need to prepare for practicing complete assessment conferences.

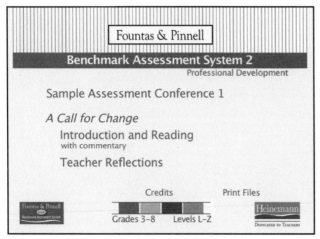

FIGURE 7.27 Sample Assessment Conference

Text Reading You will listen to each student read and discuss an independent text, an instructional text, and a hard text. Before you begin, you are instructed to print out the Recording Forms for all three texts. Next you will have the opportunity to code, score, and analyze the reading records, evaluate fluency and observe the comprehension conversations. If you wish to hear an analysis of this student's processing and understanding, choose the "commentary" segment.

Teacher Reflections Lastly, you may want to listen to the teachers' thoughtful analysis and their next steps for teaching this student.

Viewing the segments of the *Fountas & Pinnell Benchmark Assessment System DVD* will be helpful to you before you attempt your first assessment. After you have completed a few assessments, you may have some questions and will want to revisit some of the segments to review and get clarification on the procedures. Using the DVD tutorial ensures that the assessment will be administered in a standardized way.

Once you have analyzed the information you received from the assessments, you will want to refer to *The Continuum of Literacy Learning, 3–8,* (Pinnell and Fountas, Heinemann, 2011, 2008) to help you select literacy goals and books that will best meet the needs of all students across many instructional contexts. You may also find *Guided Reading* (Fountas and Pinnell, Heinemann, 1996) to be a helpful resource as you plan rich and comprehensive literacy experiences for all your students.

section 8

Frequently Asked Questions

In this section, you will find the answers to some frequently asked questions. The questions are organized into a number of categories. If you have any questions about how to use the *Benchmark Assessment System*, you may find the answer to your question in this section or you may send a question to *www.fountasandpinnell@heinemann.com*.

General

How does the* Fountas & Pinnell Benchmark Assessment System *contribute to my knowledge of students and how they develop as readers?

You will find that the comprehensive assessment procedures and the variety of tools and options provided in the *Benchmark Assessment System* are rich resources for helping you systematically examine a student's strengths and needs and begin to think about the important link between assessment and instruction. You will find detailed information about analyzing the reading behaviors of a student on an instructional-level text and linking them to specific instructional goals in the *Assessment Guide*. The Guide for Observing and Noting Reading Behaviors (found in Figure 00 of this guide (and in the *Assessment Forms Book* and *CD-ROM*) is a learning tool in itself; it focuses attention on critical reading behaviors.

The Continuum of Literacy Learning 3-8 (Pinnell and Fountas, Heinemann, 2008, 2011) is the foundation for instruction. You can make a direct link from the data gathered with the assessment to the continuum's specific behaviors to notice, teach, and support in every instructional context related to literacy.

The *Professional Development DVD* is another rich resource. It is designed to help you conduct efficient and effective assessments, learn how to interpret the results, and connect your understandings to instruction. Over time, observations made through the assessment, instruction designed to move students ahead from level to level, and follow-up assessment will deepen your understanding of literacy development.

How can the Benchmark Assessment System help upper-grade teachers learn about the reading process?

If you are an upper-grade teacher, you will find that Benchmark Assessment is the perfect starting point for learning to observe and code the reading behaviors of your students. The procedures supported by the assessment forms and the analysis training in the *Assessment Guide* and on the *Professional Development DVD* will help you observe and talk about your students' effective and ineffective behaviors and how the texts they are reading may be appropriate or inappropriate for supporting new learning.

After a few months' experience with Benchmark Assessment conferences, you will become much more knowledgeable and interested in what your students are learning about the reading process and become increasingly effective at differentiating instruction.

Is the* Fountas & Pinnell Benchmark Assessment System *a standardized test?

Yes. The administration, coding, scoring, and interpretation are standardized in procedures to get reliable results. We expect that once you get the standardized results, you will review the data to make good judgments for instruction. Good teacher decisions based on data are essential.

Is the* Fountas & Pinnell Benchmark Assessment System *an authentic assessment?

You cannot get closer to authentic assessment than with this assessment. A student reads several books, thinks and talks about them, and writes about reading. This is not only a valid assessment of the competencies you want to measure, but is a productive use of teacher and student time.

Some teachers feel that the assessment is an accountability measure for them. Do you agree?

We do not recommend that the assessment scores be used as a measure of teacher effectiveness without other contextual factors being considered. As teachers, we need to seek information about our students as well as how our teaching is impacting their learning. At the beginning of the year, the assessment gives information about the starting points of the learners. As the school year progresses, the assessment becomes a tool for measuring the growth of the students and the effectiveness of your teaching. The series of assessments conducted over several years will reflect the success of the entire school in bringing each student forward in literacy outcomes.

Can Benchmark Assessment be used with emotionally disturbed children?

We feel this system would be highly supportive for this population as it is administered individually. The books are especially engaging and the comprehension conversation is warm and supportive. The only concern might be the age-appropriateness of the books in System

1 (levels A-N) which were written with K-2 children in mind. The books in System 2 (levels L-Z) are more sophisticated in content, but are more challenging. Another component of the system that would be helpful are the 40+ optional assessments which enable teachers to make a thorough diagnosis of a student's strengths in the areas of phonics, word structure, and vocabulary.

We would like to set level goals for our students at each grade. What would you suggest?

It is not possible for us to predict where your students should be, as it depends on many factors. However, to guide you we can suggest the following: 1.) refer to Figure 1.1, the Text Gradient in this guide, 2.) refer to Figure 5.1, the Quarterly Instructional Level Expectations for Reading chart in this guide, and 3.) take a close look at *The Continuum of Literacy Learning 3–8* included in your system boxes, for specific behaviors to notice, teach, and support at Levels L–Z.

Is there a place to pose questions and get a response?

Yes, we invite you to send your comments or questions to *www.fountasandpinnell@heinemann.com* and we will respond as quickly as possible.

Understanding Levels

What does the term level mean and how are levels determined?

A level refers to the difficulty of the book in relation to other books placed along a continuum from A to Z, easiest to hardest. We examine the characteristics of a book and place it along a gradient of books in relation to each other. A level designates the books as easier than the level after (later in the alphabet) and harder than the level before it (earlier in the alphabet). We use ten characteristics to determine a level and the composite of characteristics contributes to its final designation. For a detailed explanation of each level, see *Leveled Books, K–8* (Fountas and Pinnell, Heinemann, 2006).

Do the Fountas and Pinnell Benchmark levels match the guided reading levels?

Yes. This assessment is specifically designed to match the guided reading levels described in *Leveled Books, K–8* (Fountas and Pinnell, Heinemann, 2006) and other publications by Fountas and Pinnell.

How can I use this system to match books leveled with other systems?

Fountas and Pinnell have leveled over 33,000 books which appear in both *Leveled Book List K-8* (Fountas and Pinnell, Heinemann, 2009) and on the *fountasandpinnell.com* website under the link for "F&P Leveled Books," which is updated every month. Also, many publishers place several different kinds of levels on books and/or offer correlation charts.

Administering the Assessment

How often should Benchmark Assessment be administered?

We suggest that you administer the assessment at the beginning of the year to know where to start your teaching with each student. You may also want to conduct the assessment in the middle of the year to take stock of progress, though you may already have the information from your ongoing use of reading records in instruction. Finally, at the end of the year you may want to conduct one more assessment to obtain a final record of the student's growth across the year. You may decide to administer the last assessment for the year a couple of months before the end of the year. This could provide information for instruction and could be less redundant with the first assessment in the following school year.

How long does it take to administer the assessment to a child?

At the lower levels it may take 20 minutes while it may take about 30–40 minutes when your students are reading longer texts and the conversations are more substantive. Remember that the longer books have a stopping point for oral reading. Also, fluency makes a difference. In this guide we make several suggestions on how to be efficient with your use of time.

How do you know at which level to start Benchmark Assessment so as to make the administration as time efficient as possible?

We provide several time-saving options. If you have no information on a student's previous reading, the Where-to-Start Word Test provides a rough starting level for assessment and will cut down the number of books he needs to read before you can identify an independent and an instructional level. If you do have information about a student's previous reading performance, we provide some charts in Section 2 of this guide that help determine the starting point by looking at the texts they are reading.

How can I ensure that I am conducting the assessment in a standardized manner?

The precise steps of the assessment conference are described in this book and are systematically presented on the Recording Forms for each book. The introduction is standardized and printed on the cover of the book as well as on the Recording Form. The steps of the administration, the scoring, and the analysis are all standardized. In addition, the tools supporting the assessment—the *F&P Calculator/Stopwatch* and the At-a-Glance charts provide an easy way to maintain consistency and help you internalize the steps. Further, the *Professional Development DVD* provides clear examples and plentiful practice for developing precision and consistency throughout assessment conferences.

When I am assessing a student, can I skip levels?

Yes. Your goal is to have the student read the fewest number of books that will give you the data you need as efficiently as possible. If you find a book is very easy, you may want to skip a level or more to get to one that is closer to her instructional level. The same applies when a text is very hard and you need to find an instructional level; in this case you may want to skip down one or more levels.

Should I assess both fiction and nonfiction reading?

The fiction and nonfiction book at each level are equivalent measures. You can use either text to determine a student's ability to read at that level. We recommend alternating fiction and nonfiction books as you move up the levels.

What about students who listen in on conversations during an assessment with another child? Can that affect their score?

Ideally, the administration between the teacher and student should take place at the back of the room so there is no distraction. It is unlikely that, even if a student overhears part of a conversation, it would

greatly affect her performance, but if you are concerned, you might want to consider using the alternate book at that level when assessing her.

Using the Benchmark Books

Are the benchmark books ones students may have read before?

In Benchmark Assessment, students read unseen text, or text they have not read before. You can expect the text to be a little harder than it would be if they have read it before.

Why is it important that the student not have read the books before?

On a cold reading, with only minimal introduction, you have the best opportunity to observe what a student can do independently. It is important to have this information in order to guide the reader in her independent choices and to determine what she needs to learn next.

Why is the book introduction so short? Why can't I tell the student more about the book?

Because you want to learn what the student can do independently. It is important not to tell him too much about the text in advance of reading. The introduction is scripted so that the assessment can be as standardized as possible. This standardization is necessary so that we can interpret the results for a class or a school.

Why are the System 2 books shorter than the System 1 books?

The books for System 1 while longer (16 pages), contain illustrations that give young readers picture support. The books from System 2 are shorter (4 pages), and contain limited illustrations except for nonfiction text features like diagrams and maps to support the older reader. Length is only one factor in text difficulty and it is not a significant one unless you are talking about a large difference (50 to100) in number of pages which would inevitably place a greater burden on memory. A short text can be very hard, with difficult vocabulary, complex sentences, and complex ideas. A long text can be easy, with familiar concepts and vocabulary and simple sentences. Another consideration was the amount of time required to administer the assessment. The length of the books in System 2 provides an adequate sample for assessing a more proficient reader's oral and silent reading, vocabulary, capacity to solve multi-syllabic words, and ability to interpret more sophisticated content.

Can I show a student the pictures during the introduction of the text?

We do not recommend showing the pictures during the introduction. The student may look at the front cover as you read the introduction. It is important to follow the standardized directions for the administration so your results will be consistent.

When I am assessing and the first book the student reads is too hard, what should I do?

You should judge how hard the book is and move down at least a couple of levels so you can find his independent and instructional levels.

Are there any plans to expand the number of benchmark books offered at each level?

There are no current plans to add books to the system. Two books at a level (one fiction, one nonfiction) are all that is needed. If you use a book for one assessment conference, the student will be at a different level by the next conference interval. If for some reason this is not true, you have an alternate book to use at that level. Further, if a book is too hard for a child you should discontinue the reading. You can use this book again if the student read very little of it months before.

If a student reads the same book (from fall to spring), does it change the effectiveness of the assessment?

Yes. A student should not be assessed on the same book more than once. If a student is familiar with a book it can skew the results. That is why two different books are provided at each level.

Assessment Procedures: Oral Reading
Is it permissible for a student to point while reading the text?

You should instruct students to point under the words only at levels A and B. After that, do not tell him to point or not to point. If a student is pointing beyond level C, you may want to make a note of it, as it is likely interfering with fluent, phrased reading.

If a student is reading a book that is too hard, is it necessary for her to finish it so I can determine an accuracy level?

No, you can stop the reading early. You might want to say something like, "This is a very tricky book. You can stop there." As a teacher, you have gathered the data you need and you can discontinue the testing. There is no need to have the student continue to read if the accuracy rate has gone well below 90% for Levels A–K or 95% for Levels L–Z.

What if I can't keep up with the coding and I miss some of a student's errors?

If you find you cannot keep up with the coding, ask the student to stop until you catch up. The more experienced you get in administering the assessment, the faster your coding will go.

If a student makes multiple errors on the same word, is that counted as an error each time he says it?

See Figure 2.8 of this guide for the Coding Errors and Self-Corrections chart as this is the standardized procedure. Each missed word in the book counts as one error each time it is misread. Therefore, if a student misreads the same word eight times, it counts as eight errors. This is very telling behavior as the student had eight opportunities to notice that it didn't look or sound right. The exception to this rule is proper nouns, which count as an error only one time, even if a student misreads it again and again.

The directions sometimes indicate the student should continue to read the text silently; wouldn't it be better if I listened to him read the whole book?

No, you can get an accurate picture of reading in the allotted segment. It is important to give the student the opportunity to process the text without the oral reinforcement. The oral reading also slows him down.

Do the headings count as errors if the students don't read them?

Yes, the headings count as they are included in the running words count. Other items like captions, diagram labels, etc. are not included in the running words so should not be counted as errors if students skip them.

Do I have to calculate the oral reading rate?

We recommend calculating reading rate starting at level J. We have provided you with a formula for calculating reading rate on the Recording Form. (This is also addressed in Section 2 of this guide.) You may also use the *F & P Calculator/Stopwatch* included in your system box to get a quick and accurate score.

What is the appropriate oral reading rate for each level?

We have provided ranges for reading rate. See Figure 2.23.

Why is reading rate important?

Reading rate is one indicator of whether a reader is putting groups of words together in processing the text. When a student is reading one word at a time, the reading gets bogged down and he is not likely to be able to attend to the meaning of the text. Keep in mind that reading rate is not the most important indication of fluency. Other characteristics include phrasing, pausing, word stress, and intonation. Some readers can actually read too fast.

Assessment Procedures: Fluency

At what level should I expect a student to read fluently?

You should expect a student to read with phrasing and fluency as soon as the early reading behaviors are well under control, which we expect should happen by about the end of Level B or beginning of Level C in instruction. Readers will not be reading fast with complete fluency at the early levels because they are still learning ways of processing print. You should expect, though, to see some phrasing, especially on texts that have dialogue. Begin insisting on phrased, fluent reading at level C.

Is fluency a stage of reading?

No. Fluency is not a stage of reading. At about level C, readers can read with phrasing and fluency at every level if it is within instructional or independent range.

What if I have a student who reads a level with accuracy and understanding but is not at all fluent? Should I go down a level for instruction?

That is not always the answer. We suggest using the teaching prompts and procedures provided in *Prompting Guide, Part 1* (Fountas and Pinnell,

Heinemann, 2009) to get a shift in fluency before moving down a level. Some students develop a habit of reading dysfluently and might do so even at easy levels. You'll want to look in greater depth at their reading. We suggest using the Six Dimensions Fluency Rubric found in the *Assessment Forms Book* and *CD-ROM* so that you can decide with more precision what to teach the student. Sometimes, if accuracy and understanding are there, you can teach intensively for fluency and get a shift in a short time.

Assessment Procedures: Comprehension Conversation

Why does Benchmark Assessment use a comprehension conversation instead of comprehension questions?

We have found that a comprehension conversation is the most effective way to get the best evidence of comprehension because you can paraphrase questions and probe further for student understanding.

What should I do if a student does not come up with the key understandings?

First, use the prompts provided on the Recording Form to elicit answers. You do not need to score the student lower because you had to probe for answers. Some children are not accustomed to spontaneously talking about their thinking, yet they may understand the text very well and demonstrate it when questioned. If that still doesn't work, it suggests an unsatisfactory level of understanding.

Can a student look back at the book during the comprehension conversation?

Though you should not instruct a student to do so, it is permissible for her to initiate looking back in the text. If she begins to read the text, ask her to tell the response in her own words.

If a student does look back at the book, does this affect his comprehension score?

If a student initiates looking back in the text, locates the information, and provides a correct response, you should give him credit for the answer. Looking back in the text will not affect the comprehension score unless he is simply pointing at or rereading some of the text to you. If that happens, say something like, "Tell me in your own words."

What if a student does not understand a prompt?

Be sure to rephrase the question to provide the maximum opportunity for her to understand it. Your goal is to determine whether she understood the information in the story, not whether she understood the question.

How can I keep up with the note taking during the conversation?

After you have administered the conversation one or two times, you will be able to interpret a student's comments and connect them to the key understandings provided on the Recording Form. Check the ones he has covered and take notes only on the additional information he provided (if any). Also, you can take a quick moment to make these checks right after the conversation (while the student is writing or after he leaves).

Should I "count" the "right answers" a student makes in order to come up with a comprehension score?

No. These texts vary and have different requirements in terms of key understandings (thinking within, beyond, and about the text). Look at the rubric for scoring each of these three categories, then make a holistic decision as to the extent to which the student has demonstrated thinking.

Where can I find more information about thinking within, beyond, and about the text?

First we'd refer you the *The Continuum of Literacy Learning 3-8* in your system box. You will also find very detailed descriptions in *Teaching for Comprehending and Fluency: Thinking, Talking, and Writing About Reading, K–8* (Fountas and Pinnell, Heinemann, 2006).

How can I make the comprehension conversation sound "natural"?

You will find some suggestions in Figure 2.16 of this guide.

Assessment Procedures: Writing About Reading

Why is the Writing About Reading section of the Recording Form considered optional?

The comprehension conversation should provide ample evidence of a student's comprehension of a book; in fact, It is more trustworthy than writing. Writing provides additional evidence, but you would not base your assessment on a student's ability to write. Writing about reading is a learned skill. In other words, a student might be able to read and comprehend a piece, but lack experience and skill in putting that understanding into words. Here, the problem is not comprehension, but an ability to compose her thoughts.

How does the writing part of the assessment factor into the total score?

The Writing About Reading portion of the assessment is strictly optional and is not calculated into the formula for determining instructional and independent levels. It's there to give you some extra diagnostic information about how well a student comprehended a book.

Interpreting and Reporting Results

What if a student achieves instructional or independent level at two levels?

Occasionally you will find that a student performs the same on two levels of text. Use the *higher* of the levels as your indicator.

What if a student reads a book at the instructional level and then a higher level (harder) text at the independent level?

Have the student try another more difficult text to see if the independent level was achieved because the topic was easy. If this text is hard for him, you will probably want to begin at the original instructional level. If this text is easy for him, continue until you find another instructional level and begin there. When you begin teaching, you will have the opportunity to observe him closely with other texts and can always move up or down a level and change groups if needed.

How will I know how the results from Benchmark Assessment relate to the standards for grade-level performance in our district?

Your school/district should make decisions about expected grade-level standards, taking into account your state goals. You can refer to the Quarterly Instructional Level Expectations for Reading chart (Figure 5.1 of this guide) for suggested indicators, but adjust them if you have rationales for a different standard.

Teaching Decisions

Does a student's guided reading group have to be at her instructional level?

No. The "recommended placement level," which is the recommended level for guided reading, may be a level lower or higher than the instructional level, depending on your analysis. Section 3 of this guide describes the thinking process involved in finding a placement level.

What if I have students with six or seven different placement levels? Should I have that many guided reading groups?

It is very difficult to have a large number of reading groups. It makes it hard for you to provide instruction on a regular basis because you certainly cannot see all groups every day or even over a week. As you look over your recommended placement levels, you may have to put students with slightly different instructional levels in a single group. Try to vary your interactions within the group accordingly, giving some students more support and others more challenge (for example, with writing). Most teachers find it difficult to work with more than four or five groups.

What if I have a student who reads at a level far below the rest of the class?

This student needs intervention to make accelerated progress, so the first thing to do is to try to get her some extra services. At the same time, she desperately needs classroom instruction, so you should try not to remove her from all of the teaching you are providing. If at all possible, provide enough individual support that she can participate in a group and make better progress.

What if I have a student who is so far ahead of the class that he doesn't belong in any group?

This kind of student can enjoy participating with the highest level group because he will benefit from discussion with others and there is always something more to learn. Advanced readers often read books that are easy for them. Remember that these groups are dynamic, so you can always invite the student to participate in reading some books and not others. In addition, you will want to provide challenging independent reading for him (extended through individual conferences).

What kind of teaching should I provide for students who need to make significant gains to catch up to grade level? For instance, a fourth grader beginning the year at Level H, how much growth is reasonable to expect?

Our experience suggests that daily intensive teaching as an extra intervention can make a difference to students who lag behind. Of course, progress always depends on the quality of instruction a student receives. The fourth grader described here needs *daily* intervention of an intensive nature *in addition* to good classroom instruction. If individual tutoring is available, this student should receive it for as long as needed. If not, she should participate in an intensive small group intervention lesson every day. We recommend a group size of about 3 or 4 to 1 teacher. The lessons should include daily reading of instructional level texts, writing about reading, and phonics or word work (attention to the structure of words). With this kind of regular intervention teaching, we would expect two years of growth within one year. That means that the goal for this student would be proficiently reading at about level O or P. That still would not be on grade level, so she would probably need intervention in grade 5 as well.

How does Benchmark Assessment help me with my leveled book program?

The *Fountas & Pinnell Benchmark Assessment System* is designed to help you collect reliable evidence of student competencies and reading levels so you can begin your teaching where the learners are—at the optimal instructional level and with in-depth knowledge of their reading behaviors—bringing all readers forward in their competencies. No other assessment has been directly linked to the Fountas and Pinnell levels to date, so you will also have a reliable and valid assessment to link to guided reading small-group reading instruction.

English Language Learners

Should I administer the assessment to a student who speaks very little English?

We suggest that you follow your school policy regarding the assessment of students whose first language is not English. If you would administer other standardized tests to those students, then you should administer this one. You will find that the gradient of texts will allow most children at least to begin to engage in the reading process.

How does Benchmark Assessment support my ability to conduct the assessment conference with students whose first language is not English?

You will notice that throughout this guide we have provided specific support to help you understand how language differences should be noticed in the administration and interpretation of the assessment. In addition, case studies of English language learners described in Section 5 of this guide provide real situations for you to think about and learn from.

We have a large population of English language learners in our school. When we administer Benchmark Assessment, should we accept their responses in their native language?

First, we trust that the language proficiency policy in your school/district has been applied and that the children are learning to read in English in the classroom. Your district needs to decide on the standardization of the assessment within its policies. You should tell the student that he is going to read a book in English and suggest that he try to talk with you in English. If the teacher understands the native language and determines that he is providing evidence of understanding the book, he should be given credit for the response. If none of the teachers can understand a student's response in another language, then you will need to tell him he must speak to you only in English.

Collecting and Using Data

How can I pass information along to ensure that my students' literacy growth will be documented across the years?

You will find a variety of tools in the *Benchmark Assessment System* to support the documentation of a student growth over time as well as ways to track development of groups and classes. *Student Folders* (included in each system box) provide a longitudinal graph for teachers to record progress. They are designed to be passed from teacher to teacher to hold the assessment information on one student from kindergarten to grade 8. The *Online Data Management System* provides several options for reports on individuals or classes in report or graph format. *ODMS* provides expanded tracking and reporting capabilities for both teachers and administrators in a networkable format. Detailed information can be found in Section 7 of this guide.

Is there a way for our school's Benchmark Assessment data to be linked to the district office?

Yes. The *Online Data Management System*, which is described in detail in Section 7 of this guide, allows data on individual students and classes to be accessible for teachers and administrators throughout your district.

How will I know how assessment level relates to our standards for grade level performance in our district?

Your school and your district should make decisions about expected grade level standards, taking into account your state goals. You can refer to F&P Text Level Gradient™ (Figure 1.1 of this guide) for suggested indicators, but adjust them if you have rationales for a different standard.

How can we use the Benchmark Assessment data to improve our school?

Have regular faculty meetings to examine the data within and across grade levels. Look at the general reading levels of the age cohort, but don't stop there. Use the case studies in Section 5 of this guide to help you think about some priorities for teaching students. Think across the language and literacy framework. You can teach for comprehending through interactive read aloud, minilessons, guided reading, and literature discussion. Use *The Continuum of Literacy Learning 3–8* in your system box to identify teaching goals.

section 9

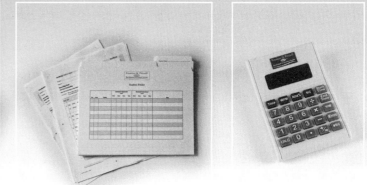

▶ Appendix A: Benchmark Books

Benchmark books are the centerpiece of *Benchmark Assessment System 2.* They provide the material for the student's oral reading from which the teacher observes many dimensions of reading behavior. There are thirty books, fifteen fiction and fifteen nonfiction, ranging from level L, the easiest, to level Z, the hardest. System 2 provides one fiction and one nonfiction book at each level.

Each fiction and nonfiction book has been written and edited to represent the designated Fountas and Pinnell level. Each represents the specific characteristics of that level. You can find very detailed analyses of texts at each level of the gradient, A–Z, in *Leveled Books for Readers, K–8: Matching Texts to Readers for Effective Teaching* (Heinemann, 2006) and *The Continuum of Literacy Learning: A Guide for Teaching PreK–8* (Heinemann, 2011).

In this section, we briefly describe the thirty benchmark books. The bulleted lists summarize important characteristics of each book. These characteristics emerged from analyzing the text to place it on the gradient. They are descriptions of what makes the book easier or harder and are related to the demands the text makes on the reader. Reading these descriptions will help you realize what the reader has to do to read the book. If the reader is successful, then you have good evidence that he can meet the demands of texts at that level.

▶ Benchmark Books

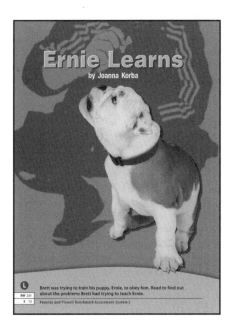

Ernie Learns
by Joanna Korba

Brett was trying to train his puppy, Ernie, to obey him. Read to find out about the problems Brett had trying to teach Ernie.
Fountas and Pinnell Benchmark Assessment System 2

dog what to do. He tried to remember more and then decided to start. Maybe that was all.

"Sit, Ernie!" Brett said.

He nudged the puppy, and the little dog sat.

Then Brett made another attempt. But Ernie just looked at him. Then Brett showed the puppy over and over how to sit. Again, Ernie forgot what to do.

"Maybe you don't like sitting," Brett said. "Let's try something new." He backed away from his dog. "Stay!" he said.

Ernie didn't stay. He didn't lie

down. And he didn't come when he was called.

Brett's mom was watching from the porch. Brett yelled, "Mom, why can't I teach Ernie anything?"

"I think you forgot an important step," Mom said. She held out some puppy treats. "You have to make him want to be good! Watch for him to do something right. Then praise him and reward him. That's how Dad and I get you to be good!" ∎

Brett grinned and said, "Aw, you know I'd be good anyway!" Mom laughed. "Puppies and people aren't all that different,"

2

3

Ernie Learns

Fiction level L

Total words: 324

Average sentence length: 6.8 words

In this story, Brett tries to train his puppy Ernie to obey him. He tries telling Ernie what to do, but nothing works. His mom suggests praising and rewarding Ernie, just like she and Dad do to get Brett to be good. The puppy treats do the trick. The story ends with Brett giving his mom a "happy bark."

Features of this text are:

❑ variation in sentence length with some sentences over fifteen words long

❑ mostly one- and two-syllable words

❑ dialogue, both simple and split, between two speakers

❑ simple story line

❑ paragraphs, marked by indentation

❑ play on language at the end.

Hang On, Baby Monkey
by Donna Latham

A baby monkey is born and hangs on to his mother's back. Read to find out how the other monkeys help the mother care for her newborn monkey.

The baby grabs the fur on his mother's belly and begins to feed. The baby is snug against his mother's warm body. Later, the baby curls his long tail, arms, and legs around his mother.

The First Weeks

For a few weeks, the baby rides on his mother's back. The mother carries, feeds, and grooms her baby. She keeps the baby safe from snakes, hawks, and big cats.

Sometimes, the baby monkey loses his grip and falls to the rain forest floor. A monkey from the troop climbs down the tree and

A baby capuchin clings to his mother's back.

picks up the baby. Back with his mother, the baby hangs on again.

After a month, the baby begins to learn about the world. He moves away from his mother. But he only goes as far as his tail will let him! The baby holds on to his mother using his long tail.

Caring for the baby is hard work! Other monkeys in the troop

2

3

Hang On, Baby Monkey

Nonfiction level L

Total words: 292

Average sentence length: 10.6 words

This text provides information about how a monkey troop takes care of their young. The text is presented in three sections in temporal sequence, with headings. Each section tells about a part of the baby monkey's life. An important main idea is that the monkeys in a troop help each other as members of a family would. The baby monkey survives by hanging on to his mother; he rides on his mother's back at first and then stays close to her by holding on with his tail.

Features of this text are:

- ❏ three sections with headings
- ❏ told in temporal sequence
- ❏ monkey troop compared to family
- ❏ themes of survival and animals depending on each other
- ❏ varied sentence length, most ten to twelve words long
- ❏ simple words, mostly two syllables
- ❏ paragraphs set off by indentation
- ❏ photographs with captions
- ❏ map with legend
- ❏ glossary.

▶ Benchmark Books

was responsible enough to get a dog.

"Great! How can I prove I'm responsible? I'll do anything!"

"First, you should call the animal shelter and ask them how much it costs to get a dog. Then you'll have to save the money."

"I can certainly do that!" I said.

I called the shelter. I found out it costs one hundred and forty dollars to get a puppy and seventy dollars to get a dog. I decided to get a grown dog!

How long would it take me to save seventy dollars? I started to do the math.

My allowance was seven dollars a

week, if I did all my chores. I never used to save any of it. Now I'd have to save a whole lot. ■

With seven dollars a week, I'd have seventy dollars in ten weeks. But that was too long to wait!

I asked Mom about doing some extra jobs for her. She agreed to pay me three dollars for each one. She said I could clean the garage, vacuum the car, paint the kitchen door, brush all the cobwebs out of the basement (yuck!) . . .

"Okay, Mom, I think that's enough for now!" I said.

The next few weeks were really hard. I did all my chores, even

---

Saving Up

Fiction level M

Total words: 394

Average sentence length: 8.6 words

Danny wants to get a dog, but he has to prove to his mom that he is responsible. He undertakes two responsibilities: finding out how much a dog would cost, and earning the money. Danny meets his goal by doing extra chores and saving the seventy dollars. He names his new dog Buck.

Features of this text are:

- ❏ straightforward story told in chronological sequence
- ❏ told in first-person narrative
- ❏ dialogue between two characters, some unassigned
- ❏ mostly simple or compound sentences
- ❏ some strings of verb clauses set off by commas
- ❏ joke at the end
- ❏ full range of punctuation, including dashes
- ❏ humor at the end.

City Hawks

by Maryann Dobeck

Pale Male is a red-tailed hawk. He made a nest on the ledge of an apartment building in New York City. Read to find out what happened.

M
RW 214
B 15
Fountas and Pinnell Benchmark Assessment System 2

people had the nest and the spikes taken away.

That made other people mad. They marched outside the building. They held up signs and yelled, "Bring back the nest!" They called city leaders. They fought so hard for Pale Male that the spikes were put back up. Before long, Pale Male and his mate were back. Now, New York is home to the city hawks for as long as they want to stay.

Tall buildings are across from Central Park.

4

Glossary

binoculars	special kind of glasses for looking at things that are far away
chest	the front part of the body, from the neck to the stomach
ledge	a narrow shelf or surface

City Hawks

Nonfiction level M

Total words: 325

Average sentence length: 9.4 words

This book tells the story of Pale Male, a red-tailed hawk who built a nest on the ledge of a fancy apartment building across from Central Park in New York City. The hawk found a mate and raised several families, becoming famous in the process. A controversy arose when people living in the building got tired of being watched by people with binoculars. The nest was taken down, but marching protesters soon had it up again for good. Information is organized into three sections with headings. Drawings and photographs are included.

Features of this text are:

- ❏ organized into three sections with headings, in chronological order
- ❏ journalistic style with a summary lead
- ❏ presentation of two perspectives: people who live in the building and do not want others observing them and people who want Pale Male to have his nest
- ❏ author's perspective supporting Pale Male
- ❏ mostly simple or compound sentences
- ❏ mostly one- or two-syllable words
- ❏ no technical vocabulary
- ❏ glossary.

She watered the flowers in her mother's garden in the summer.

This was one chore that Vanessa didn't mind doing because it was a chance to watch the butterflies in the flower garden along the fence in the backyard.

One morning, as Vanessa was watering the flowers, a bright yellow-and-black butterfly fluttered into her yard. "That butterfly looks just like one in my book," Vanessa thought to herself. Up, up, then down, down it floated on the breeze.

"Where will it land?" she wondered.

The graceful butterfly swooped down to sip nectar from the tallest red flower in the garden. "I've got to catch it!" Vanessa thought. But when she tiptoed closer, the little beauty quickly lifted back up into the air. "Oh! Please don't fly away!" she said under her breath.

As if it heard her wish, the butterfly landed on a pink lily. Vanessa stood very still. "A butterfly catcher must be patient," she said to herself. ■

2

3

Vanessa's Butterfly

Fiction level N

Total words: 299

Average sentence length: 9.9 words

Vanessa, whose name means "butterfly," loves butterflies. She studies them and loves to watch them in her flower garden. One day Vanessa sees a beautiful yellow-and-black butterfly and wants to catch it. The more she watches it, the more she appreciates its beauty. Realizing that the butterfly needs to be free, Vanessa decides to be a butterfly watcher instead of a butterfly catcher.

Features of this text are:

❑ story lead providing background to support Vanessa's love of butterflies

❑ foreshadowing of the end with the information that her favorite story was *The Butterfly Catcher*

❑ descriptive language showing the butterfly's movement (*floated on the breeze, swooped*)

❑ character development (Vanessa's change of mind)

❑ some long sentences with twenty or more words

❑ mostly one- and two-syllable words.

What Are Guide Dogs?

Guide dogs help blind people get from place to place and lead independent lives. With a guide dog, blind people can go to the grocery store, ride the bus, or take a trip on a plane. Guide dogs are allowed in places where most other dogs are not.

Not just any dog can be a guide dog. A guide dog needs many months of training at a special school.

At school they learn to behave quietly, especially in public. Guide dogs have to focus on helping their owners. They are taught to ignore other things, such as interesting smells and other animals.

Guide dogs help their owners cross streets safely.

They also learn to keep still and quiet in busy places, such as shopping malls or offices. Most dogs would have a very hard time doing that!

Dogs At Work

If you see a guide dog doing its job, remember not to pet or talk to it. Guiding is very hard to do. It requires a dog's full attention. ■

A guide dog wears a special harness, called a lead harness.

Dogs at Work

Nonfiction level N

Total words: 313

Average sentence length: 11.4 words

This book explains the role of guide dogs in helping blind people. The text includes an introduction and two sections with headings. An important main idea is that guide dogs require special training. Photographs with captions and a glossary are included.

Features of this text are:

- ❏ starts with a question that compares guide dogs to best friends
- ❏ details what guide dogs know how to do
- ❏ provides a special meaning for the word *independent*
- ❏ most sentences ten to twenty words
- ❏ some technical vocabulary such as *harness* and *handler*
- ❏ photographs with captions
- ❏ glossary.

▶ Benchmark Books

The New Girl
by Moira Glass

Nora's mother works in the Army and her family has to move to a new place. Read to find out what happens when Nora tries to make new friends.

A month later, Nora walked into her new school. Her sneakers squeaked on the shiny, polished floors. She was not surprised that the other kids turned, stared, and whispered, but didn't say hello. "No one ever talks to the new girl," she told herself.

At lunch, Nora looked around the crowded cafeteria. At every table kids were eating lunch with their special friends, talking and laughing. No kids invited Nora to sit with them. Only one girl smiled at Nora. She was sitting by herself looking lonely and nervous. "She's probably new, too," Nora thought, so she just ignored her. Nora dreamed of being in a group of friends, just as she was in her old school.

That night she told her mother about her terrible day. "Did you talk to anyone?" her mother asked. Nora shook her head. "All the kids ignored me." ■

"I'm sorry, honey," Mom said. "But remember, to get you have to give." She was always coming up with sayings that sounded like they belonged on bumper stickers. "There must be one other kid at your school who could use a friend," Mom added. "Maybe you should try making the first move."

The next day Nora saw the girl who had smiled at her the day before. This time Nora smiled back, and before long they were talking. The girl's name was Liz, and this was her seventh school in five years. She was an Army kid, too!

2

3

The New Girl

Fiction level O

Total words: 402

Average sentence length: 9.0 words

Nora's mom is in the Army, and Nora is unhappy because her family has to move again. The first day at her new school is difficult. The only friendly person is another girl, who smiles at her, but Nora ignores her. When she returns home, her mother advises her that "to get you have to give." Nora follows this advice and makes a friend of the other new girl, also an Army kid.

Features of this text are:

- ❑ assumption of background information (military families moving)
- ❑ setting requiring inference (feeling of a newcomer) and understanding of the importance of peer group
- ❑ some two-syllable words
- ❑ some adjectives in strings, set off by commas
- ❑ most sentences complex (with at least two clauses)
- ❑ variety in vocabulary related to dialogue (*grumbled, complained*)
- ❑ dialogue among three characters
- ❑ simple foreshadowing
- ❑ passage of time
- ❑ meaning of slogans or "sayings"
- ❑ character development (learning a simple lesson).

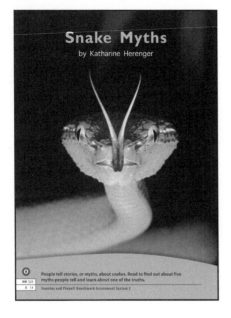

Snake Myths
by Katharine Herenger

People tell stories, or myths, about snakes. Read to find out about five myths people tell and learn about one of the truths.

Fountas and Pinnell Benchmark Assessment System 2

Snakes' eyes are protected by a layer of clear scales.

Myth 2

Snakes' tongues can be dangerous. That's another misunderstanding. In fact, only a snake's fangs are harmful. A snake flicks its tongue to smell the air. It can use smells to figure out which way its prey is moving or whether an enemy is near. If a snake flicks its tongue at you, it's just trying to figure out if you're something good to eat. (Don't worry—snakes rarely eat people!)

2

Poisonous snakes have two large fangs in the upper front part of the mouth.

Myth 3

Some people think that snakes feel wet and slimy. But a snake's skin is really very dry and smooth. This smoothness makes a snake's skin look shiny and wet. The way a snake's scales move, sliding along the ground, may also make them look slimy. ■

Myth 4

Snakes can bend and twist and slither and slide this way and that. Many people think they have no bones. But snakes do

3

Snake Myths

Nonfiction level O

Total words: 351

Average sentence length: 10.2 words

This book introduces five commonly held myths about snakes: (1) snakes hypnotize their prey; (2) snakes' tongues are dangerous; (3) snakes feel wet and slimy; (4) snakes have no bones; and (5) most snakes are poisonous. Each myth is introduced, then the evidence to the contrary is presented. The main idea of the text is that snakes do not want to harm people.

Features of this text are:

- ❑ introduction provides the main idea of the book
- ❑ information organized into five myths and a conclusion
- ❑ clear organization within sections—presentation of myth first, followed by evidence to the contrary
- ❑ photographs with captions
- ❑ some three- and four-syllable words (*fascination, hypnotize*)
- ❑ vocabulary (such as *myth*) defined within the text
- ❑ parenthetical material set off by commas in a few sentences
- ❑ glossary.

▶ Benchmark Books

Plenty of Pets

by Stephanie Herbek

Nate loved animals and really wanted a pet. He was allergic to all kinds of animals, so he was feeling sorry for himself. Read to find out what made him feel better.

Fountas and Pinnell Benchmark Assessment System 2

The bell rang, and Nate grabbed his backpack and headed home in a downpour. His neighbor, Mrs. Gonzalez, pulled up beside him in her minivan. "Hop in," she said. "It's a deluge out there!" Even before the door closed, Nate's nose started to tickle.

"Achoo!" he sneezed loudly. "Achoo! Achoo!" Rubbing his red, itchy eyes, Nate croaked, "Is there an animal in here?"

"Just Daisy!" Mrs. Gonzalez said sheepishly, as a pudgy bulldog poked its head over the front seat. Nate walked home.

A sniffling Nate woke up Saturday morning feeling sorry for himself. "Why do I have to be allergic to everything?" he fretted as he trudged downstairs.

His mom smiled. "I have exciting news!" she exclaimed. "My friend Dr. Hung, who works at the aquarium, could use your help with the animals on Saturdays. How about it?" ■

"Thanks, Mom, but the idea of sneezing all day doesn't appeal to me," said Nate.

"You're allergic to animals that have fur or feathers," Mom pointed out, "not to marine animals that live in the water."

Nate felt nervous as they drove to the aquarium, but after he met Dr. Hung, his anxiety melted away. Within minutes, they were standing next to a huge saltwater pool. "Meet our Pacific white-sided dolphins, Nate," said Dr. Hung. "They're ready for their lunch!"

Dr. Hung handed Nate a pair of floppy rubber gloves and a heavy pail

2

3

Plenty of Pets

Fiction level P

Total words: 404

Average sentence length: 9.0 words

Nate is disappointed that he can't bring home his classroom's hamster because he is allergic to everything with fur or feathers. His mom arranges for him to help Dr. Hung in the aquarium on Saturday and he discovers that dolphins, especially one named Splash, will eat from his hand. He has a wonderful time. When he gets home, another surprise is waiting. His mom gives him a pet fish, which he names Little Splash.

Features of this text are:

- ❏ varied sentence length, with some sentences fifteen to twenty words
- ❏ many complex sentences
- ❏ divided dialogue
- ❏ mostly familiar vocabulary, with a few difficult words such as *sheepishly*, *beluga*, *fretted*, and *sneeze-free* (coined for humor)
- ❏ straightforward story with clear problem and resolution
- ❏ third-person narrative
- ❏ words to signal passage of time: *later*, *after*, day of the week
- ❏ little or no character development.

Animal Instincts

by D. M. Longo

Ⓟ An instinct is something you are born ready to do. Read to find out about the instincts dogs and cats have.

RW 213
R 13 Fountas and Pinnell Benchmark Assessment System 2

seem odd to us. Yet our family pets are behaving in exactly the same way as their ancestors did thousands of years ago.

The Pack Is Back

The dogs you know are probably household pets and live indoors. Wild dogs live in packs—groups in which animals live, work, and hunt together. Dogs in a pack depend on one another to survive, so pack instinct is very strong. The leader of the pack is the smartest dog. The other dogs in the pack obey the leader. This instinct is one reason that pet dogs are such devoted family members. Dogs regard their human families as their packs

and one family member as the leader of the pack. ■

Sebastian is a pet dog. Why does he enjoy chasing cars? He is following his predator instinct. A predator is an animal that hunts for its food. Like a predator, Sebastian runs after anything that moves quickly, like a rabbit—or a car!

Dogs love to run.

2   3

Animal Instincts

Nonfiction level P

Total words: 355

Average sentence length: 10.4 words

Focusing on cats and dogs, this text explains the origins of some common behaviors of these pets. Belonging to a "pack," for example, makes dogs devoted family members, and their predator instinct leads them to chase cars. Cats pounce on anything that moves because of the instinctual behavior of hunting. The text is presented with an introduction and three sections with headings.

Features of this text are:

❏ comparison of animal and human instinctual behaviors

❏ some technical terms *(instinctual, instinct, pack, predator)* all defined within the text

❏ examples to illustrate points

❏ photograph with caption

❏ glossary.

A SECRET HOME
by Sarah Wolbach

Lenny and Beth go on a hiking expedition through Mint Canyon with their Aunt Maddy. Read to find out what they learned about spiders on their hike.

Fountas and Pinnell Benchmark Assessment System 2

As they followed the winding trails, Aunt Maddy pointed out all kinds of plants and wildlife. They stopped for a water break. Then Lenny shouted, "Look out for the spider!" and Beth froze. It was obvious to Aunt Maddy that the kids were scared of spiders.

"Has a spider ever harmed either of you?" Aunt Maddy asked. Both kids shook their heads. "Sounds like you suffer from arachnophobia (uh RAK nuh FOE bee uh)—an extreme fear of spiders."

"Aren't spiders dangerous?" Lenny asked. "I heard about a boy who got really sick from a spider bite."

Aunt Maddy nodded. "Sure, some spiders, like the black widow, are dangerous." ■

"Yes," Lenny said excitedly, "that's the kind that bit that boy."

"Well," Aunt Maddy replied, "you'd

certainly want to avoid black widows, but most spiders won't hurt you. They want to avoid you as much as you want to avoid them."

They walked for a while, and then Aunt Maddy stopped. "Take a look down there," she said, gesturing toward the ground.

Beth and Lenny stared downward but didn't see anything except dirt and a few small rocks. They stood very still for a few minutes, and along came a furry spider about the size of a quarter. Aunt Maddy whispered, "That's a trap-door spider. Don't worry. It won't hurt you at all."

As the three of them watched, the spider used its two front legs to flip open a small, perfectly formed trap door in the earth. The spider then disappeared under the ground, pulling the door shut behind it. Beth

2

3

A Secret Home

Fiction level Q

Total words: 481

Average sentence length: 9.4 words

Lenny and Beth go with their Aunt Maddy on a lengthy hike through a dusty canyon. Both children are afraid of spiders and have some misconceptions about them. Aunt Maddy points out an interesting spider, the trap-door, and the children become so interested in it that they overcome their fear.

Features of this text are:

❑ foreshadowing of an "adventure" in the opening paragraph

❑ some very short sentences in the dialogue; most sentences ten to twenty words

❑ technical word, *arachnophobia*, with pronunciation guide in parentheses

❑ content information about spiders

❑ character development as shown by children's becoming interested in spiders

❑ turning point on page 4 when children become interested in the trap-door spider.

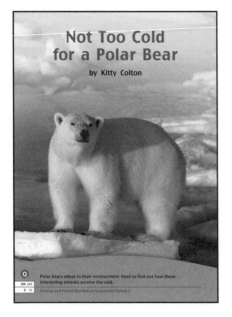

Not Too Cold
for a Polar Bear

by Kitty Colton

Polar bears adapt to their environment. Read to find out how these interesting animals survive the cold.

Fountas and Pinnell Benchmark Assessment System 2

polar bear. The polar bear is the largest of the eight species, or kinds, of bears. Polar bears live only in very cold climates like the Arctic region.

The word Arctic tells you that the polar bear's environment is icy cold. In the winter, temperatures can drop to minus 50 degrees. As if that's not enough reason to shiver, polar bears also spend a great deal of time in the icy Arctic Ocean. Polar bears are the largest predators on land. They mainly hunt and eat seals, and because seals are usually found in the ocean, polar bears are often found in or near the ocean, too. They are excellent swimmers.

Polar bears are classified as marine mammals.

2

Surviving the Cold

How do polar bears survive all that cold? Polar bears are very well adapted to life in the frozen Arctic. A polar bear's entire body, even the bottoms of its feet, is covered in fur. The fur protects it from the cold. The top layer of fur is called guard hair. Guard hair sticks together when it's wet. The wet hair is a barrier that protects polar bears from the cold water. ■

Below the guard hairs is a downy undercoat of fur that gives polar bears another layer of warmth. Underneath their fur, polar bears have black skin. The black

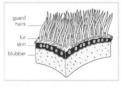

Amazing fact: Beneath its fur, a polar bear has black skin. The dark color absorbs the heat of the sun.

3

Not Too Cold for a Polar Bear

Nonfiction level Q

Total words: 393

Average sentence length: 12.5 words

An opening question frames the central idea of this text—that some animals have ways of surviving very cold weather. The book focuses on how polar bears are adapted to live in the Arctic region. Organized into two sections, the text provides specific details about how the characteristics of the polar bear's body work together to provide protection. It ends on a humorous note by showing how polar bears cool off when they get too hot.

Features of this text are:

- ❏ opens with posing a question
- ❏ two sections with headings
- ❏ first section with general information about polar bears and their environment
- ❏ second section with specific details about the polar bear's body
- ❏ technical vocabulary (for example, guard hair, blubber)
- ❏ variable sentence length but some with over twenty words
- ❏ photographs with captions
- ❏ drawing with cutaway of skin
- ❏ glossary.

▶ Benchmark Books

The Election
by Roy W. Sorrels

Jill was running for class president. Read to find out what happened when she gave her campaign speech in the auditorium.

RW 214
R 12 Fountas and Pinnell Benchmark Assessment System 2

Jill bolted upright in bed, feeling dazed.

Jill nodded slowly. "I'm okay," she said in an unconvincing voice. "What time is it?"

"Time to get ready to deliver your speech for class president," her mother said, smiling.

As the memory of her dream came flooding back, Jill felt a fresh wave of panic. "Mom, I don't know if I can do it. The thought of standing in front of all those people makes me feel sick!"

Jill's mother sat down next to her and smiled. "You know, Jill, sometimes I have to give speeches at big meetings." Jill's mother was a heart surgeon, an expert in her field. "I used to feel as frightened as you are now."

Jill asked, "How did you get over your fears?" ■

"Well," her mother began, "when I have to get up in front of hundreds of strangers, I focus on one friendly face I know. Then I imagine that the two of us are sitting across a table from each other and talking about work."

"And do you stop being scared?"

"Well, not completely. It's normal to feel nervous about something that's new to you. But if you can find the courage to do it anyway, it won't feel so scary the next time. You can do it—I'm sure of it."

Later that morning, Jill walked slowly across the auditorium stage and stood behind the podium. She took a deep breath and scanned the faces in the crowd. There, in the second row, was her friend Eduardo. He smiled at her encouragingly. Jill imagined herself talking directly to Eduardo, exactly as her mother had suggested.

2

3

The Election

Fiction level R

Total words: 492

Average sentence length: 11.1 words

This story begins with a dream in which Jill is speaking to her sixth-grade class and draws a blank. As she jolts awake, she realizes that she is afraid to speak to her class as a candidate for class president. Her mother gives her some good advice (looking for one friendly face). Jill tries the technique, relaxes, and feels very good by the end of the speech.

Features of this text are:

❑ requires reader to understand that the first paragraph was only a dream

❑ requires understanding of the setting and its contribution to the character's feelings

❑ mostly familiar vocabulary with a few difficult words (*podium, unconvincing*)

❑ most sentences between ten and twenty words

❑ full range of punctuation including dash and ellipses

❑ description of internal feelings of the central character and how and why they change

❑ requires reader to infer why Jill would be a good president and to predict the outcomes of the election.

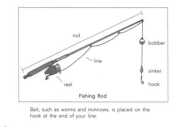

professionals call it.) Terminal tackle consists of hooks and sinkers for the end of your line. The hook holds your bait—whatever you use to attract the fish. The sinker is a small weight that pulls your hook into the water so it doesn't float on the surface.

If you go fishing in a lake, you might want some colorful bobbers. Bobbers are little balls tied to the line about two or three feet above the hook and sinker. If your bobber is bobbing, that means a fish is nibbling at your line! If you are fishing in a stream, you'll need wading boots and

Bait, such as worms and minnows, is placed on the hook at the end of your line.

a net. For deep-sea fishing, you'll need a sturdy boat!

The most important item of all is the bait. Worms are the top choice because they attract almost any fish. Another favorite bait is minnows—small fish used to catch larger fish. ■

Other Supplies

Taking along a few other items can make your fishing expedition a lot more comfortable. You will want to take insect repellent, sunblock, a hat, and sunglasses. A first-aid kit is a must. And don't forget snacks, including plenty of water or juice! If you plan to be out in a boat, always take a life jacket.

And speaking of snacks and boats—don't bring any bananas on a fishing boat! For hundreds of years, people have banned bananas from fishing boats. They believed the fruit brings bad luck. This superstition probably began in the 1700s. Back then, several ships carrying bananas disappeared

Fishing Smarts

Nonfiction level R

Total words: 513

Average sentence length: 11.7 words

The important idea in this book—that fishing is more complicated than it appears—is introduced in the first paragraph. The text has three sections with headings. Information about equipment and supplies is presented in the first two sections. In the last section, there is a response to the superstitions surrounding fishing, which were introduced in section two. The text ends with an implicit suggestion to "catch and release" the fish.

Features of this text are:

- ❏ technical words, most of which are defined within the text (*tackle, reel, spool, terminal tackle, hooks and sinkers, bobber, sinker*)
- ❏ familiar vocabulary
- ❏ requires understanding of the context
- ❏ requires understanding of the historical reference to superstitions in the 1700s
- ❏ information on equipment and supplies in the first two sections
- ❏ information about fishing "know-how" in the third section
- ❏ implicit suggestion to "catch and release" fish
- ❏ photographs with captions
- ❏ diagram of fishing rod with labels
- ❏ glossary.

▶ Benchmark Books

"How 'bout you?" I casually asked.

"Already ate," he answered, just as casually.

He lied to me, and I lied to him. Ever since Dad lost his job and the money dried up, we lied and kept secrets. The façade helps us make it easier for each other.

Effortlessly, I told another one. "Dad? Anthony asked me to stay over again. OK?"

"An opportunity to sleep in a bed? Go for it." ■

Not to mention a home-cooked supper and breakfast. It was easier for Dad, too. Then he didn't have to feed me.

"Heads up!" said Dad. He lobbed over a brown bag. In the bag was my standard lunch: a peanut-butter sandwich and an apple.

"Thanks," I said as I hopped on my bike.

Dad told me where he'd be job-hunting that day, in case I needed him. "Come here right after school tomorrow," he said. "It's moving day." To be as inconspicuous as possible, we moved the van a lot.

I had an unauthorized stop to make on the way to school—one of those secrets I mentioned earlier. Dad didn't know that every Tuesday morning I earned a couple of bucks unloading produce behind Cardozo's Market. I used the money for school supplies that I couldn't bear to ask my dad to buy.

I worked for twenty minutes before I got up the nerve to ask, "Mr. Cardozo . . . I was wondering. Any chance you could hire me permanently?"

"I wish I could, Ray, but what I really need is a full-time produce manager. If you were older and out of school . . ." He shook his head sympathetically.

I got things settled with Anthony. Then all through math I thought about that job at Cardozo's. So during lunch period, I hand-lettered a flyer:

HELP WANTED
PRODUCE MANAGER
CARDOZO'S MARKET
THIRD AND CENTRAL PARKWAY

2   3

Could Be Worse

Fiction level S

Total words: 589

Average sentence length: 9.6 words

This book tells the story of Ray and his father, who are homeless. Ray's father is unemployed, and they live in a battered van. The story begins with the retelling of a joke about a man for whom everything goes wrong. He says, "It could be worse. At least it's not raining." Just then, it starts to pour. This joke is important because it represents Ray's and his dad's life at this point. They don't have enough money even to eat, but they both lie—putting on a good face, each to the other. Ray takes action against his problem by working a few hours in a market. Learning that the market needs a full-time produce manager, Ray finds a way to let his dad know. His dad gets the job. At the end, Ray's dad says, "It's not going to make us millionaires. But it could be worse." This comment echoes back to the joke at the beginning, but this time, it isn't raining.

Features of this text are:

- ❑ begins and ends with reference to the joke, "It could be worse . . ."
- ❑ first-person narrative
- ❑ varied sentence length, some very short, but several more than twenty words long
- ❑ wide range of punctuation, including semicolon and ellipses
- ❑ mostly familiar vocabulary but several difficult words (*unauthorized, permanently, opportunity, professional*)
- ❑ use of rain as a symbol of trouble
- ❑ requires understanding that Ray and his dad lied to protect each other
- ❑ requires understanding of the setting.

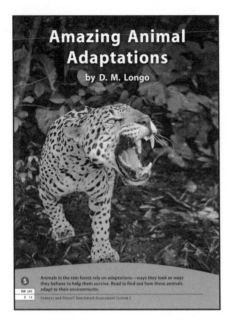

Amazing Animal Adaptations

by D. M. Longo

Animals in the rain forest rely on adaptations—ways they look or ways they behave to help them survive. Read to find out how these animals adapt to their environments.

Fountas and Pinnell Benchmark Assessment System 2

Its coloring, powerful jaws, and swimming abilities make the jaguar a fearsome predator. Its coloring allows it to blend in with tree trunks.

blends in with its surroundings. Its camouflage allows the jaguar to sneak up on its prey. Jaguars aren't exactly picky eaters—they eat animals, both large and small. Jaguars have large heads and powerful jaws that allow them to be fearsome hunters. They are also skilled swimmers, able to snatch fish, turtles, and even small alligators from the water in the wet rain forests where they live.

The Giant Anteater

The anteater curls into a ball in the hollow of a tree to hide from the jaguar. The anteater has wiry, gray hair with stripes of black and white across its back and throat. ∎

2

Sticky saliva coats the anteater's tongue. This adaptation makes it easy to slurp up ants and termites.

The anteater is one of the oddest-looking beasts in the animal world. Its strange appearance is an example of how animals adapt to their environments. With its huge claws, the anteater can rip into ants' nests. Its long, pointy snout lets it poke its head into holes. The anteater's tongue is about two feet long. Using its long tongue, the anteater slurps up ants effortlessly.

The Red-Eyed Tree Frog

The red-eyed tree frog uses an adaptation, sticky toe pads, to cling to the underside of wet leaves. The toe pads are like suction cups that let the frog hold on tight. Its bright

3

Amazing Animal Adaptations

Nonfiction level S

Total words: 423

Average sentence length: 14.2 words

This highly descriptive text provides information about how animals in the rain forest behave in ways that allow them to survive. The information is presented in five sections. The beginning is a suspenseful description of a jaguar, an anteater, and a red-eyed tree frog going about their night lives. The three following sections provide details about each of the three animals. The text is written in present tense. The important idea is summarized in the last section—that all living things are adapted to their environments.

Features of this text are:

❑ introduces the main idea with a description of the three animals going about their nocturnal lives

❑ details on the three animals in three sections

❑ summarizes the main idea at the end

❑ key vocabulary words related to the concept (*adaptation, camouflage, environment, predators*)

❑ varied sentence length, with most between ten and twenty words

❑ photographs with captions

❑ glossary.

▶ Benchmark Books

"Get a Horse!"
by Roy W. Sorrels

It was 1904, and Ethan's father brought home an automobile. Read to find out how Ethan and the others felt about the new Model A Ford.

Fountas and Pinnell Benchmark Assessment System 2

coat, gloves, a leather cap, and a pair of goggles for protection.

The year was 1904, and everybody in Detroit had been talking about the horseless carriage that Henry Ford had invented. Ford called it the automobile, because it moved on its own. No horse was required. Ford said that the automobile was going to replace the horse and carriage, but most people didn't believe it. People had been riding in horse-drawn carriages and wagons for hundreds of years, and it was a great way to get around. ■

The automobile pulled up in front of the house enveloped in a cloud of dust. As the driver removed his cap and goggles, Ethan thought, "Oh no!" Seeing that the driver was his father, Ethan wanted to sink down into his shoes in embarrassment.

The crowd was chanting, "Get a horse! Get a horse!"

But Ethan's dad seemed unconcerned; in fact, he looked very pleased with himself. "What do you think, Ethan? I thought I'd surprise you and your mother. Want to go for a spin in our new Model A?" His father helped him clamber onto the seat next to him.

The motor wheezed, rattled, and roared into action. They whizzed down the street in a cloud of dust while barking dogs and laughing children chased them. The chickens in front of Mr. Grant's house flapped, squawked, and scurried out of the way.

Ethan's hair blew into his eyes as the Model A roared down the winding dirt road.

Ethan was slightly frightened to be riding in an automobile, but he was having a lot of fun, too. He was even a little disappointed when Father shouted that it was time to go home.

That night, Ethan's mother said, "Tom, everybody in town thinks you're crazy!"

"Not everybody," replied Ethan's father. "I predict that before long everyone will be driving an automobile."

Ethan had to admit that riding with his father had been exciting. He never thought he'd ever go as fast as 20 miles an hour! But he was worried about one thing.

"Dad," he said, "what's going to happen to Chester?" Chester was the aging horse they'd had for as long as Ethan could remember. "Are we still going

2

3

"Get a Horse!"

Fiction level T

Total words: 551

Average sentence length: 12.5 words

The story takes place in 1904, when Henry Ford's automobile was a new invention and many people ridiculed the horseless carriage. In the beginning of the story, Ethan is embarrassed when his father drives a Model A home. After riding in it, however, Ethan decides that he likes going as fast as 20 miles an hour. After his worries about Chester, the aging horse owned by the family, are alleviated, Ethan asks for another ride.

Features of this text are:

❏ requires understanding of the setting and attitudes of people at the time

❏ character change in attitude

❏ requires reader to infer Ethan's feelings and the reasons for them (initial embarrassment and worry about Chester the horse)

❏ words like *trousers* and *carriage* that are not commonly used today and/or had different meanings in 1904

❏ descriptive words

❏ varied sentence length, with some complex sentences of more than twenty words.

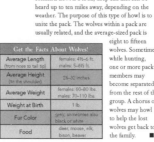

Why Do Wolves Howl?
by Gabriel Kidd

Some people have misconceptions about wolves and their howls. Read to find out about the many types of howls and the reasons for each of them.

Types of Howls

There are several types of wolf howls, each with its own particular purpose. The most common howl is a loud, deep call that can be heard up to ten miles away, depending on the weather. The purpose of this type of howl is to unite the pack. The wolves within a pack are usually related, and the average-sized pack is eight to fifteen wolves. Sometimes, while hunting, one or more pack members may become separated from the rest of the group. A chorus of wolves may howl to help the lost wolves get back to the family. ■

Get the Facts About Wolves!	
Average Length (from nose to tail tip)	females: 4½–6 ft. males: 5–6½ ft.
Average Height (to the shoulder)	26–32 inches
Average Weight	females: 60–80 lbs. males: 70–110 lbs.
Weight at Birth	1 lb.
Fur Color	grey; sometimes also black or white
Food	deer, moose, elk, bison, beaver

Reasons for Howls

It's common for wolves to howl before setting out to hunt for food. The purpose of this howl may be to excite pack members and help them bond. It's as if they are a team preparing to compete. But once the hunt starts, the wolves are silent. Howling during a hunt would only alert the potential prey that it is in danger.

The howling begins again after a successful hunt. These howls seem to sound satisfied! Again, it's as if the wolf team has just scored a major victory!

Wolves communicate not only within a pack, but between packs as well. Packs can howl back and forth for hours. This may be their way of defending their territory from neighboring packs. These howls warn other packs to keep their distance.

Wolves also howl when they feel lonely or isolated, or are seeking mates. This type of howl has a different sound; it rises and falls, dragging out at the end.

Even six-month-old wolf pups know where, when, and to whom they should howl.

2   3

Why Do Wolves Howl?

Nonfiction level T

Total words: 532

Average sentence length: 13.8 words

This text describes wolves' howls as a kind of language that they use to communicate with each other. After an introduction that outlines the misconceptions about wolves, the information is presented in three sections: (1) types of howls; (2) reasons for howls; and (3) howls are unique. It seems that wolves howls identify one another. No two wolves within a pack howl on the same note at the same time.

Features of this text are:

- ❑ begins with contrasting misconceptions about the real reasons wolves howl

- ❑ information presented with an introduction and three sections with headings

- ❑ varied sentence length with most between ten and twenty words

- ❑ many different words to describe wolves' howls

- ❑ ending paragraph referring back to beginning

- ❑ chart providing general facts about wolves (information not in the body of the text)

- ❑ photographs with captions

- ❑ glossary.

▶ Benchmark Books

Soon, Marta reaches her favorite lookout at the summit of a high mesa. She spots a majestic golden eagle that is circling overhead, high above the valley. The sun on her face is a constant reminder that the desert will be sweltering soon. She checks her watch, then tells Sniffles, "It's time to head home, boy." As they make their careful way back downhill, the eagle lets out a screech in the silent blue sky. Warily, Marta stops and searches the desert below. ■

Sniffles turns to stare at Redcliff Mountain towering behind them. Without warning, the hound dashes uphill. "Sniffles, come back!" Marta calls out, but her dog has vanished into the hillside.

More apprehensive than angry, Marta checks her watch again and sets off to search for her pet. She backtracks to the spot where the trail splits. One path twists up the steep, jagged sides of Eagle Rock Canyon while the other disappears into a tangled patch of needle-sharp cacti. Marta's watch reads 8:00 a.m. The temperature is climbing, and the air is hot, dry, and still.

"Sniiiifffles! Where aaaare you?" Marta calls.

This time, she hears her dog barking from a cliff about twenty yards up the canyon. "Come down here, Sniffles!" she yells. "It's getting late!"

The hound is barking furiously now. "What is it, boy?" Marta asks with a shaky voice, as she climbs the wind-worn slope apprehensively. There, on the ledge, only Sniffles' tail is visible; the rest of him is hidden in the darkness of a foot-wide opening in the canyon wall. They will certainly be late getting back now, Marta thinks anxiously.

As Marta edges cautiously along the narrow ledge to grab her dog, Sniffles slips deeper inside the shadowy cave. Moments later, a shrill yelp pierces the air, and a furry flash bolts out of the cave. The dog sends Marta stumbling back, and she falls to the ground, sending pebbles clattering over the ledge into the deep canyon below. Frightened by her close call, Marta struggles to get to her feet just as a gray cloud of bats bursts from the cave. "Sniffles! Wait for me!" she cries, scrambling and sliding down the rocky slope behind her dog.

The startled explorers kick up dust all the way down the canyon trail and they never look back, not once.

Marta will remember the cave later, when she encounters a threat more dangerous than the desert and closer than she ever imagined.

Canyon Mystery

Fiction level U

Total words: 587

Average sentence length: 12.3 words

This text is the first chapter of a longer story, inviting the reader to predict the events that will follow, events that are foreshadowed by the girl's father's urgent admonition to return early, no matter what. Marta and her dog Sniffles are exploring a valley in New Mexico. Marta loves the beauty of the mesa. Suddenly Sniffles barks and runs away. They discover a cave with bats. The chapter ends with the idea that Marta will remember the cave later when she encounters a threat more dangerous than the desert.

Features of this text are:

- ❑ parallel between the danger in the desert and the implied threat communicated by Marta's father
- ❑ present-tense, third-person narrative
- ❑ varied sentence length but many more than twenty words
- ❑ some distortion of words in print for dramatic effect *("Where aaaare you?")*
- ❑ requires reader to envision the setting in order to understand danger
- ❑ requires reader to connect first paragraph with the last in order to predict what may come in the subsequent chapters.

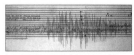

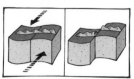

Scientists describe the seismograph's measurements with numbers. Since the 1930s, they have used a system called the Richter [RIK-ter] scale. If an earthquake measures below 3.0 on the Richter, people usually can't feel it. Earthquakes over 5.0 on the scale can cause damage, while a measurement of 7.0 is evidence of a major earthquake.

A pen attached to a seismograph draws an image that shows the magnitude of an earthquake.

What Causes Earthquakes?

How and why do all these earthquakes occur? Earth has many different layers. Its outermost layer is called the crust and is made up of huge sections called tectonic plates. Below the crust is another layer, called the mantle, which is made up of softer rock. When tectonic plates push against each other, a huge amount of force or pressure builds up.

Eventually, the force causes the plates to shift on top of the mantle in different ways: they can push toward each other, pull away from each other, or simply slide past each other. These movements are usually so small that people aren't aware of them, but when tectonic plates collide, there's no mistaking what has occurred—an earthquake!

Plate movements can cause Earth's crust to crack, causing a break called a fault. Along the Pacific Coast of the United States lies a 700-mile-long fault. The rocks below the earth's surface frequently shift or break along this fault, making the state of California vulnerable to many earthquakes.

Rocks below the earth's surface can shift along a fault.

Some Famous Earthquakes

A major earthquake jolted San Francisco on April 18, 1906. It caused a huge fire and the destruction of 28,000 buildings. Many people were killed or injured in this terrible quake. Scientists believe this earthquake may have registered as high as 8.3 on the Richter scale.

Earthquakes

Nonfiction level U

Total words: 501

Average sentence length: 15.0 words

This text begins with information about the destructive power of earthquakes and communicates the important idea that earthquakes occur across the planet every day, but the majority of them are so slight that people don't even know they are happening. The next three sections describe how to measure earthquakes, the causes of earthquakes, and some famous earthquakes. An important idea in the final section is that earthquakes are so dangerous because they cannot be clearly predicted.

Features of this text are:

❑ information presented with an introduction and four sections with headings

❑ requires inference that the tectonic plates are constantly moving

❑ requires understanding of historical information

❑ some technical vocabulary (*fault, Richter scale, seismologists, tectonic plates, tremors*)

❑ pronunciation guide in parentheses for technical words

❑ photographs with captions

❑ diagrams illustrating the shifting along a fault

❑ chart detailing famous earthquakes

❑ glossary.

▶ Benchmark Books

A Call for Change
by Sarah Wolbach

The Daily Tribune

Kids are hanging out...
...downtown, with nothing...
...where to go...
...if we...

Police...
want k...
on the...
city s...
Woul...
if we...

Obviously, I hope that our mayor and city council members will see merit in my ideas and take action to implement them.

My concern is the lack of facilities available for young people like me to stay safely occupied and productive during the hours we are not in school. It is a fact that young people in Charlottesville spend only 20% of their time in school—six hours a day, 180 days per year. What they do with the other 80% is one of the most significant questions facing our community. ■

Kids are hanging out downtown, with nothing to do and nowhere to go. Business owners don't want kids like me in their shops. They say that shoplifting is a problem and that groups of unruly kids scare off their other customers. Police officers don't want kids loitering idly on the streets or in the city square. Consider this: Would we be hanging around bothering people if we had something better to do? It's not likely.

My suggestion is to rehabilitate the old Plainview Middle School, which has been closed for years, and open a community center to offer social, recreational, and educational activities for kids. If adults want kids to spend their time productively, they should be willing to offer rich and challenging activities to help us learn, explore our talents, and develop positive relationships with peers and adults. And the center can offer opportunities for adults, too. That way, everybody wins!

And while we're on the subject, I wouldn't be surprised if plenty of those "unruly" kids wanted to serve their community right now. I would like to see the mayor set up a youth board. This group of committed teens could identify youth issues within the city. The board would then work together with the mayor and city and state officials to identify resources, develop solutions, and make improvements.

I know some people will say that this city has budget problems, and that there's not even enough money to repair the potholes in the streets. But here is my question: Can this city afford not to do this? It's true that it will cost money to pay for the services I propose. Many adults are just flat against raising taxes. To them I say this: We are your neighbors. We are part of this community that we all share. The problem I described belongs to all of us, because all of us care about the kind of city we live in. The future of your youth is in your hands. Do the right thing! Give me and other kids the programs we need to stay safe, learn, and grow into successful adults that everyone can be proud of.

2   3

A Call for Change

Fiction level V

Total words: 479

Average sentence length: 15.6 words

This fictional text presents a persuasive essay calling for a change in a community. The challenge in this text is that the genre appears to be informational (essay) even though it is fictional. At the beginning, a brief introduction sets the scene by providing the information that Rachel is the winner of an eighth-grade essay contest. It foreshadows the idea that Rachel has a forceful personality. The essay outlines a problem—that kids are hanging around downtown with nothing to do. It also makes a concrete proposal—to rehabilitate the old middle school and open a community center to provide educational and recreational opportunities for kids.

Features of this text are:

❑ persuasive essay—nonfiction format although fictional

❑ requires inference to understand Rachel's personality

❑ requires understanding of the problem and the specific proposal by Rachel to solve it

❑ parenthetical material set off by dashes in the middle of sentences

❑ many multisyllabic words, including some with five syllables

❑ requires understanding of the art of persuasion and ability to find examples in the text.

Tsunamis:
Mighty Ocean Waves
by George Capaccio

A man named Ari Afrizal survived a tsunami in 2004. Read to learn about his story and these powerful and treacherous waves.

Fountas and Pinnell Benchmark Assessment System 2

With no food or water, Ari clung to a piece of wood for five days. When he spotted an abandoned fishing raft, Ari mustered what little strength he had left and climbed on. Once on the raft, he discovered a few bottles of fresh water. Later, he spotted some coconuts drifting in the ocean, snatched them up, and, because he had no tools, cracked them open with his teeth! Miraculously, Ari was able to survive for two more weeks on nothing but coconuts and water. As each day passed, Ari began to doubt that he would survive.

He could see many ships sailing along the horizon, but none of them could see him. Finally, a ship caught sight of Ari, rescued him, and delivered him home safely. He was dehydrated but lucky to be alive. ■

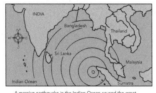

A massive earthquake in the Indian Ocean caused the great tsunami of 2004.

What Happened

Ari's amazing story began on December 26, 2004, when an earthquake off the coast of Sumatra in the Indian Ocean

produced a series of powerful waves called a tsunami. *Tsunami* is a Japanese word meaning "harbor wave." The 2004 tsunami pulsed across the ocean and slammed violently against the coastlines of more than a dozen countries, leaving hundreds of thousands of people dead and more than a million homeless.

What Are Tsunamis?

Tsunamis are incredibly powerful, and their waves become even more treacherous when they enter harbors or bays. They can travel at the speed of a jet airliner, cross the Pacific Ocean in a single day, and attain heights of over 100 feet.

What Causes Tsunamis?

Earthquakes that are just below the ocean floor cause the floor to rise and fall; when that happens, they have the potential to trigger tsunamis. Like ripples in a pond, tsunamis reverberate from the earthquake zone. The waves continually pile up behind each other; as they reach shallow water, their speed decreases, while their height increases. Their maximum height depends partly on the characteristics of the shoreline they are moving toward.

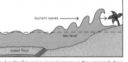

The height of tsunami waves increases as they approach shore.

2

3

Tsunamis: Mighty Ocean Waves

Nonfiction level V

Total words: 515

Average sentence length: 16.8 words

This text begins with the story of Ari Afrizal, an Indonesian man who survived for almost three weeks in the ocean during the 2004 tsunami. This dramatic tale is followed by four sections describing this specific tsunami and then defining and explaining the causes of the giant waves. The book ends with a short section explaining that the only way for people to protect themselves from tsunamis is to head for higher ground.

Features of this text are:

- ❑ presents information in four sections with headings
- ❑ begins with a real story, adding drama to the text
- ❑ varied sentence length with some more than twenty-five words
- ❑ some technical vocabulary (*tsunami, aftershock, reverberate*)
- ❑ smaller font than previous levels
- ❑ photographs with captions
- ❑ maps and drawings with labels
- ❑ chart detailing dates and deadly tsunamis
- ❑ glossary.

▶ Benchmark Books

How I Spent My Summer Vacation
by Lynea Bowdish

The writer, a girl named Kim, tells about her trip to Thailand. Read to find out what she learned and how she felt when she returned.

Fountas and Pinnell Benchmark Assessment System 2

After nearly two days of seemingly endless travel, we finally arrived at our assigned village. There we were greeted by our hosts, seventeen-year-old Daw and her older brother Aran.

Aran took Dad to the site of the school he'd been helping rebuild, while Daw showed Mom and me the temporary school. Mom would instruct the children—mostly orphans—in English. I felt absolutely useless: I couldn't teach or build. Had I traveled so far to do nothing? ■

But Daw had plans for me. "We're going to the beach, Kim," Daw said to me the next morning, and I thought, "Great—I love the beach."

"Twice a day the tide comes in and leaves what it took in December," she said, as she handed me a pair of gloves. "Our job is to clean it up." Of course. I felt like an idiot.

At the beach, Daw gave me a plastic bag and began walking along the high tide line. The last high tide had deposited its debris: chunks of metal, wood, and plastic; cups, cans, and ropes. I knew that thousands of bodies had never been recovered, and I prayed that none had washed ashore last night. It was difficult work: bending, stooping, filling the bags, and hauling them up on the beach where the tide couldn't pull them back.

In the following days, we spent the majority of our time collecting garbage. When we'd rest on the sand, gazing out to sea, I tried to imagine what it felt like to watch a looming, 33-foot wall of water crashing towards me, what it felt like to be swallowed up by the wave, and what it would be like never to see my family again.

When Daw talked, she admitted that she got weary from the backbreaking work. But she kept at it in honor of those who were lost. After that, so did I.

One morning I found a shoe. It was a child's shoe—tiny and worn. I collapsed and cried. I cried for the thousands who lost their lives in Thailand on that horrifying day. And I cried because I knew then how profoundly lucky I was to be able to help the survivors. Daw put her arms around me and held on.

I don't know how many bags of garbage we collected, but I do know that Daw and I talked and laughed as we worked and that the two weeks flew by. When we said goodbye, it was Daw's turn to cry. I took off my locket and fastened it around her neck. It was a symbol of survival. It testified to life going on, even after disaster strikes.

I touched my neck often as we made our way home and thought about the great-grandmother I barely knew. Even without her locket, we were linked in some way, heart to heart. So were Daw and I now.

I don't know if I accomplished anything meaningful, but I do know that I learned something about myself; maybe someday I'll be able to put a name to it. Meanwhile, I'm going to ask Dad if we can go back next year.

2

3

How I Spent My Summer Vacation

Fiction level W

Total words: 659

Average sentence length: 13.6 words

This story, told in first person as if in a diary entry, describes Lynea's experience volunteering in Thailand to help with disaster relief after the 2004 tsunami. Initially, Lynea doesn't want to go, but having no other option, she accompanies her parents on the trip. She wears the locket that her great-grandmother gave her—the only thing that was saved when an earthquake devastated her family's pension in Italy many years ago. This locket comes to be a symbol of survival as Lynea learns more about the human disaster and about herself.

Features of this text are:

- ❏ begins with a date as in a diary entry
- ❏ first-person narrative
- ❏ character development in that Lynea changes as she realizes the gravity of the situation
- ❏ turning point when Lynea finds the student's shoe and breaks down and cries for the thousands who lost their lives
- ❏ use of the locket as a symbol of survival
- ❏ sophisticated subject matter
- ❏ visual images of the crashing of thirty-three-foot walls of water
- ❏ many sentences with fifteen to twenty or more words
- ❏ mostly familiar vocabulary.

OBITUARY
Coretta Scott King 1927–2006
by Gabriel Kidd

This is an obituary for Coretta Scott King. Read to learn about the important things she did in her lifetime.

The Civil Rights Movement

After they married, the Kings returned to Alabama, and in 1955, the year the couple's first child was born, Dr. King gained national attention by playing a leading role in the Montgomery Bus Boycott.

King encouraged African Americans to boycott the bus company because the buses in Montgomery were segregated. The boycotters walked instead of riding the buses. It was the beginning of one of the most important periods in American history—the Civil Rights Movement.

Coretta Scott King, the widow of civil rights activist Martin Luther King, Jr., has died. She was 78.

Through the early 1960s, many different groups worked for equality for African Americans. Throughout the United States, many of these efforts were met with violence. Martin Luther King, Jr. wanted to draw national attention to civil rights and to the need for strong federal policies that would erase discrimination. In 1963, he organized a march on Washington, D.C.; thousands of people joined the march. A year later, President Johnson signed the Civil Rights Act of 1964. The following year, Congress passed the Voting Rights Act of 1965. Although the movement could not overcome all the barriers African Americans faced, it was very successful.

Dr. King was assassinated in 1968 in Memphis, Tennessee, just before a planned march in support of African-American sanitation workers. According to the Reverend Jesse Jackson, Mrs. King organized his funeral and then went to Memphis and finished the march. "She was a staunch freedom fighter," he said.

Continuing the Struggle

Left with four children to raise alone, Coretta Scott King took up her husband's efforts. She led the campaign for a national holiday in his honor and also founded the Martin Luther King, Jr., Center for Nonviolent Social Change in Atlanta.

Established in 1968 by Coretta Scott King, the King Center is the official, living memorial dedicated to carrying on the legacy of Dr. Martin Luther King, Jr. and to educating the world about his life and work.

Coretta Scott King never stopped fighting for equality for all Americans. She became an important voice in other social and political issues as well, working for women's rights and becoming involved in the struggle against apartheid in South Africa.

On her passing, Massachusetts Senator Ted Kennedy said this about Mrs. King: "I believe what Coretta Scott King would want us to do is continue this march toward progress when it comes to disability rights, women's rights, civil rights—and not retreat from it."

Obituary: Coretta Scott King 1927–2006

Nonfiction level W

Total words: 589

Average sentence length: 19.8 words

The genre of this text is a newspaper article, an obituary of Coretta Scott King. It contains information about Coretta's birth, life, and death, including her role as wife of Dr. Martin Luther King. One of the main ideas of the article is that Coretta not only supported her husband's causes but continued his work after his death. The article includes quotes about Mrs. King, including comments on her never-ending fight for equality.

Features of this text are:

❑ begins with date and summary of King's life and death

❑ inset quote from Coretta Scott King

❑ information presented in three sections with headings

❑ requires understanding of the format of an obituary

❑ requires understanding of the setting

❑ words to be understood in context (*discrimination, Civil Rights, assassinated, boycott*)

❑ varied sentence length with some sentences more than thirty words

❑ requires understanding of Coretta's continuation of the campaign for equality

❑ photo with caption

❑ timeline

❑ glossary.

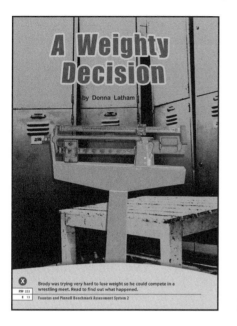

A Weighty Decision

by Donna Latham

Brody was trying very hard to lose weight so he could compete in a wrestling meet. Read to find out what happened.

Fountas and Pinnell Benchmark Assessment System 2

Brody's head was a block of cement as he tilted to tie his shoes. His heart was a bass drum, pounding an intense beat in his chest. Dizziness body-slammed him; his knees buckled, and he clumsily flailed his bulky arms to regain his balance.

"Dude, you look like an astronaut exiting the mothership for an extravehicular moonwalk," Jason Liang, Brody's best friend, wisecracked from the doorway. "I thought you wrestled in the lightweight division; you're bulked up like a heavyweight!"

"Bite your tongue," Brody said with a grunt.

"Hey, I have the parentmobile. Want to grab a pizza?" ■

Brody jammed his trembling hands into his pockets. "Thanks, but I'm heading out for a run. I need to sweat off five pounds to drop weight for the meet, so pizza's out."

"I'll run with you, but take off that crazy ski mask, dude. I have a reputation to uphold around here. And leave that nauseatingly vile yellow stuff behind, okay?" Jason grunted, as they thundered out the door. Side by side they loped—effortless movement for Jason, grueling for Brody—enjoying the easy silence forged from a lifelong friendship.

"Five pounds, huh?" asked Jason.

"If I get my weight down to 135 but don't lose any muscle mass, I should be able to demolish those guys from Madison." Smiling weakly, Brody flexed his layered arm before abruptly doubling over.

"Brody!"

"Leg cramp," Brody growled, teeth clenched against the pain. "Been getting them on and off."

"Dude, you've got to drink something. I think you might be dehydrated. Wish I hadn't told you to leave that nasty, yellow juice at home."

Brody, hobbling painfully, avoided Jason's piercing gaze.

"You're the only person I've mentioned this to. I'm thinking about taking over-the-counter diet pills. Don't give me that look; they're herbal."

"Oh, that's a brilliant strategy! You want alien substances in your body? I thought you were the big athlete, dedicated to fitness."

"Coach Wozniak expects us to make weight, but lately, it's gotten harder and harder for me. Coach says we should eat healthy foods and exercise, but if I do that I just keep putting on the pounds. I'm getting desperate!"

"So the goal is to be the reigning champion of stupidity? I thought it was to be your personal best...."

Jason stopped talking, lost in thought as he remembered his cousin Leora who was hospitalized for an eating disorder when she was 16. What a nightmare that was. "C'mon man, let's go back. I need to show you something."

At home, Brody stripped off his extra layers and downed a big glass of juice while Jason searched the Internet.

"OK, smart guy, listen to this." Jason read aloud from the screen: "Over-the-counter diet pills can be hazardous. They can trigger cardiac and renal failure, as well as cause slow muscle recovery and a host of additional dangerous side effects."

Jason turned and looked Brody straight in the eye and told him Leora's story.

"Leora got better and later became a nutritionist, so she's up on the research studies in all the medical journals. She can explain to you why diet pills aren't a healthy way to lose weight. All I know is, keep doing what you've been doing and the only opponent you'll be wrestling is the Grim Reaper—even with no diet pills."

2

3

A Weighty Decision

Fiction level X

Total words: 682

Average sentence length: 11.8 words

In this story, Brody faces a significant decision—trying with all possible means to lose weight for the wrestling tournament or following his best friend's advice to take care of his health. He makes his decision based on his best friend Jason's account of his cousin Leora's eating disorder. The two boys also find information on the Internet that leads Brody to decide to protect his health.

Features of this text are:

❑ requires reader to recognize internal conflict in a character

❑ requires inference to recognize main character's motivations

❑ requires close attention to detail to learn that the main character is only thinking of taking diet pills, not actually taking them

❑ colloquial dialogue between teen characters

❑ extensive use of figurative language (opponent as a mound of clothing; head as *block of cement; wrestling with the Grim Reaper*)

❑ some very difficult vocabulary (*leviathan, nauseatingly, concoction, nutritionist*) but no technical words

❑ many long sentences, some with more than thirty words

❑ full range of punctuation including dashes and ellipses.

▶ Benchmark Books

The Internet: Getting Connected
by George Capaccio

The Internet is a network of networks for communication. Read to learn about its history and how it works.

RW 213
R 13 Fountas and Pinnell Benchmark Assessment System 2

E-Mail

When computer users send an e-mail they are initiating a series of electronic pulses. For these digital signals to be transmitted and received, they must first be broken down into very small packets by the sender's Internet Service Provider (ISP). Each packet of data contains information about its origin and destination. A set of instructions called the Transmission Control Protocol (TCP) performs the function of creating data packets. ■

The Internet Protocol (IP) makes sure the packets are sent to the right place via the router, a network device that determines the next point to which a data packet should be forwarded. When the packets reach their destination, the TCP reassembles them into the original message.

History of the Internet

You may think that the Internet is a recent phenomenon, but according to some historians, it was developed by the U.S. Department of Defense in the 1960s as a civil defense tool during the Cold War. The prospect of a nuclear war created a perceived need for an efficient communications network that would be less vulnerable than existing systems. A network like the Internet might survive the devastation of a nuclear holocaust or similar disaster.

The Internet Today

Today's Internet consists of several different kinds of information systems, each of which was developed independently. Probably the most widely used and most influential of these multiple systems are e-mail and the World Wide Web.

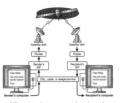

Billions of e-mail messages are exchanged every day.

For several decades, the Internet was viewed as unappealing in appearance and impractical for use by the general public; then, however, computer scientists began integrating leading technological developments like URLs (Uniform Resource Locators) and hypertext. By 1990, it was possible for the Internet to display not only words but also a whole range of multimedia. By the mid-nineties, inventions like Web browsers and search engines had turned the Web into an easy-to-use and exciting feature of the whole Internet experience. A visually uninspiring tool before the World Wide Web came into use, the Internet came alive with color, graphics, live pictures, as well as audio and video streaming. Users have "virtually" at their fingertips, virtually every kind of information they might want to seek. Public consumption has exploded, and this dynamic tool continues to evolve.

2

3

The Internet: Getting Connected

Nonfiction level X

Total words: 659

Average sentence length: 20.1 words

This text explains how the Internet works and provides information about its interesting history. For example, the Internet has been around since the 1960s when (according to some historians) it was created by the U.S. Department of Defense as a civil defense tool. Information is presented in five sections with headings. The Internet is defined and described, along with explanations as to why it has become so popular recently.

Text characteristics

- ❑ requires understanding of historical information; for example, *civil defense, Cold War*
- ❑ some information in chronological order
- ❑ requires readers to predict uses of the Internet
- ❑ long sentences, many more than thirty words
- ❑ many longer multisyllabic words
- ❑ includes technical vocabulary (*protocol, electronic pulses, digital, data packet, hypertext*)
- ❑ the word *virtually* used with two different definitions for a play on words
- ❑ pie graph with key
- ❑ diagram with labels to show how e-mail works
- ❑ drawing with legend to show hypertext
- ❑ glossary.

▶ Benchmark Books

Saying Goodbye

Fiction level Y

Total words: 711

Average sentence length: 13.6

This story, told in first-person narrative, begins with the central character talking directly to his friend Gerald, who died in an accident six months earlier. It then flashes back to the time of the accident and then forward to the present. Luis depended on Gerald, who always reassured and encouraged him. Gradually, Luis realizes that he needs to move on with his life, although he will always remember his friend.

Features of this text are:

- ❑ first-person narrative
- ❑ changes from present tense to past and back to present
- ❑ uses flashback
- ❑ turning point on page 3 with e-mail from Celine
- ❑ changes audience—from addressing Gerald to addressing the reader
- ❑ mature content
- ❑ varied sentence length with most fifteen to twenty-five words
- ❑ includes figurative language (*death slashes into our lives like a blade slashes skin*)
- ❑ many multisyllabic and/or difficult words (*prescient, philosophical, perspective*)
- ❑ some Spanish words.

▶ Benchmark Books

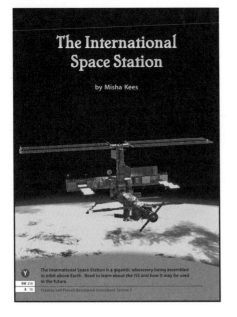

The International Space Station

by Misha Kees

The International Space Station is a gigantic laboratory being assembled in orbit above Earth. Read to learn about the ISS and how it may be used in the future.

RW 216

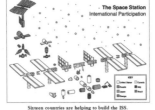

in a space station—in close quarters with others and without access to the outdoor world—for such long periods of time.

More than 100,000 scientists and technical experts from 16 countries have participated in the extensive efforts to complete the space station. More than 40 space shuttle flights will be required to transport all of the space station's components into space for assembly.

The Space Station
International Participation

Sixteen countries are helping to build the ISS.

Life Aboard the ISS

Currently, three crew members can live on the ISS at any given time. The scientists spend the majority of their time performing experiments in the space station's six science laboratories. Their research initiatives include studies of ways to create more effective medicines and lighter and more durable metals that can be used in space; additionally,

they invent and test new robots that can perform specialized functions in space.

The scientists perform many experiments focusing on the human body; for example, they are examining the long-term effects of living in a weightless environment. As a result of studying human cells in such an environment, scientists have uncovered new information about human growth; for example, that cells develop differently in space, a finding that has potential for accelerating progress in the search for solutions to combat deadly diseases such as cancer.

The space station is also used to help astronauts prepare for future space missions by providing a facility for them to learn how to live and work away from Earth. If astronauts can remain safe and healthy while in residence on the ISS, they will be able to do the same while traveling to other destinations in the solar system.

The scientists living on the space station spend the majority of their time working on experiments, but they also devote at least two hours each day to physical fitness. Exercise is a critical factor as we contemplate life in space because muscles and bones deteriorate more rapidly in the weightless environment. Of course, the scientists need to sleep and eat, too, so the ISS is equipped with sleeping bunks, a shower, a kitchen, and other comforts of home, though it's no luxury hotel. And astronauts who face prospective voyages in space must also wrestle with the prospect not only of living in close quarters with a small group of people, but also of spending long periods of time away from their homes and families and the beloved places on Earth that they must leave behind; experimenting with life on the space station will help them develop ways to cope with the ordeal.

2   3

The International Space Station

Nonfiction level Y

Total words: 662

Average sentence length: 27.8 words

This book describes the International Space Station (ISS) that is now being assembled in orbit. The information is presented in three sections with headings. First, the station is described, along with its purposes. Then, life aboard the ISS is described, including what it is like to live in space and the kinds of experiments scientists can do there. Some significant issues are presented—the problems related to living in close quarters with a small group of people and leaving families for a long period of time. The last section presents problems to be solved.

Features of this text are:

❏ informational text presented in three sections with headings

❏ many long sentences, most fifteen to twenty-five words

❏ some technical words and many difficult multisyllabic words (*gravity, environmental, adaptations, psychologically, contemplating, initiatives, prospective*)

❏ use of acronyms

❏ photograph with caption

❏ diagram with legend

❏ glossary.

▶ Benchmark Books

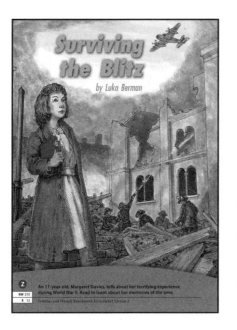

Surviving the Blitz

by Luka Berman

An 11-year-old, Margaret Davies, tells about her terrifying experience during World War II. Read to learn about her memories of the time.

Z
RW 215
R 12   Fountas and Pinnell Benchmark Assessment System 2

itself were cracking open. The dank shelter flooded each time it rained, forcing us to hide instead under the stairs in our house, like mice in the wainscoting. ∎

The cat that stalked us was fearsome, indiscriminate, deadly, and could strike at any moment, yet my parents always remained calm and comforting, somehow managing to make the most gut-deep fright tolerable, even as bombs blasted and we cowered in the dark.

When we mice emerged, shaken, from hiding, we might find the neighbors' house or the house down the street gone, the people who had lived there wailing in the middle of the road, tearing at their hair and their clothes; or we might see even worse—scenes of carnage that are burned into my brain and that I do not choose to pass on to innocent readers.

The Blitz turned Hell loose on our world, and yet, when I think back, I'm struck by how life carried on, even amidst the chaos.

Father kept up his shipbuilding business, while Mother worked part-time at a factory that made detonators for our own bombs.

My younger sisters and I continued to attend school, although air raids interrupted classes for hours. Our teachers tried valiantly to continue our lessons inside the air-raid shelter, but I can attest that concentration is impossible when the ground is groaning and shaking and Death is dropping from the sky. As time passed, fewer and fewer brave souls showed up for classes.

The Blitz brought shortages of everything, including food. Before work, Mother stood in a long queue, sometimes for hours, to buy our family's ration of meat, cheese, eggs, butter, and sugar. Fruits like bananas and

oranges disappeared from our diets altogether, while the weekly ration of "sweets" was 2 ounces—just one miniscule bar of chocolate for the entire family!

The cinema in our neighborhood was transformed into a crater by a direct hit, but my sisters and I discovered ingenious ways to amuse ourselves. I spent hours staring at the sky and soon became an expert at identifying aircraft, including my favorite, the de Haviland *Mosquito*, a light bomber too fast for the Luftwaffe to intercept. (I admit, it never crossed my mind that these planes might be bombing youngsters much like myself, but in Germany.) My sisters played in bomb sites as I hunted for shrapnel to collect as souvenirs.

We got accustomed to the war—even the bombs. Believe it or not, there were times when I didn't even think about them.

But those intervals never lasted long. Our family spent most evenings huddled around the wireless (radio, to you), hungrily devouring news about the war. Neither we nor anyone we knew then owned a television.

Thousands were left homeless, but—miraculously—our little house remained standing, and—miraculously—my family and I were physically unharmed. The only scars we carry with us from the Blitz are the deep scars of memory.

2   3

Surviving the Blitz

Fiction level Z

Total words: 639

Average sentence length: 21.6 words

This fictional text is written as a memoir. Told in first-person narrative, past tense turning to present at the end, the memories of Margaret Davies are recounted. She was only 11 years old in 1940 when the Blitz began and bombs fell for 57 days. Margaret describes the experience, using the metaphor of a cat to represent the lightning war and that of mice hiding in the wainscoting to represent the terrified Londoners. Readers will infer two important ideas: that people can get used even to this kind of experience and try to go on with their daily lives as usual; and even though Margaret and her family were not physically harmed, they will always carry the scars of terror.

Features of this text are:

- ❑ written as a memoir, although fictional
- ❑ knowledge of historical content required
- ❑ begins with a question and answer that sum up the content
- ❑ many long sentences, some forty or more words
- ❑ descriptive language
- ❑ many sophisticated words (*pulverizing, indiscriminate, tolerable, valiantly, concentration, queue, wireless*)
- ❑ figurative language (*the cat that stalked us, deep scars of memory*)
- ❑ German and French words in italics.

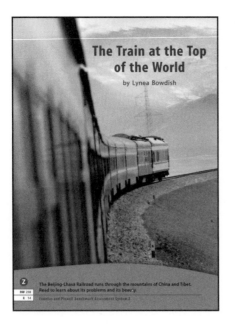

The Train at the Top of the World

by Lynea Bowdish

The Beijing-Lhasa Railroad runs through the mountains of China and Tibet. Read to learn about its problems and its beauty.

Fountas and Pinnell Benchmark Assessment System 2

The Train at the Top of the World

Nonfiction level Z

Total words: 646

Average sentence length: 23.4 words

This text provides information about the Beijing-Lhasa Railroad, the highest railroad in the world (between 13,123 and 16,640 feet above sea level). The railroad was extremely difficult to build and its life may be temporary since it is built on fragile permafrost. Passengers see unbelievable vistas from the train but at the same time must be protected by special tinted windows (to protect them from ultraviolet rays) and often must be given oxygen. The railroad opened trade between two regions that were difficult to access prior to its construction. Information is presented in three sections with headings.

Features of this text are:

- ❑ text presented in three sections with headings
- ❑ many long sentences, some more than forty words
- ❑ many difficult multisyllable words (*permafrost, riveted, ultraviolet, unprecedented, terrain, potentially*)
- ❑ map with key
- ❑ photographs with captions
- ❑ chart providing information about mountain sickness
- ❑ glossary.

▶ Appendix B: Using the F & P Calculator/Stopwatch

Using the *F & P Calculator/Stopwatch* will facilitate taking a reading record on each student. This device is easy to use in conjunction with the Recording Form, which can be printed out from the *Assessment Forms Book* or *CD-ROM*. The following are the instructions for using the calculator/stopwatch in abbreviated form. In Section 2 of this guide, you can see how to integrate this tool into the administration of the assessment conference.

1. Press **RW** and enter the number of running words (RW) in the text on the calculator/stopwatch.

2. Press **Start Time*** on the calculator as the child begins oral reading. Press **End Time** when the reading is complete.

3. Press **#Errors** and enter the number of errors on the calculator.

4. Press **#SC** and enter the number of self-corrections on the calculator.

5. Press **Time*** to get **Elapsed Minutes or Seconds**.

6. Press **WPM** to see **Words per Minute**.

7. Press **Accur.%** for **Percentage of Accuracy**.

8. Press **SC** to get the **Self-Correction Ratio**.

* Recommended Starting at Level J

▶ Appendix C: Suggested Criteria for the Use of Optional Literacy Assessments

The following are reasonable criteria for use in observing change over time in literacy competencies. The show learning progressing across areas, but development of concepts and understandings will depend on the school or district curriculum standards and the type of instruction offered students. You may adjust these criteria to fit your district decisions. Revisions or updates to this document can be found on *www.fountasandpinnell.com*.

Fountas and Pinnell Benchmark Assessment System—Grade 3

Optional Assessment	Description	Beginning of Year (Aug.–Sept.)	1st Interval Assessment (Nov.–Dec.)	2nd Interval Assessment (Feb.–Mar.)	End of Year (May–June)
HIGH FREQUENCY WORDS					
Reading High-Frequency Words—100 *Individual* Score = 100	Students read 100 high frequency words (Lists 1, 2, 3, 4, and 5. **Notice:** speed, word substitutions (similar visual features), good attempts, letter/sound relationships the reader controls	1 = 100 2 = 100 3 = <100 4 = <100	1 = 100 2 = 100 3 = <100 4 = <100	1 = 100 2 = 100 3 = <100 4 = <100	1 = 100 2 = 100 3 = <100 4 = <100
Reading High-Frequency Words—200 *Individual* Score = 200	Students read 200 high frequency words (Lists 1, 2, 3, 4, and 5. **Notice:** speed, word substitutions (similar visual features), good attempts, letter/sound relationships the reader controls	1 = 200+ 2 = 175-199 3 = 150-174 4 = <150	1 = 200 2 = 200 3 = 175-199 4 = <175	1 = 200 2 = 200 3 = <200 4 = <200	1 = 200 2 = 200 3 = <200 4 = <200
PHONICS					
Phonograms I Score = 80	Students read words with simple phonogram patterns (Lists 1, 2, 3, and 4. **Notice:** evidence of awareness of patterns, particular patterns that are not known	1 = 80 2 = 80 3 = 60-79 4 = <60	1 = 80 2 = 80 3 = <80 4 = <80	1 = 80 2 = 80 3 = <80 4 = <80	1 = 80 2 = 80 3 = <80 4 = <80
Phonograms II **List 1** *Individual* Score = 18	Students read words with phonogram patterns. **Notice:** score, speed, patterns	1 = 7+ 2 = 6 3 = 3-5 4 = <3	1 = 11+ 2 = 10 3 = 7-9 4 = <7	1 = 13+ 2 = 12 3 = 10-11 4 = <10	1 = 18 2 = 18 3 = 15-17 4 = <15

Key
Exceeds Expectations
Meets Expectations
Approaches Expectations: Needs Short-Term Intervention
Does Not Meet Expectations: Needs Intensive Intervention

Fountas and Pinnell Benchmark Assessment System— Grade 3 *continued*

Optional Assessment	Description	Beginning of Year (Aug.–Sept.)	1st Interval Assessment (Nov.–Dec.)	2nd Interval Assessment (Feb.–Mar.)	End of Year (May–June)
PHONICS, *continued*					
Phonograms II List 2 *Individual* Score = 18	Students read words with phonogram patterns. **Notice:** score, speed, patterns	1 = 7+ 2 = 6 3 = 3-5 4 = <3	1 = 11+ 2 = 10 3 = 7-9 4 = <7	1 = 15+ 2 = 14 3 = 11-13 4 = <11	1 = 17+ 2 = 16 3 = 13-15 4 = <13
Phonograms II List 3 *Individual* Score = 24	Students read words with phonogram patterns. **Notice:** score, speed, patterns	1 = 9+ 2 = 8 3 = 4-7 4 = <4	1 = 13+ 2 = 12 3 = 9-11 4 = <9	1 = 19+ 2 = 18 3 = 13-17 4 = <13	1 = 21+ 2 = 20 3 = 15-19 4 = <15
Phonograms II List 4 *Individual* Score = 24	Students read words with phonogram patterns. **Notice:** score, speed, patterns	1 = 9+ 2 = 8 3 = 3-7 4 = <3	1 = 13+ 2 = 12 3 = 7-11 4 = <7	1 = 19+ 2 = 18 3 = 9-17 4 = <9	1 = 21+ 2 = 20 3 = 15-19 4 = <15
Phonograms II List 5 *Individual* Score = 25	Students read words with phonogram patterns. **Notice:** score, speed, patterns	1 = 9+ 2 = 8 3 = 3-7 4 = <3	1 = 13+ 2 = 12 3 = 7-11 4 = <7	1 = 19+ 2 = 18 3 = 13-17 4 = <13	1 = 21+ 2 = 20 3 = 15-19 4 = <15
Phonograms II List 6 *Individual* Score = 25	Students read words with phonogram patterns. **Notice:** Score, speed, patterns	1 = 9+ 2 = 8 3 = 3-7 4 = <3	1 = 13+ 2 = 12 3 = 7-11 4 = <7	1 = 19+ 2 = 18 3 = 13-17 4 = <13	1 = 21+ 2 = 20 3 = 15-19 4 = <15
Consonant Blends *Individual* Score = 14	Students read words, marking the consonant blends, or words with two or three consonant sounds together. **Notice:** ability to use consonant blends to attempt word; number of words with consonant blends student can read; awareness of consonant blends as shown in incorrect attempts.	1 = 14 2 = 14 3 = <14 4 = <14	1 = 14 2 = 14 3 = <14 4 = <14	1 = 14 2 = 14 3 = <14 4 = <14	1 = 14 2 = 14 3 = <14 4 = <14

Key

Exceeds Expectations

Meets Expectations

Approaches Expectations: Needs Short-Term Intervention

Does Not Meet Expectations: Needs Intensive Intervention

Optional Assessment	Description	Beginning of Year (Aug.–Sept.)	1st Interval Assessment (Nov.–Dec.)	2nd Interval Assessment (Feb.–Mar.)	End of Year (May–June)
PHONICS, *continued*					
Vowel Clusters List 1 *Individual* Score = 23	Students read words with vowels that appear together and represent one sound (simple vowel clusters *ee, ea, ai, oo*). **Notice:** score, knowledge of vowel clusters shown in attempts, vowel clusters the reader controls	1 = 23 2 = 22 3 = 18-21 4 = <18	1 = 23 2 = 22 3 = 18-21 4 = <18	1 = 23 2 = 22 3 = 18-21 4 = <18	1 = 23 2 = 22 3 = 18-21 4 = <18
Vowel Clusters List 2 *Individual* Score = 20	Students read words with vowels that appear together and represent one sound (a greater variety of vowel clusters including combinations with *w*). **Notice:** score, knowledge of vowel clusters shown in attempts, vowel clusters the reader controls	1 = 19+ 2 = 18 3 = 15-17 4 = <15	1 = 20 2 = 20 3 = 17-19 4 = <17	1 = 20 2 = 20 3 = <20 4 = <20	1 = 20 2 = 20 3 = <20 4 = <20
Vowel Clusters List 3 *Individual* Score = 14	Students read words with vowels that appear together and represent one sound (vowel clusters with *r*). **Notice:** score, knowledge of vowel clusters shown in attempts, vowel clusters the reader controls	1 = 13+ 2 = 12 3 = 9-11 4 = <9	1 = 14 2 = 14 3 = 11-13 4 = <11	1 = 14 2 = 14 3 = <14 4 = <14	1 = 14 2 = 14 3 = <14 4 = <14
WORD STRUCTURE					
Suffixes I *Individual* Score = 10	Students read words with more complex suffixes. **Notice:** score, particular suffixes recognized (even in incorrect attempts), speed	1 = 10 2 = 10 3 = 6-9 4 = <6	1 = 10 2 = 10 3 = <10 4 = <10	1 = 10 2 = 10 3 = <10 4 = <10	1 = 10 2 = 10 3 = <10 4 = <10
Suffixes II *Individual* Score = 15	Students read words with more complex suffixes. **Notice:** score, particular suffixes recognized (even in incorrect attempts), speed	1 = 5+ 2 = 4 3 = 2-3 4 = <2	1 = 7+ 2 = 6 3 = 4-5 4 = <4	1 = 9+ 2 = 8 3 = 6-7 4 = <6	1 = 11+ 2 = 10 3 = 8-9 4 = <8

Key
Exceeds Expectations
Meets Expectations
Approaches Expectations: Needs Short-Term Intervention
Does Not Meet Expectations: Needs Intensive Intervention

Fountas and Pinnell Benchmark Assessment System— Grade 3 *continued*

Optional Assessment	Description	Beginning of Year (Aug.–Sept.)	1st Interval Assessment (Nov.–Dec.)	2nd Interval Assessment (Feb.–Mar.)	End of Year (May–June)
WORD STRUCTURE, *continued*					
Prefixes *Individual* Score = 12	Students read words with prefixes. **Notice:** number of words read correctly, prefixes student recognizes, speed	1 = 6+ 2 = 5 3 = 3-4 4 = <3	1 = 8 2 = 7 3 = 5-6 4 = <5	1 = 9+ 2 = 8 3 = 6-7 4 = <6	1 = 10+ 2 = 9 3 = 7-8 4 = <7
Compound Words *Individual* Score = 38	Students read compound words and identify the two words that have been put together. **Notice:** score, evidence in attempts that the reader notices parts of words	1 = 38 2 = 38 3 = <38 4 = <38	1 = 38 2 = 38 3 = <38 4 = <38	1 = 38 2 = 38 3 = <38 4 = <38	1 = 38 2 = 38 3 = <38 4 = <38
Syllables in Longer Words Score = 30	Students demonstrate that they understand the concept of syllables, can hear syllable breaks, can count the number of syllables in a word, and have a beginning understanding of where to divide a word when hyphenating. **Notice:** score, speed of identification, particular syllables that are hard	1 = 5+ 2 = 4 3 = 2-3 4 = <2	1 = 7+ 2 = 6 3 = 4-5 4 = <4	1 = 9+ 2 = 8 3 = 6-7 4 = <6	1 = 11+ 2 = 10 3 = 8-9 4 = <8
Grade 3 Word Features Test *Individual* Score = 30	Students read 30 words, which include a variety of features. **Notice:** words read correctly, evidence of understanding word features in incorrect attempts	1 = 16+ 2 = 15 3 = 11-14 4 = <11	1 = 21+ 2 = 20 3 = 15-19 4 = <15	1 = 26+ 2 = 25 3 = 20-24 4 = <20	1 = 30 2 = 30 3 = 25-29 4 = <25
VOCABULARY					
Concept Words: Time Score = 24	Students read concept words. (Alternatively, they select words from a larger group of words.) They tell how they are alike. **Notice:** score, evidence of noticing connections	1 = 21+ 2 = 20 3 = 15-19 4 = <15	1 = 24 2 = 24 3 = 20-23 4 = <20	1 = 24 2 = 24 3 = <24 4 = <24	1 = 24 2 = 24 3 = <24 4 = <24

Key
Exceeds Expectations
Meets Expectations
Approaches Expectations: Needs Short-Term Intervention
Does Not Meet Expectations: Needs Intensive Intervention

Optional Assessment	Description	Beginning of Year (Aug.–Sept.)	1st Interval Assessment (Nov.–Dec.)	2nd Interval Assessment (Feb.–Mar.)	End of Year (May–June)
VOCABULARY, *continued*					
Concept Words: Color Score = 24	Students read concept words. (Alternatively, they select words from a larger group of words.) They tell how they are alike. **Notice:** score, evidence of noticing connections	1 = 23+ 2 = 20-22 3 = 16-19 4 = <16	1 = 23+ 2 = 22 3 = 18-21 4 = <18	1 = 23+ 2 = 22 3 = 18-21 4 = <18	1 = 24 2 = 24 3 = 20-23 4 = <20
Concept Words: Weather Score = 21	Students read concept words. (Alternatively, they select words from a larger group of words.) They tell how they are alike. **Notice:** score, evidence of noticing connections	1 = 21 2 = 21 3 = 18-20 4 = <18	1 = 21 2 = 21 3 = <21 4 = <21	1 = 21 2 = 21 3 = <21 4 = <21	1 = 21 2 = 21 3 = <21 4 = <21
Concept Words: Transportation Score = 24	Students read concept words. (Alternatively, they select words from a larger group of words.) They tell how they are alike. **Notice:** score, evidence of noticing connections	1 = 24 2 = 24 3 = 18-23 4 = <18	1 = 24 2 = 24 3 = 18-23 4 = <18	1 = 24 2 = 24 3 = <24 4 = <24	1 = 24 2 = 24 3 = <24 4 = <24
Concept Words: Action Words (Verbs) Score = 12	Students read concept words. (Alternatively, they select words from a larger group of words.) They tell how they are alike. **Notice:** score, evidence of noticing connections	1 = 12 2 = 12 3 = 9-11 4 = <9	1 = 12 2 = 12 3 = <12 4 = <12	1 = 12 2 = 12 3 = <12 4 = <12	1 = 12 2 = 12 3 = <12 4 = <12
Concept Words: Describing Words (Adjectives) Score = 15	Students read concept words. (Alternatively, they select words from a larger group of words.) They tell how they are alike. **Notice:** score, evidence of noticing connections	1 = 15 2 = 15 3 = 11-14 4 = <11	1 = 15 2 = 15 3 = <15 4 = <15	1 = 15 2 = 15 3 = <15 4 = <15	1 = 15 2 = 15 3 = <15 4 = <15

Key
Exceeds Expectations
Meets Expectations
Approaches Expectations: Needs Short-Term Intervention
Does Not Meet Expectations: Needs Intensive Intervention

Optional Assessment	Description	Beginning of Year (Aug.–Sept.)	1st Interval Assessment (Nov.–Dec.)	2nd Interval Assessment (Feb.–Mar.)	End of Year (May–June)
VOCABULARY, *continued*					
Concept Words: Describing Words (Adverbs) Score = 12	Students read concept words. (Alternatively, they select words from a larger group of words.) They tell how they are alike. **Notice:** score, evidence of noticing connections	1 = 12 2 = 12 3 = 8-11 4 = <8	1 = 12 2 = 12 3 = <12 4 = <12	1 = 12 2 = 12 3 = <12 4 = <12	1 = 12 2 = 12 3 = <12 4 = <12
Concept Words: Calendar Score = 16	Students read concept words. (Alternatively, they select words from a larger group of words.) They tell how they are alike. **Notice:** score, evidence of noticing connections	1 = 16 2 = 16 3 = <16 4 = <16	1 = 16 2 = 16 3 = <16 4 = <16	1 = 16 2 = 16 3 = <16 4 = <16	1 = 16 2 = 16 3 = <16 4 = <16
Concept Words: Motion Score = 20	Students read concept words. (Alternatively, they select words from a larger group of words.) They tell how they are alike. **Notice:** score, evidence of noticing connections	1 = 20 2 = 20 3 = 15-19 4 = <15	1 = 20 2 = 20 3 = <20 4 = <20	1 = 20 2 = 20 3 = <20 4 = <20	1 = 20 2 = 20 3 = <20 4 = <20
Concept Words: Number Score = 25	Students read concept words. (Alternatively, they select words from a larger group of words.) They tell how they are alike. **Notice:** score, evidence of noticing connections	1 = 25 2 = 25 3 = 20-24 4 = <20	1 = 25 2 = 25 3 = <25 4 = <25	1 = 25 2 = 25 3 = <25 4 = <25	1 = 25 2 = 25 3 = <25 4 = <25
Concept Words: Ordinal Score = 20	Students read concept words. (Alternatively, they select words from a larger group of words.) They tell how they are alike. **Notice:** score, evidence of noticing connections	1 = 13+ 2 = 12 3 = 8-11 4 = <8	1 = 15+ 2 = 15 3 = 12-14 4 = <12	1 = 19+ 2 = 18 3 = 14-17 4 = <14	1 = 20 2 = 20 3 = 18-19 4 = <18

Key
Exceeds Expectations
Meets Expectations
Approaches Expectations: Needs Short-Term Intervention
Does Not Meet Expectations: Needs Intensive Intervention

Optional Assessment	Description	Beginning of Year (Aug.–Sept.)	1st Interval Assessment (Nov.–Dec.)	2nd Interval Assessment (Feb.–Mar.)	End of Year (May–June)
VOCABULARY, *continued*					
Synonyms I Score = 15	Students read and identify words that mean the same or almost the same thing. **Notice:** evidence of understanding the concept of synonyms; number of pairs identified; known synonym pairs	1 = 11+ 2 = 10 3 = 4-9 4 = <4	1 = 13+ 2 = 12 3 = 8-11 4 = <8	1 = 15 2 = 15 3 = 12-14 4 = <12	1 = 15 2 = 15 3 = <15 4 = <15
Synonyms II List 1 Score = 12	Students read and identify words that mean the same or almost the same thing. **Notice:** evidence of understanding of the concept of synonyms; number of pairs students can identify; known synonym pairs	1 = 3+ 2 = 2 3 = 1 4 = <1	1 = 5+ 2 = 4 3 = 2-3 4 = <2	1 = 6+ 2 = 5 3 = 3-4 4 = <3	1 = 7+ 2 = 6 3 = 4-5 4 = <4
Synonyms II List 2 Score = 12	Students read and identify words that mean the same or almost the same thing. **Notice:** evidence of understanding of the concept of synonyms; number of pairs students can identify; known synonym pairs	1 = 3+ 2 = 2 3 = 1 4 = <1	1 = 5+ 2 = 4 3 = 2-3 4 = <2	1 = 6+ 2 = 5 3 = 3-4 4 = <3	1 = 7+ 2 = 6 3 = 4-5 4 = <4
Synonyms II List 3 Score = 12	Students read and identify words that mean the same or almost the same thing. **Notice:** evidence of understanding of the concept of synonyms; number of pairs students can identify; known synonym pairs	1 = 3+ 2 = 2 3 = 1 4 = <1	1 = 5+ 2 = 4 3 = 2-3 4 = <2	1 = 6+ 2 = 5 3 = 3-4 4 = <3	1 = 7+ 2 = 6 3 = 4-5 4 = <4
Antonyms I Score = 15	Students read and identify words that mean the opposite or almost the opposite. **Notice:** evidence of understanding the concept of antonyms	1 = 15 2 = 15 3 = 11-14 4 = <11	1 = 15 2 = 15 3 = <15 4 = <15	1 = 15 2 = 15 3 = <15 4 = <15	1 = 15 2 = 15 3 = <15 4 = <15

Key	
Exceeds Expectations	
Meets Expectations	
Approaches Expectations: Needs Short-Term Intervention	
Does Not Meet Expectations: Needs Intensive Intervention	

Optional Assessment	Description	Beginning of Year (Aug.–Sept.)	1st Interval Assessment (Nov.–Dec.)	2nd Interval Assessment (Feb.–Mar.)	End of Year (May–June)
VOCABULARY, *continued*					
Antonyms II List 1 Score = 15	Students read and identify words that mean the opposite or almost the opposite. **Notice:** evidence of understanding the concept of antonyms	1 = 4+ 2 = 3 3 = 2 4 = <2	1 = 7+ 2 = 6 3 = 4-5 4 = <4	1 = 10+ 2 = 9 3 = 7-8 4 = <7	1 = 13+ 2 = 12 3 = 9-11 4 = <9
Antonyms II List 2 Score = 15	Students read and identify words that mean the opposite or almost the opposite. **Notice:** evidence of understanding the concept of antonyms	1 = 4+ 2 = 3 3 = 2 4 = <2	1 = 7+ 2 = 6 3 = 3-5 4 = <3	1 = 10+ 2 = 9 3 = 6-8 4 = <6	1 = 13+ 2 = 12 3 = 9-11 4 = <9
Vocabulary in Context: Levels M, N, O, P Score = 0–15 on rubric	Students use context to correctly identify the meaning of 5 words selected from a benchmark book at their instructional level or independent level. **Notice:** number of words known or almost known; ability to use context; ability to articulate meaning, score, evidence of thinking Rubric: 1) Did not respond or said "I don't know." 2) Made a response that is in some way related to the meaning of the word (any definition). 3) Responded with a definition that is approximately the meaning of the word (same definition as used in the text). 4) Responded with a full definition of the word (precise definition used in the text).	Level M 1 = 12-15 2 = 9-11 3 = 4-8 4 = <4	Level N 1 = 12-15 2 = 9-11 3 = 4-8 4 = <4	Level O 1 = 12-15 2 = 9-11 3 = 4-8 4 = <4	Level P 1 = 12-15 2 = 9-11 3 = 4-8 4 = <4

Key
Exceeds Expectations
Meets Expectations
Approaches Expectations: Needs Short-Term Intervention
Does Not Meet Expectations: Needs Intensive Intervention

Optional Assessment	Description	Beginning of Year (Aug.–Sept.)	1st Interval Assessment (Nov.–Dec.)	2nd Interval Assessment (Feb.–Mar.)	End of Year (May–June)
HIGH-FREQUENCY WORDS					
Reading High-Frequency Words *Individual* Score = 200	Students read 200 high-frequency words (Lists 1, 2, 3, 4, and 5; page 244 in B2 forms book). **Notice:** speed, word substitutions (similar visual features), good attempts, letter/sound relationships the reader controls	1 = 200 2 = 200 3 = 175-199 4 = <175	1 = 200 2 = 200 3 = <200 4 = <200	1 = 200 2 = 200 3 = <200 4 = <200	1 = 200 2 = 200 3 = <200 4 = <200
PHONICS					
Phonograms II List 1 *Individual* Score = 18	Students read words with phonogram patterns. **Notice:** score, speed, patterns	1 = 18 2 = 18 3 = 15-17 4 = <15	1 = 18 2 = 18 3 = <18 4 = <18	1 = 18 2 = 18 3 = <18 4 = <18	1 = 18 2 = 18 3 = <18 4 = <18
Phonograms II List 2 *Individual* Score = 18	Students read words with phonogram patterns. **Notice:** score, speed, patterns	1 = 17+ 2 = 16 3 = 13-15 4 = <15	1 = 18 2 = 18 3 = 16-17 4 = <16	1 = 18 2 = 18 3 = <18 4 = <18	1 = 18 2 = 18 3 = <18 4 = <18
Phonograms II List 3 *Individual* Score = 24	Students read words with phonogram patterns. **Notice:** score, speed, patterns	1 = 21+ 2 = 20 3 = 15-19 4 = <15	1 = 24 2 = 24 3 = 20-24 4 = <20	1 = 24 2 = 24 3 = <24 4 = <24	1 = 24 2 = 24 3 = <24 4 = <24
Phonograms II List 4 *Individual* Score = 24	Students read words with phonogram patterns. **Notice:** score, speed, patterns	1 = 21+ 2 = 20 3 = 15-19 4 = <15	1 = 22+ 2 = 22 3 = 19-21 4 = <19	1 = 22+ 2 = 22 3 = 19-21 4 = <19	1 = 22+ 2 = 24 3 = 20-23 4 = <20

Key
Exceeds Expectations
Meets Expectations
Approaches Expectations: Needs Short-Term Intervention
Does Not Meet Expectations: Needs Intensive Intervention

Optional Assessment	Description	Beginning of Year (Aug.–Sept.)	1st Interval Assessment (Nov.–Dec.)	2nd Interval Assessment (Feb.–Mar.)	End of Year (May–June)
PHONICS, *continued*					
Phonograms II List 5 *Individual* Score = 25	Students read words with phonogram patterns. **Notice:** score, speed, patterns	1 = 21+ 2 = 20 3 = 15-19 4 = <15	1 = 23+ 2 = 22 3 = 18-21 4 = <18	1 = 23+ 2 = 22 3 = 20-21 4 = <20	1 = 25 2 = 25 3 = 20-24 4 = <20
Phonograms II List 6 *Individual* Score = 25	Students read words with phonogram patterns. **Notice:** score, speed, patterns	1 = 21+ 2 = 20 3 = 15-19 4 = <15	1 = 23+ 2 = 22 3 = 18-21 4 = <18	1 = 23+ 2 = 22 3 = 20-21 4 = <20	1 = 25 2 = 25 3 = 20-24 4 = <20
Vowel Clusters List 1 *Individual* Score = 23	Students read words with vowels that appear together and represent one sound (simple vowel clusters (*ee, ea, ai, oo*). **Notice:** score, knowledge of vowel clusters shown in attempts, vowel clusters the reader controls	1 = 23 2 = 23 3 = 19-22 4 = <19	1 = 23 2 = 23 3 = <23 4 = <23	1 = 23 2 = 23 3 = <23 4 = <23	1 = 23 2 = 23 3 = <23 4 = <23
Vowel Clusters List 2 *Individual* Score = 20	Students read words with vowels that appear together and represent one sound (a greater variety of vowel clusters including combinations with *w*). **Notice:** score, knowledge of vowel clusters shown in attempts, vowel clusters the reader controls	1 = 20 2 = 20 3 = <20 4 = <20	1 = 20 2 = 20 3 = <20 4 = <20	1 = 20 2 = 20 3 = <20 4 = <20	1 = 20 2 = 20 3 = <20 4 = <20
Vowel Clusters List 3 *Individual* Score = 14	Students read words with vowels that appear together and represent one sound (vowel clusters with *r*). **Notice:** score, knowledge of vowel clusters shown in attempts, vowel clusters the reader controls	1 = 14 2 = 14 3 = <14 4 = <14	1 = 14 2 = 14 3 = <14 4 = <14	1 = 14 2 = 14 3 = <14 4 = <14	1 = 14 2 = 14 3 = <14 4 = <14

Key
Exceeds Expectations
Meets Expectations
Approaches Expectations: Needs Short-Term Intervention
Does Not Meet Expectations: Needs Intensive Intervention

Optional Assessment	Description	Beginning of Year (Aug.–Sept.)	1st Interval Assessment (Nov.–Dec.)	2nd Interval Assessment (Feb.–Mar.)	End of Year (May–June)
WORD STRUCTURE					
Suffixes II *Individual* Score = 15	Students read words with more complex suffixes. **Notice:** score, particular suffixes recognized (even in incorrect attempts), speed	1 = 11+ 2 = 10 3 = 8-9 4 = <8	1 = 13+ 2 = 12 3 = 9-11 4 = <9	1 = 15 2 = 15 3 = 13-14 4 = <14	1 = 15 2 = 15 3 = <15 4 = <15
Prefixes *Individual* Score = 12	Students read words with prefixes. **Notice:** number of words read correctly, prefixes student recognizes, speed	1 = 10+ 2 = 9 3 = 7-8 4 = <7	1 = 11+ 2 = 10 3 = 8-9 4 = <8	1 = 12 2 = 11 3 = 9-10 4 = <9	1 = 12 2 = 12 3 = 11 4 = <11
Syllables in Longer Words *Individual* Score = 30	Students demonstrate that they understand the concept of syllables, can hear syllable breaks, can count the number of syllables in a word, and have a beginning understanding of where to divide a word when hyphenating. **Notice:** score, speed of identification, particular syllables that are hard	1 = 11+ 2 = 10 3 = 8-9 4 = <8	1 = 15+ 2 = 14 3 = 11-13 4 = <11	1 = 21+ 2 = 20 3 = 17-19 4 = <17	1 = 23+ 2 = 22 3 = 18-21 4 = <18
Grade 4 Word Features Test *Individual* Score = 30	Students read 30 words, which include a variety of features. **Notice:** words read correctly, evidence of understanding word features in incorrect attempts	1 = 16+ 2 = 15 3 = 11-14 4 = <11	1 = 21+ 2 = 20 3 = 15-19 4 = <15	1 = 26+ 2 = 25 3 = 20-24 4 = <20	1 = 30 2 = 30 3 = 25-29 4 = <25
VOCABULARY					
Synonyms II List 1 *Individual* Score: 12	Students read and identify words that mean the same or almost the same thing. **Notice:** evidence of understanding of the concept of synonyms; number of pairs students can identify; known synonym pairs	1 = 12 2 = 12 3 = 9-11 4 = <9	1 = 12 2 = 12 3 = <12 4 = <12	1 = 12 2 = 12 3 = <12 4 = <12	1 = 12 2 = 12 3 = <12 4 = <12

Key
Exceeds Expectations
Meets Expectations
Approaches Expectations: Needs Short-Term Intervention
Does Not Meet Expectations: Needs Intensive Intervention

Optional Assessment	Description	Beginning of Year (Aug.–Sept.)	1st Interval Assessment (Nov.–Dec.)	2nd Interval Assessment (Feb.–Mar.)	End of Year (May–June)
VOCABULARY, *continued*					
Synonyms II List 2 Score = 12	Students read and identify words that mean the same or almost the same thing in List 2. **Notice:** evidence of understanding of the concept of synonyms; number of pairs students can identify; known synonym pairs	1 = 12 2 = 12 3 = 9-11 4 = <9	1 = 12 2 = 12 3 = <12 4 = <12	1 = 12 2 = 12 3 = <12 4 = <12	1 = 12 2 = 12 3 = <12 4 = <12
Synonyms II List 3 Score = 12	Students read and identify words that mean the same or almost the same thing in List 3. **Notice:** evidence of understanding of the concept of synonyms; number of pairs students can identify; known synonym pairs	1 = 12 2 = 12 3 = 9-11 4 = <9	1 = 12 2 = 12 3 = <12 4 = <12	1 = 12 2 = 12 3 = <12 4 = <12	1 = 12 2 = 12 3 = <12 4 = <12
Antonyms II List 1 Score = 15	Students read and identify words that mean the opposite or almost the opposite. **Notice:** score, evidence of understanding of the concept	1 = 15 2 = 15 3 = <15 4 = <15	1 = 15 2 = 15 3 = <15 4 = <15	1 = 15 2 = 15 3 = <15 4 = <15	1 = 15 2 = 15 3 = <15 4 = <15
Antonyms II List 2 Score = 15	Students read and identify words that mean the opposite or almost the opposite. **Notice:** score, evidence of understanding of the concept	1 = 13+ 2 = 12 3 = 9-11 4 = <9	1 = 15 2 = 15 3 = <15 4 = <15	1 = 15 2 = 15 3 = <15 4 = <15	1 = 15 2 = 15 3 = <15 4 = <15
Homophones II List 1 Score = 20	Students read a sentence and write the correct homophone in the blank space. They choose from 2 or 3 words. **Notice:** score, ease, known homophones, difficult homophones	1 = 11+ 2 = 10 3 = 7-9 4 = <7	1 = 13+ 2 = 12 3 = 9-11 4 = <9	1 = 15+ 2 = 14 3 = 11-13 4 = <11	1 = 17+ 2 = 16 3 = 13-15 4 = <13

Key
Exceeds Expectations
Meets Expectations
Approaches Expectations: Needs Short-Term Intervention
Does Not Meet Expectations: Needs Intensive Intervention

Optional Assessment	Description	Beginning of Year (Aug.–Sept.)	1st Interval Assessment (Nov.–Dec.)	2nd Interval Assessment (Feb.–Mar.)	End of Year (May–June)
VOCABULARY, *continued*					
Homophones II List 2 Score = 20	Students read a sentence and write the correct homophone in the blank space. They choose from 2 or 3 words. **Notice:** score, ease, known homophones, difficult homophones	1 = 11+ 2 = 10 3 = 7-9 4 = <7	1 = 13+ 2 = 12 3 = 9-11 4 = <9	1 = 15+ 2 = 14 3 = 11-13 4 = <11	1 = 17+ 2 = 16 3 = 13-15 4 = <13
Homophones II List 3 Score = 20	Students read a sentence and write the correct homophone in the blank space. They choose from 2 or 3 words. **Notice:** score, ease, known homophones, difficult homophones	1 = 9+ 2 = 8 3 = 5-7 4 = <5	1 = 11+ 2 = 10 3 = 7-9 4 = <7	1 = 13+ 2 = 12 3 = 9-11 4 = <9	1 = 15+ 2 = 14 3 = 11-13 4 = <11
Homographs Score = 12	Students read aloud sentence pairs that have homographs **Notice:** ability to pronounce words accurately to reflect meaning; speed, score; ability to read specific words	1 = 5+ 2 = 4 3 = 2-3 4 = <2	1 = 7+ 2 = 6 3 = 4-5 4 = <4	1 = 9+ 2 = 8 3 = 6-7 4 = <6	1 = 11+ 2 = 10 3 = 8-9 4 = <8
Vocabulary in Context Levels P, Q, R, S Score = 0–12 on rubric	Students use context to correctly identify the meaning of 5 words selected from a benchmark book at their instructional level or independent level. **Notice:** number of words known or almost known; ability to use context; ability to articulate meaning, score, evidence of thinking	Level P 1 = 12-15 2 = 9-11 3 = 4-8 4 = <4	Level Q 1 = 12-15 2 = 9-11 3 = 4-8 4 = <4	Level R 1 = 12-15 2 = 9-11 3 = 4-8 4 = <4	Level S 1 = 12-15 2 = 9-11 3 = 4-8 4 = <4

Rubric:

  0) Did not respond or said "I don't know.

  1) Made a response that is in some way related to the meaning of the word (any definition).

  2) Responded with a definition that is approximately the meaning of the word (same definition as used in the text).

  3) Responded with a full definition of the word (precise definition used in the text).

Key

Exceeds Expectations

Meets Expectations

Approaches Expectations: Needs Short-Term Intervention

Does Not Meet Expectations: Needs Intensive Intervention

Optional Assessment	Description	Beginning of Year (Aug.–Sept.)	1st Interval Assessment (Nov.–Dec.)	2nd Interval Assessment (Feb.–Mar.)	End of Year (May–June)
WORD STRUCTURE					
Syllables in Longer Words Score = 30	Students demonstrate that they understand the concept of syllables, can hear syllable breaks, can count the number of syllables in a word, and have a beginning understanding of where to divide a word when hyphenating. **Notice:** score, speed of identification, particular syllables that are hard	1 = 23+ 2 = 22 3 = 18-21 4 = <18	1 = 26+ 2 = 25 3 = 21-24 4 = <21	1 = 29+ 2 = 28 3 = 25-27 4 = <25	1 = 30 2 = 30 3 = 27-29 4 = <27
Grade 5 Word Features Test *Individual* Score = 30	Students read 30 words, which include a variety of features. **Notice:** words read correctly, evidence of understanding word features in incorrect attempts	1 = 16+ 2 = 15 3 = 11-14 4 = <11	1 = 21+ 2 = 20 3 = 15-19 4 = <15	1 = 26+ 2 = 25 3 = 20-24 4 = <20	1 = 30 2 = 30 3 = 25-29 4 = <25
VOCABULARY					
Homophones II List 1 Score = 20	Students read a sentence and write the correct homophone in the blank space. They choose from 2 or 3 words. **Notice:** score, ease, known homophones, difficult homophones	1 = 17+ 2 = 16 3 = 13-15 4 = <13	1 = 19+ 2 = 18 3 = 15-17 4 = <15	1 = 20 2 = 20 3 = 17-19 4 = <17	1 = 20 2 = 20 3 = <20 4 = <20
Homophones II List 2 Score = 20	Students read a sentence and write the correct homophone in the blank space. They choose from 2 or 3 words. **Notice:** score, ease, known homophones, difficult homophones	1 = 17+ 2 = 16 3 = 13-15 4 = <13	1 = 19+ 2 = 18 3 = 15-17 4 = <15	1 = 20 2 = 20 3 = 17-19 4 = <17	1 = 20 2 = 20 3 = <20 4 = <20
Homophones II List 3 Score = 20	Students read a sentence and write the correct homophone in the blank space. They choose from 2 or 3 words. **Notice:** score, ease, known homophones, difficult homophones	1 = 17+ 2 = 14-16 3 = 9-13 4 = <9	1 = 19+ 2 = 16-18 3 = 11-15 4 = <11	1 = 20 2 = 18-19 3 = 15-17 4 = <15	1 = 20 2 = 20 3 = <17-19 4 = <17

Key
Exceeds Expectations
Meets Expectations
Approaches Expectations: Needs Short-Term Intervention
Does Not Meet Expectations: Needs Intensive Intervention

Optional Assessment	Description	Beginning of Year (Aug.–Sept.)	1st Interval Assessment (Nov.–Dec.)	2nd Interval Assessment (Feb.–Mar.)	End of Year (May–June)
VOCABULARY, *continued*					
Homographs Score = 12	Students read aloud sentence pairs that have homographs. **Notice:** ability to pronounce words accurately to reflect meaning; speed, score; ability to read specific words	1 = 11+ 2 = 10 3 = 7-9 4 = <7	1 = 12 2 = 12 3 = 9-11 4 = <9	1 = 12 2 = 12 3 = <12 4 = <12	1 = 12 2 = 12 3 = <12 4 = <12
Vocabulary in Context **Levels S, T, U, V** Score = 0–12 on rubric	Students use context to correctly identify the meaning of 5 words selected from a benchmark book at their instructional level or independent level. **Notice:** number of words known or almost known; ability to use context; ability to articulate meaning, score, evidence of thinking Rubric: 0) Did not respond or said "I don't know. 1) Made a response that is in some way related to the meaning of the word (any definition). 2) Responded with a definition that is approximately the meaning of the word (same definition as used in the text). 3) Responded with a full definition of the word (precise definition used in the text).	Level S 1 = 12-15 2 = 9-11 3 = 4-8 4 = <4	Level T 1 = 12-15 2 = 9-11 3 = 4-8 4 = <4	Level U 1 = 12-15 2 = 9-11 3 = 4-8 4 = <4	Level V 1 = 12-15 2 = 9-11 3 = 4-8 4 = <4

Key
Exceeds Expectations
Meets Expectations
Approaches Expectations: Needs Short-Term Intervention
Does Not Meet Expectations: Needs Intensive Intervention

Optional Assessment	Description	Beginning of Year (Aug.–Sept.)	1st Interval Assessment (Nov.–Dec.)	2nd Interval Assessment (Feb.–Mar.)	End of Year (May–June)
WORD STRUCTURE					
Syllables in Longer Words Score = 30	Students demonstrate that they understand the concept of syllables, can hear syllable breaks, can count the number of syllables in a word, and have a beginning understanding of where to divide a word when hyphenating. **Notice:** score, speed of identification, particular syllables that are hard	1 = 30 2 = 30 3 = 27-29 4 = <27	1 = 30 2 = 30 3 = <30 4 = <30	1 = 30 2 = 30 3 = <30 4 = <30	1 = 30 2 = 30 3 = <30 4 = <30
Grade 6 Word Features Test *Individual* Score = 30	Students read 30 words, which include a variety of features. **Notice:** words read correctly, evidence of understanding word features in incorrect attempts	1 = 16+ 2 = 15 3 = 11-14 4 = <11	1 = 21+ 2 = 20 3 = 15-19 4 = <15	1 = 26+ 2 = 25 3 = 20-24 4 = <20	1 = 30 2 = 30 3 = 25-29 4 = <25
VOCABULARY					
Homophones II List 1 Score = 20	Students read a sentence and write the correct homophone in the blank space. They choose from 2 or 3 words. **Notice:** score, ease, known homophones, difficult homophones	1 = 20 2 = 20 3 = 17-19 4 = <17	1 = 20 2 = 20 3 = <20 4 = <20	1 = 20 2 = 20 3 = <20 4 = <20	1 = 20 2 = 20 3 = <20 4 = <20
Homophones II List 2 Score = 20	Students read a sentence and write the correct homophone in the blank space. They choose from 2 or 3 words. **Notice:** score, ease, known homophones, difficult homophones	1 = 20 2 = 20 3 = 17-19 4 = <17	1 = 20 2 = 20 3 = <20 4 = <20	1 = 20 2 = 20 3 = <20 4 = <20	1 = 20 2 = 20 3 = <20 4 = <20
Homophones II List 3 Score = 20	Students read a sentence and write the correct homophone in the blank space. They choose from 2 or 3 words. **Notice:** score, ease, known homophones, difficult homophones	1 = 20 2 = 20 3 = 17-19 4 = <17	1 = 20 2 = 20 3 = <20 4 = <20	1 = 20 2 = 20 3 = <20 4 = <20	1 = 20 2 = 20 3 = <20 4 = <20

Key
Exceeds Expectations
Meets Expectations
Approaches Expectations: Needs Short-Term Intervention
Does Not Meet Expectations: Needs Intensive Intervention

Optional Assessment	Description	Beginning of Year (Aug.–Sept.)	1st Interval Assessment (Nov.–Dec.)	2nd Interval Assessment (Feb.–Mar.)	End of Year (May–June)
VOCABULARY, *continued*					
Homographs	Students read aloud sentence pairs that have homographs. **Notice:** ability to pronounce words accurately to reflect meaning; speed, score; ability to read specific words	1 = 20 2 = 20 3 = 17-19 4 = <17	1 = 20 2 = 20 3 = <20 4 = <20	1 = 20 2 = 20 3 = <20 4 = <20	1 = 20 2 = 20 3 = <20 4 = <20
Greek and Latin Word Roots I Score = 6	Students correctly identify the meanings of Greek and Latin roots by looking at a list of words that include each root. **Notice:** ability to read and understand words; ability to identify what each list has in common; known roots and almost known roots; evidence of understanding of the concept of historical roots of words	1 = 2+ 2 = 2 3 = 1 4 = <1	1 = 3+ 2 = 3 3 = 2 4 = <2	1 = 4+ 2 = 4 3 = 3 4 = <3	1 = 5+ 2 = 5 3 = 4 4 = <4
Vocabulary in Context **Levels V, W, X, Y** Score = 0–12 on rubric	Students use context to correctly identify the meaning of 5 words selected from a benchmark book at their instructional level or independent level. **Notice:** number of words known or almost known; ability to use context; ability to articulate meaning, score, evidence of thinking Rubric: 0) Did not respond or said "I don't know. 1) Made a response that is in some way related to the meaning of the word (any definition). 2) Responded with a definition that is approximately the meaning of the word (same definition as used in the text). 3) Responded with a full definition of the word (precise definition used in the text).	Level V 1 = 12-15 2 = 9-11 3 = 4-8 4 = <4	Level W 1 = 12-15 2 = 9-11 3 = 4-8 4 = <4	Level X 1 = 12-15 2 = 9-11 3 = 4-8 4 = <4	Level Y 1 = 12-15 2 = 9-11 3 = 4-8 4 = <4

Key

Exceeds Expectations
Meets Expectations
Approaches Expectations: Needs Short-Term Intervention
Does Not Meet Expectations: Needs Intensive Intervention

Optional Assessment	Description	Beginning of Year (Aug.–Sept.)	1st Interval Assessment (Nov.–Dec.)	2nd Interval Assessment (Feb.–Mar.)	End of Year (May–June)
WORD STRUCTURE					
Grade 7/8 Word Features Test *Individual* Score = 30	Students read 30 words, which include a variety of features. **Notice:** words read correctly, evidence of understanding word features in incorrect attempts	1 = 16+ 2 = 15 3 = 11-14 4 = <11	1 = 21+ 2 = 20 3 = 15-19 4 = <15	1 = 26+ 2 = 25 3 = 20-24 4 = <20	1 = 30 2 = 30 3 = 25-29 4 = <25
VOCABULARY					
Greek and Latin Word Roots I Score = 6	Students correctly identify the meanings of Greek and Latin roots by looking at a list of words that include each root. **Notice:** ability to read and understand words; ability to identify what each list has in common; known roots and almost known roots; evidence of understanding of the concept of historical roots of words	1 = 5+ 2 = 4 3 = 2-3 4 = <2	1 = 6 2 = 6 3 = <6 4 = <6	1 = 6 2 = 6 3 = <6 4 = <6	1 = 6 2 = 6 3 = <6 4 = <6
Greek and Latin Word Roots II Score = 6	Students correctly identify the meanings of Greek and Latin roots by looking at a list of words that include each root. **Notice:** ability to read and understand words; ability to identify what each list has in common; known roots and almost known roots; evidence of understanding of the concept of historical roots of words	1 = 5+ 2 = 4 3 = 2-3 4 = <2	1 = 5+ 2 = 4 3 = 2-3 4 = <3	1 = 6 2 = 6 3 = 4-5 4 = <4	1 = 6 2 = 6 3 = 5 4 = <5

Key
Exceeds Expectations
Meets Expectations
Approaches Expectations: Needs Short-Term Intervention
Does Not Meet Expectations: Needs Intensive Intervention

Optional Assessment	Description	Beginning of Year (Aug.–Sept.)	1st Interval Assessment (Nov.–Dec.)	2nd Interval Assessment (Feb.–Mar.)	End of Year (May–June)
VOCABULARY, *continued*					
Analogies I Score = 8	Students identify the relationship between two words and choose another pair of words the exhibits the same relationship. **Notice:** evidence of understanding analogy; words the student understands and almost understands; whether a student can identify relationships between words	1 = 5+ 2 = 4 3 = 2-3 4 = <2	1 = 6+ 2 = 5 3 = 3-4 4 = <3	1 = 7+ 2 = 6 3 = 4-5 4 = <4	1 = 8 2 = 7 3 = 5-6 4 = <5
Analogies II Score = 8	Students identify the relationship between two words and choose another pair of words the exhibits the same relationship. **Notice:** evidence of understanding analogy; words the student understands and almost understands; whether a student can identify relationships between words	1 = 5+ 2 = 4 3 = 2-3 4 = <2	1 = 6+ 2 = 5 3 = 3-4 4 = <3	1 = 7+ 2 = 6 3 = 4-5 4 = <4	1 = 8 2 = 7 3 = 5-6 4 = <5

Vocabulary in Context Levels Y, Z
Score = 0–12 on rubric
	Students use context to correctly identify the meaning of 5 words selected from a benchmark book at their instructional level or independent level.
	
	Notice: number of words known or almost known; ability to use context; ability to articulate meaning, score, evidence of thinking
	
	Rubric:
	  0) Did not respond or said "I don't know.
	  1) Made a response that is in some way related to the meaning of the word (any definition).
	  2) Responded with a definition that is approximately the meaning of the word (same definition as used in the text).
	  3) Responded with a full definition of the word (precise definition used in the text).
		Level Y
		1 = 12-15
		2 = 9-11
		3 = 4-8
		4 = <4
			Level Y
			1 = 12-15
			2 = 9-11
			3 = 4-8
			4 = <4
				Level Z
				1 = 12-15
				2 = 9-11
				3 = 4-8
				4 = <4
					Level Z
					1 = 12-15
					2 = 9-11
					3 = 4-8
					4 = <4

Key
Exceeds Expectations
Meets Expectations
Approaches Expectations: Needs Short-Term Intervention
Does Not Meet Expectations: Needs Intensive Intervention

Fountas and Pinnell Benchmark Assessment System—Grade 8

Optional Assessment	Description	Beginning of Year (Aug.–Sept.)	1st Interval Assessment (Nov.–Dec.)	2nd Interval Assessment (Feb.–Mar.)	End of Year (May–June)
WORD STRUCTURE					
Grade 7/8 Word Features Test *Individual* Score = 30	Students read 30 words, which include a variety of features. **Notice:** words read correctly, evidence of understanding word features in incorrect attempts	1 = 30 2 = 30 3 = 27-29 4 = <27	1 = 30 2 = 30 3 = <30 4 = <30	1 = 30 2 = 30 3 = <30 4 = <30	1 = 30 2 = 30 3 = <30 4 = <30
VOCABULARY					
Greek and Latin Word Roots I Score = 6	Students correctly identify the meanings of Greek and Latin roots by looking at a list of words that include each root. **Notice:** ability to read and understand words; ability to identify what each list has in common; known roots and almost known roots; evidence of understanding of the concept of historical roots of words	1 = 6 2 = 6 3 = <6 4 = <6	1 = 6 2 = 6 3 = <6 4 = <6	1 = 6 2 = 6 3 = <6 4 = <6	1 = 6 2 = 6 3 = <6 4 = <6
Greek and Latin Word Roots II Score = 6	Students correctly identify the meanings of Greek and Latin roots by looking at a list of words that include each root. **Notice:** ability to read and understand words; ability to identify what each list has in common; known roots and almost known roots; evidence of understanding of the concept of historical roots of words	1 = 6 2 = 6 3 = <6 4 = <6	1 = 6 2 = 6 3 = <6 4 = <6	1 = 6 2 = 6 3 = <6 4 = <6	1 = 6 2 = 6 3 = <6 4 = <6

Key
Exceeds Expectations
Meets Expectations
Approaches Expectations: Needs Short-Term Intervention
Does Not Meet Expectations: Needs Intensive Intervention

Optional Assessment	Description	Beginning of Year (Aug.–Sept.)	1st Interval Assessment (Nov.–Dec.)	2nd Interval Assessment (Feb.–Mar.)	End of Year (May–June)
VOCABULARY, *continued*					
Analogies I Score = 8	Students identify the relationship between two words and choose another pair of words the exhibits the same relationship. **Notice:** evidence of understanding analogy; words the student understands and almost understands; whether a student can identify relationships between words	1 = 8 2 = 7 3 = 5-6 4 = <5	1 = 8 2 = 8 3 = 6-7 4 = <6	1 = 8 2 = 8 3 = <8 4 = <8	1 = 8 2 = 8 3 = <8 4 = <8
Analogies II Score = 8	Students identify the relationship between two words and choose another pair of words the exhibits the same relationship. **Notice:** evidence of understanding analogy; words the student understands and almost understands; whether a student can identify relationships between words	1 = 8 2 = 7 3 = 5-6 4 = <5	1 = 8 2 = 8 3 = 6-7 4 = <6	1 = 8 2 = 8 3 = <8 4 = <8	1 = 8 2 = 8 3 = <8 4 = <8
Vocabulary in Context Level Z Score = 0–12 on rubric	Students use context to correctly identify the meaning of 5 words selected from a benchmark book at their instructional level or independent level. **Notice:** number of words known or almost known; ability to use context; ability to articulate meaning, score, evidence of thinking	Level Z 1 = 11+ 2 = 10 3 = 8-9 4 = <8	Level Z 1 = 11+ 2 = 11 3 = 9-10 4 = <9	Level Z 1 = 12 2 = 12 3 = 10-11 4 = <10	Level Z 1 = 12 2 = 12 3 = <12 4 = <12

Rubric:

0) Did not respond or said "I don't know.

1) Made a response that is in some way related to the meaning of the word (any definition).

2) Responded with a definition that is approximately the meaning of the word (same definition as used in the text).

3) Responded with a full definition of the word (precise definition used in the text).

Key
Exceeds Expectations
Meets Expectations
Approaches Expectations: Needs Short-Term Intervention
Does Not Meet Expectations: Needs Intensive Intervention

▶ GLOSSARY

Accuracy (as in oral reading) or **accuracy rate** The percentage of words the student reads aloud correctly

Analyzing a reading record
Looking at errors, self-corrections, and sources of information to plan instruction

Annual Record of Reading Progress
A graph showing a student's progress through reading levels across one grade or year; located in *Assessment Forms Book and CD-ROM*

Appeal (in benchmark reading assessment)
A reader's verbal or nonverbal request for help

Assessment at-a-Glance
A chart containing a brief summary of the steps in administering the Benchmark Assessment (see inside front cover or *Assessment Forms Book* and *CD-ROM*)

Assessment conference
A one-on-one teacher-student Benchmark Assessment session

Assessment Summary Form
The form that combines the results of multiple benchmark book readings from the Recording Forms and guides identification of Benchmark independent, instructional, and recommended placement levels; located in *Assessment Forms Book* and *CD-ROM*

Basal reading program
A multigrade series, usually of textbook anthologies, with an established scope and sequence of skills

Benchmark book
The leveled text a student reads during Benchmark Assessment

Bi-annual Assessment Summary
A form that compiles Assessment Summary Form results from assessment conferences conducted two times during a school year; located in the *Assessment Forms Book* and *CD-ROM*

Class Record
A chart containing a class list on which to record students' independent and/or instructional levels in order to see a group's reading levels in relation to each other; located in the *Forms Book* and *CD-ROM*

Code (a reading record)
Using a copy of the text from the benchmark book, you record a student's oral reading errors, self-corrections, and other behaviors

Coding and Scoring Errors at-a-Glance
A chart containing a brief summary of how to code and score oral reading errors (see inside back cover and *Assessment Forms Book* and *CD-ROM*)

Comprehension (as in reading)
The process of constructing meaning while reading a text

Comprehension conversation
Part Two of the Recording Form in which the student shares his understanding of the text

Core reading program (see basal reading program)

Diagnostic assessment
A reading assessment designed to identify strengths and weaknesses in knowledge of specific language elements

Error
A reader's response that is not consistent with the text and that is *not* self-corrected

F & P Calculator/Stopwatch
A device that will calculate the reading time, reading rate, accuracy rate, and self-correction rate for a reading

Fiction
A story created from the imagination

Fluency (as in reading)
The way an oral reading sounds, including phrasing, intonation, pausing, stress, rate, and integration of the first five factors

Font
The style and size of type (alphabet characters) in a printed piece

Genre
A category of texts that share a particular form, common attributes, or content

Gradient of reading difficulty (see text gradient)

Guide for Observing and Noting Reading Behaviors
Lists questions a teacher should ask himself or herself about the ways a student is processing or problem solving texts; located in the *Assessment Forms Book* and *CD-ROM*

Hard reading level
The level at which the student reads a text orally with less than 90% accuracy (levels A–K) or less than 95% accuracy (levels L–Z)

Holistic scoring
A score that reflects overall performance rather than counting items

Independent reading level
The level at which the student reads a text with 95% or higher accuracy and excellent or satisfactory comprehension (levels A–K) or 98% or higher accuracy with excellent or satisfactory comprehension (levels L–Z)

Individual instruction
One teacher working with one student

Insertion (as in error in reading)
A word added during oral reading that is not in the text

Instructional reading level
At levels A–K, the level at which the student reads the text with 90–94% accuracy and excellent or satisfactory comprehension; or 95% or higher accuracy and limited comprehension. At levels L–Z, the level at which the student reads the text with 95–97% accuracy and excellent or satisfactory comprehension; or 98% or higher accuracy and limited comprehension.

Interactive read-aloud
The teacher reading aloud to a group of students and inviting them to think and talk about the text before, during, and after reading

Intervention
Intensive additional instruction for students not progressing as rapidly as expected; usually one-on-one tutoring or small-group (one-on-three) teaching

Key understandings (in benchmark books)
Important ideas within (literal), beyond (implied), or about (determined through critical analysis) the text that are necessary to comprehension

Leveled books
Texts designated along a gradient from level A (easiest) to level Z (hardest)

Literature discussion
Students talking to each other about a text, either in a small group or with the whole class

Longitudinal Record of Reading Progress
A graph showing a student's progress through reading levels across multiple grades; located in the *Assessment Forms Book* and *CD-ROM* and on *Student Folders*

M (meaning)
One of three sources of information that readers use (MSV: meaning, language structure, visual information). Meaning, the semantic system of language, refers to meaning derived from words, meaning across a text or texts, and meaning from personal experience or knowledge.

Minilesson
A brief, focused lesson on any aspect of reading or writing, usually involving the whole class or a small group

Nonfiction
A text whose primary purpose is to convey information and facts that are accurate

Omission (as in error)
A word left out or skipped during oral reading

Optional assessments
A selection of Phonics and Word Analysis plus Vocabulary Assessments designed to target specific areas of literacy knowledge; located in the *Assessment Forms Book* and *CD-ROM*

Oral reading (in Benchmark Assessment) Part One of the Recording Form during which the student reads a text aloud while the teacher codes the reading

Phonics
The study and teaching of letters and their related sounds as they function within words

Phonics and Word Analysis Assessments
A set of optional assessments that evaluates letter knowledge, early literacy concepts, high-frequency words, phonological awareness, letter-sound relationships, and word structure; located in the *Assessment Forms Book* and *CD-ROM*

Preprimer
A beginning text used to teach reading; usually the first books read in a basal reading program

Primer
An early reading text; follows preprimers and precedes the grade 1 text in a basal reading program

Processing (as in reading)
The mental operations involved in constructing meaning from written language

Prompt (in Benchmark Assessment)
A question, direction, or statement designed to encourage the student to say more about a topic during a comprehension conversation

Quarterly Assessment Summary
A form that compiles Assessment Summary results from assessment conferences conducted four times during a school year; located in the *Assessment Forms Book* and *CD-ROM*

Reading graph
A graph that charts a student or students' progress through leveled books (see the Annual Record of Reading Progress and the Longitudinal Record of Reading Progress)

Reading interview
An optional assessment containing questions to gain information about a student's reading preferences and reading history; located in the *Assessment Forms Book* and *CD-ROM*

Reading Rate (WPM)
The number of words a student reads per minute, either orally (as in Benchmark Assessment) or silently

Reading record (in Benchmark Assessment)
The transcript of the text on which oral reading is coded

Recording Form
The form on which oral reading, the comprehension conversation, and the writing about reading assessment for a text are coded and scored. There is a Recording Form for each book in the *Benchmark Assessment System*. All are located in the *Assessment Forms Book* and *CD-ROM*.

Recommended Placement level
The level the teacher, after taking into consideration all data gathered through Benchmark Assessment, decides is appropriate for reading instruction

Repetition (in oral reading)
The reader saying a word, phrase, or section of the text more than once

Rubric
A scoring tool that relies on descriptions of response categories for evaluation

Running words (in Benchmark Assessment)
The number of words read aloud and coded during Part One Oral Reading

S (structure)
One of three sources of information that readers use (MSV: meaning, language structure, visual information). Language structure refers to the way words are put together in phrases and sentences (syntax or grammar).

Scoring and Analysis at-a-Glance
A brief summary of the steps in scoring the three parts of a Benchmark Assessment: oral reading, comprehension conversation, and writing about reading; located in the *Assessment Forms Book* and *CD-ROM*

Scoring a reading record (in Benchmark Assessment)
Counting coded errors and self-corrections, which allows you to calculate *accuracy rate* and *self-correction ratio* on the Recording Form. The form also provides space for a general *fluency score* (levels C–L) and *reading rate* (levels J–N).

Searching
The reader looking for information in order to read accurately, self-correct, or understand a text

Self-correction
The number of errors the reader corrects himself

Shared and performance reading
The teacher and students reading together (or in parts) a text that they know well

Silent reading
The reader reading the text to herself without orally voicing the words.

Six Dimensions Fluency Rubric
A rubric for evaluating oral reading fluency on six dimensions: pausing, phrasing, stress, intonation, rate, and the combination of these, integration; located in the *Forms Book* and *CD-ROM*

Small-group reading instruction
The teacher working with students brought together because they are similar enough in reading development to teach in a small group; guided reading

Sounding out (in Benchmark Assessment)
Pronouncing the sounds of the letters in a word as a step in reading the word (usually all the sounds in sequence)

Spelling aloud (in Benchmark Assessment)
Naming the letters in a word rather than reading the word

Standardized
Remaining essentially the same across multiple instances

Substitution (as in error in reading)
The reader reading aloud one (incorrect) word for another

Text gradient
A twenty-six-point (A–Z) text-rating scale of difficulty in which each text level, from the easiest at level A to the most challenging at level Z, represents a small but significant increase in difficulty over the previous level. The gradient correlates these levels to grade levels.

Told (in Benchmark Assessment)
The teacher telling the reader a word he cannot read

Tri-annual Assessment Summary
A form that compiles Assessment Summary results from assessment conferences conducted three times during a school year; located in the *Assessment Forms Book* and *CD-ROM*

V (visual information)
One of three sources of information that readers use (MSV: meaning, language structure, visual information). Visual information refers to the letters that represent the sounds of language and way they are combined (spelling patterns) to create words; visual information at the sentence level includes punctuation.

Vocabulary
Words and their meanings

Vocabulary Assessments
A set of optional assessments that evaluates a student's word knowledge (concept words, vocabulary in context), understanding of word relationships (synonyms,

antonyms, roots, analogies), and ability to derive the precise meaning of words in the context of a short book (vocabulary in context); located in the *Assessment Forms Book* and *CD-ROM*

Where-to-Start Word Test
A graded list of increasingly difficult words. The number of words the student reads aloud accurately is converted into an approximate level for beginning Benchmark Assessment. Located in the *Assessment Forms Book* and *CD-ROM*.

Whole-group instruction
The teacher teaching a lesson to an entire class or a large part of it

Writing
Students engaging in the writing process and producing pieces of their own writing in many genres

Writing about reading
Students responding to reading a text by writing and sometimes drawing

You Try It (in Benchmark Assessment)
A teacher prompt that directs a student to make an attempt at reading a word during oral reading

▶ Index